Formative Spirituality

Volume Two

HUMAN
FORMATION

Formative Spirituality

Volume Two

HUMAN FORMATION

·ADRIAN VAN KAAM·

CROSSROAD · NEW YORK

1985

The Crossroad Publishing Company
370 Lexington Avenue, New York, NY 10017

Library of Congress Cataloging in Publication Data

Van Kaam, Adrian L., 1920–
Human formation.
(Formative spirituality ; v. 2)
Bibliography: p. 253
Includes index.
1. Spiritual life—Catholic authors. 2. Christian
education—Philosophy. 3. Disposition (Philosophy)
4. Christianity—Psychology. 5. Catholic Church—
Education. I. Title. II. Series: Van Kaam, Adrian L.,
1920-   . Formative spirituality ; v. 2.
BX2350.2.V18   1985   248   84–29241
ISBN 0–8245–0578–6

Contents

v

Preface

This second volume of the series on formation science is about the theory of formation dispositions. These dispositions are an integral part of the human formation of life and world. They coform the *immediate* foundation of life as empirically lived by people. The material to be covered is so extensive and complex that it requires treatment in two volumes. This volume deals mainly with the theoretical foundations of disposition formation. Without these foundations it would be impossible to develop a frame of reference broad enough to integrate the formation wisdom and knowledge of humanity. Volume Three to be published soon will be titled *Formation of the Human Heart.*

At the core of human formation is the "core form" of life, symbolized by the human heart and its enduring dispositions. In this volume we shall discuss the core form at length, along with its basic disposition of awe as lived in the modes of reverence, marvel, wonder, respect, appreciation, and esteem of self, others, and world. These considerations will set the stage for the next volume on the "formation of the heart."

In Volume Two we continue our task of suggesting foundations for a formation science that can complement the functional insights gained by information sciences as well as by other arts and sciences. Formation science is about distinctively human formation, often referred to as "spiritual formation" by various religious and ideological formation traditions.

Distinctively human formation is that aspect of human development that can never be duplicated by even the most sophisticated machine. Since formation science utilizes the formationally relevant facts and insights gained by information science as well as by the other arts and sciences, it is able to clarify the role of such relevant data in the overall distinctively human formation of life and world.

It is our hope that this second volume, like Volume One, will facilitate participation in the ongoing search for the foundations of a formation science that can enlighten human progress in the midst of the exciting revolution initiated by information sciences and the new directions being set for our shared history on this planet, especially in the realm of justice, peace, and mercy for all formation segments of the world population.

Acknowledgments

It is my pleasant duty to express my gratefulness to my colleague and successor as director of the Institute of Formative Spirituality, Dr. Susan Annette Muto, a well-respected author in the field of formative spirituality, for her tireless editing of this book and her valuable suggestions for improvement. I am indebted to Father Richard Byrne OCSO, Ph.D., executive director of the Institute, for his careful reading of the manuscript and his insightful advice. Their willingness to spend time in behalf of this work is even more admirable in view of their ever increasing responsibilities at the Institute.

I also thank the graduate assistants of the Institute who helped in the preparation of the bibliography and index. They are Judy Joehrendt, Annetta Wallace, Sister Mary Josephine Torborg, and Susan Stangl. All did a marvelous job, with great patience and precision. Our excellent typist, Eve Bauer; the administrative facilitator of publications, Helen Douglas; and the other members of the Institute staff deserve recognition for their dedication to this series.

CHAPTER 1

Introduction to Formation Dispositions

V olume One of this series on formation science advanced the idea that humans are called to a distinctive form of life that should be unique and yet compatible with the situations in which they find themselves. In Volume Two we are interested in what it is that gives such a life-form coherence and consistency. Is it perhaps the acts that weave our days together? It seems improbable that they could provide a sufficient explanation because, taken by themselves, they constitute only a collection of unrelated events. What creates continuity in life is not particular acts as such. The secret of life's cohesion seems to reside in a flexible constellation of lasting dispositions that form the foundation of these acts. Together they dispose us to act coherently and in tune with the direction we have chosen to follow.

Dispositions as Secondary Foundational Life-Form

The unique configuration of lasting dispositions functions as our actual life-form at this moment of our formation history. Taken together, these dispositions constitute our secondary foundational life-form and supersede our primary foundational life-form, which remains in some measure hidden in the depth of our preformation. Ideally, this secondary foundation should approximate the direction of the primary insofar as the latter has disclosed itself.

Dispositions of the Dimensions of the Human Form of Life

The dispositions that dispose us to give and receive form in life could be called formation dispositions, or form dispositions. A form disposition is first of all a distinctive, relatively lasting, human formation direction of life. This direction can be an enduring orientation of one of the basic formation potencies of the human life-form, which were described in Volume One as the transcendent, functional, vital and historical dimensions of life. For instance, we may have cultivated a transcendent disposition for

1

aesthetic contemplation, a functional one for the management of family finances, a vital for physical exercise, a sociohistorical for world unification. Our life as a whole is a tissue of such dimensional dispositions. They give it cohesion and consistency, and they make it identifiable.

A disposition thus finds its main source in one or the other dimension of life. Each distinctively human disposition, however, when fully developed and integrated, manifests elements that are also influenced by the other dimensions. Consider the functional disposition for skillful management of family finances. When consonant with our life as a whole, it will be motivated by transcendent loving care for our family; it will suggest precautions for vital health that enable us to give our best to this management without unnecessary exhaustion of our formation energy; it will take into account the sociohistorical conditions under which we have to plan our expenditures.

Particular Propensity and Facility

Each form disposition endows the dimension concerned with a propensity and a facility to give form to life in some particular fashion. It favors a specific type of form reception and form donation. The energy flow in our life is channeled by our dispositions in preferred directions. For example, the appraisal power of our mind may have developed a disposition for apprehension and appraisal of formation opportunities in all situations, whether they are pleasing or displeasing. This alertness for opportunities facilitates an appreciative outlook on life. Hence we will be inclined a priori to invest our formation energy in positive approaches. We will be less inclined to disperse this force in depreciative appraisals when we are faced with life's afflictions. We are less prone to excessive complaining under trying conditions.

Pliability

A formative disposition connotes pliability, that is, the absence of rigidity or fixation. This means that it can give birth to a wide variety of acts. Appreciation of potential opportunities, for instance, can be justified, expressed, and implemented in a variety of ways. When illness strikes, we may appreciate it because of the warning it gives us in regard to an unhealthy style of life or because of the opportunity it offers for rest and recollection, for detachment from immoderate concerns, for identification with the suffering of others.

The list of opportunities to be disclosed by the appreciation disposition is virtually endless. We would like to stress here that pliability of the acts of a disposition rates high in formative spirituality. It fosters a flexible approach to all events in service of our spiritual unfolding.

Reiteration Fosters Consonance

A form disposition is thus a directive and creative power that channels our formative energy. It implies concrete and skillful incarnation of its direction in our daily activities. These acts anchor dispositions more and more concretely in our life. Such reiterated acts, if adapted effectively to different situations, strengthen, enhance, and expand the disposition. A vital disposition for swimming, for instance, is improved by recurrent exercise in different strokes under a variety of conditions, such as speed training, solo or team swimming, and swimming in the ocean.

Formation science is especially concerned with the consonance of dispositions. It is not enough that a disposition enable us to give form consistently to our life in an effective fashion. It must be in consonance with who we most deeply are within ourselves and in relation to other aspects of our formation field, especially to the formation traditions to which we are committed and to the formation mystery.

Contemporary Meaning of Habit Formation

Formation science includes and complements the significant contributions of one of its auxiliary sciences, experimental psychology. Experimental psychology prefers the term *habit* to that of *disposition*. It has given us a keen understanding of the kind of habit formation fostered by vital-functional form directives that operate reactively in relative isolation from the spirit dimension of life. Because a functionalistic lifestyle prevails among many people inside and outside our main Western formation traditions, this insight has been of immense practical value for our understanding of human behavior. It helps us to see how mechanistic habit may inhibit distinctively human growth. The meticulous investigations of experimental psychologists enlighten us in our search for ways to set people free from an exclusive concentration on habits that are mechanistic and external. They also help us to promote the formation of useful routines.

Because of the functional bent of our society, the word *habit* has acquired static connotations. Hence, formation science prefers the term *form disposition*. Form disposition connotes both the humanly directive and the incarnational-learning aspects of this propensity to specific action. These two elements complement one another and constitute together a form disposition. Behavioral training and human formation can and do supplement one another.

Sources and Dynamics of Form Dispositions

From what do form dispositions emerge? How can they foster human formation? Can they lead to deformation? Can they be reformed? To answer such questions we must understand the nature and dynamics of consonant form dispositions as well as their sources in the human life-form, its formation field, and their mutual interaction.

Generally speaking, we acquire a form disposition by reiterating a particular act or series of acts over a period of time. If we engage long enough in acts of kindness toward people, we may develop a disposition for kindness. Formation science does not investigate all possible types of dispositions. Its main concern is with dispositions that are humanly formative and consonant. The disposition for kindness is formative, humanly speaking, if it helps us to form human relationships based on respect and good will toward others. It would be deformative if it were merely a ploy to make others serve our interests. The same disposition is consonant if it is in tune with who we are called to be, if it helps us to realize the hidden foundational life-form we are meant to realize. To display kindness in ways that are artificial in view of our real intentions would be dissonant.

Consonance would also imply that our disposition is attuned to the formation mystery insofar as it has manifested itself to our transcendent presence. Consonance means, moreover, that the disposition is sufficiently pliable to adapt itself to our concrete formation field and that it is in tune with the consonant basic form traditions to which we have freely committed ourselves. This renders the acts of a disposition compatible, compassionate, and effective.

We can illustrate these requirements in our example of the formation of a disposition for consonant kindness. We would be disposed to be kind because we believe in the presence of the formation mystery in others. We would express our kindness congenially in the masculine or feminine, poetic or prosaic, silent or verbal, effusive or laconic fashion that is typically and honestly ours at this stage of our formation. We would adapt our expression to the people toward whom we are trying to be kind: children, adults, intimate friends, fellow players in the locker room, people filled with joy or sorrow. We would also take into account the wisdom and inspiration of our form traditions in our exercise of kindness.

Position of Form Dispositions among the Formation Powers

Before proceeding farther, it is necessary to situate our considerations of form dispositions within the larger structure of distinctively human formation as articulated in Volume One of this series.

We have seen that the central dynamic of formation is our transcendent aspiration after a life-form that truly fulfills our best aspirations. How do form dispositions serve this fulfillment? What is their position among the other powers of formation in our life? To answer these questions, let us look again at the different formation powers.

We turn first of all to the remote source of formation, our foundational life-form, the hidden nobility deep within us that is waiting to be released. This unknown sphere is not passive. It radiates formation energy into each person's life. Our striving to evolve and grow is rooted in this hidden source of being and becoming. All our formation powers spring from the radiation of the image or form we are called to realize in life. This call is nourished by the energy flow of the formation mystery. It is the innermost secret of our soul, our silent dignity to be disclosed over a lifetime.

The proximate sources of daily formation are auxiliary to this realization of our inner form. They enable its disclosure and incarnation in our empirical life and world. This proximate potency resides in our spirit. The transcendent form potency enlightens our mind, will, memory, anticipation, and imagination. Enlightened in this way, they give rise to transcendent dispositions. Other auxiliary formation powers abide in our mind, will, memory, anticipation, and imagination as *functional*. They assist the spirit in its concrete implementation of what has been disclosed as consonant for our life direction. Finally, these proximate sources of formation establish their influence in the empirical life-forms we gradually develop: the core, current, apparent, and actual forms of life.

Other powers of formation are the so-called servant formation powers: people, events, and things in our formation field that foster growth in countless ways. They interact with the formation sources within us. The servant sources themselves are nurtured and directed by the mystery of formation and its epiphanies.

Dispositions as Powers of Indispensable Facilitation

What is the place of the form dispositions in this scheme of formation powers? We could call them "powers of indispensable facilitation." They channel the orientation and energy of our formation powers in the appropriate directions, doing so consistently and smoothly, firmly and gently. They ensure a pleasing continuity of effective acts that foster consonant formation. They relieve our central powers of formation from having to become engaged in each particular act of formation. They are, so to speak, authorized and delegated by these powers to continue the direction invested in these dispositions.

Dispositions insure an economy of energy. They leave the basic form powers free for important new challenges, apprehensions, appraisals, and decisions, as well as for the formation or reformation of dispositions, if desired. These powers do not have to lose time, as it were, to appraise and decide in every instance whether and how to be kind, prayerful, honest, dedicated, fair, firm, playful and so on. The structures and powers of formation are in need of such dispositions. Without them it would be impossible to be effective in an enduring, concrete way. Dispositions are indispensable bridges between the structures of formation and our formation field.

Such structures as those of apprehension, appraisal, and decision are not initially oriented toward specific formation acts. They are only endowed with a general orientation proper to their own nature. The power of appraisal, for instance, is by and large turned toward assessing our formation field in terms of consonant life- and world-formation. It is only during one's formation history that this potency to appraise becomes specialized in the assessment of specific aspects of the field, such as people's character, political situations, transcendent symbols, functional opportunities. In each of these cases, the basic direction of the appraisal power has acquired dispositions that differentiate its fundamental orientation into specific acts of appraisal. In other words, to be able to appraise a specific realm of life, the general appraisal orientation must be disposed in that direction by a corresponding directive disposition. The same disposition principle applies to all formation powers and structures.

Preformed, Acquired, and Infused Formation Dispositions

From our description, it is evident that the number and kind of form dispositions is virtually unlimited. Our form potencies and structures can be specialized in numerous directions and corresponding dispositions. Nevertheless we can make some main distinctions.

First of all, from the viewpoint of their origin, we can distinguish *preformed, acquired,* and *infused* form dispositions. (Infused dispositions will be discussed in a later volume on form traditions.) *Preformed* refers to dispositions that result from our biogenetic, organismic, and vital infraformation. The *organic infraformation* of bodily cells, tissues, organs, and systems provides the basis for the emergence of an original structuring of vital pulsions, needs, and strivings of varying intensity.

Following closely upon organic infraformation is *vital infraformation*. It is the infrafocal (or infraconscious) preformation of the vital pulsions by a process of interformative exchanges with significant persons, events, and things in the earliest life situations. Insofar as these dispositions are due to the original organismic givenness, they are preformed; insofar as they are influenced by interformation, they are acquired. They have an in-between status. To the degree that they are attributable to interformation, they usually manifest formative influences of other people in addition to the features of the preformed organismic dispositions with which such dispositions remain intimately interwoven. This can be ascribed to the fact that infants and children are mainly form-receptive, impressionable, and susceptible. Their first mode of acquisition is by way of situational osmosis. Acquisitional activity by free adoption is at a minimum in these earliest phases of life.

Acquired dispositions are formed, maintained, and expanded through an increasingly consistent exercise of the corresponding consonant acts. For example, the disposition of gentleness is not ours at once. We have to acquire it by acts of gentleness, not performed once or twice but numerous times, and, finally, regularly and without fail. These acts have to be exercised in a formative fashion if they are to establish a consonant disposition. This means that the way in which we are gentle should be more than an automatic and convenient imitation of a pleasing style of interaction in certain circles. To be truly formative, we need to go deeper than that. These acts should give form to our inner life as well as to our outer expressions. The latter constitute an essential element of a formative disposition, for the genuine expression of gentleness will strengthen it as a proximate form disposition in our life. By the same token, the lack of repeated expression tends to diminish the strength and availability of any disposition, including gentleness.

Reiteration versus Repetition

The preceding example suggests that there is a difference between formative exercise and functional repetition. Formative exercise fosters the development of proximate form dispositions as humanly formative. In regard to the higher human dispositions, mere functional repetition, without growth in insight and personal presence, is self-defeating. It prevents the unfolding of the inner depth of proximate higher dispositions. If they remain peripheral, they cannot become truly formative and consonant.

Formative exercise of our higher dispositions is marked by freedom and flexibility, not mere repetition. This is not to say that there is no room for functional repetition in the formation of higher dispositions, but that the basic condition for human formation requires that such repetition become subservient to our free inner aspirations.

Returning to our example, people who strive for gentleness may engage in functional repetition of its acts, even when their corresponding inner aspiration seems minimal. Their genuine intention to acquire gentleness legitimates their functional repetition of gentle acts, even if their hearts cannot yet be in its expression consistently. For these reasons, formation science prefers the term *reiteration* to that of *repetition*.

In this connection, we should mention that mere routine dispositions are needed for the indispensable functional-technical articulation of our life. Their automatic repetition can free us for social-functional and transcendent presence and for the higher formative dispositions that incarnate this presence in the inner and outer spheres of our formation field. Such repetition should be fostered not for its own sake, but for the freedom it grants.

We all are familiar with the liberating effect of routine actions, such as ways of dressing, eating, cleaning, writing. These are based on automatic functional-technical dispositions acquired early in life. Without them we could not live effectively. There is no place, however, for merely automatic repetition in our higher, distinctively human dispositons. A disposition for social presence, for instance, would become deformed if we were to allow it to deteriorate into mere mechanical acts of social concern. It would no longer be a social-presence disposition. Sooner or later other people would sense this absence of distinctive humanness. Indeed, mere mechanistic repetition tends to undermine any distinctively human disposition.

Disposition Radiation

Interformation accounts for the social radiation of dispositions. All formation is interformation. The form we give to our life and world via our dispositions affects others; the dispositions of others affect us in turn. Our presence radiates, indicating to others how we are disposed. This radiation can be negative or positive, deformative or formative. Appreciative dispositions, for example, may prevail among those that enhance our appraisal power. Accordingly, we radiate positive, affirmative, and hope-filled moods and feelings. If, on the contrary, depreciative dispositions dominate our appraisals, our radiation will be negative and discouraging. It would nurture any existing feelings of form impotence in people around us.

We are responsible for our social radiation. Positive radiation can be more beneficial than any other social gift. We may try to improve the lot of the disadvantaged by physical works of mercy, which is, of course, a praiseworthy endeavor. But what happens if we do these works in a depreciative and gloomy mood? Our pretense of interest will be less influential than our negative radiation. In spite of our functional care, we may leave many people more gloomy than they would have been without our bleak appearance on the scene. Disposition radiation affects our family, friends, students, employers, employees, and colleagues in similar fashion.

We may find ourselves engaged at times in a so-called "battle of radiation." This can happen when we interact with people whose presence radiates depreciative dispositions. Our own appreciative dispositions may try by spontaneous radiation to dispel the dark moodiness of others. At times one or the other may win out. At stake here is a struggle between pervasive moods engendered by opposite dispositions.

Foundational Dispositions Coform Consonant Dispositions

The science of formation has identified a number of foundational dispositions conducive to consonant life formation. First is the central disposition of awe, giving rise to the foundational dispositional triad of faith, hope, and consonance. Subordinate to these are the dispositions of privacy, communion, openness, appreciation, affirmation, confirmation, joyousness, gentleness, firmness, congeniality, compatibility, compassion, competence, and effectiveness. These dispositions are called foundational since our life formation revolves around them. They influence in some measure the development of any consonant formative disposition whatsoever. Later we will consider them in more detail. We only want to mention here that all of them are the result of a progressive emergence, which refers in turn to a basic principle of all formation, namely, its gradual, ongoing nature.

Living and Stilted Formative and Deformative Dispositions

Dispositions that are distinctively human are alive and dynamic. They are free, pliable, and creative. They endow life with verve and flair, yet they may lose their dynamism. This happens when our life goes sour. We become disenchanted. Our dispositions begin to lose their elasticity. Their inspirational and aspirational roots shrivel. Only their peripheral expression may be repeated in parched and sterile routines. Instead of human presence, flexibly expressed in behavior, we end up with dull, stilted routines, depleted of their transcendent roots, their sparkle all but gone.

Different from these, and often worse, are deformative dispositions. What if we have developed a disposition to exaggerate all events out of proportion? This deformative approach presents us and others with a distorted picture of what is really going on in our formation field. It is difficult to respond to that field effectively. Our distorted perceptions and responses incline us to give and receive form dissonantly and deceptively. Deformation of apprehension, appraisal, affirmation, reaction, and response is the result of this disposition.

All of us have developed some deformative dispositions. The crucial question is whether we are aware of them and willing to reform them. Otherwise they will keep interfering with the consonant flow of formation. They tend to bind up energy that could be used beneficially in consonant formative dispositions. We will return later to this question. For now, suffice it to say that fixation of formation energy in dissonant dispositions vitiates the open-endedness of human formation. Our formation powers may become encapsulated. If this happens, the dammed-up flow of form energy leads to exaltation of that disposition.

People may form a disposition within which only financial success, uncommitted sexual freedom, ascetic overexertion, or functional-emotional piety can make them happy. This favored aspect of their life is blown up beyond reasonable proportions. The frantic pursuit of such objectives blots out attention that should be given to other form directives. It devours their energy and prevents any other mode of form giving and form reception.

This tendency to fashion dissonant form dispositions may become pervasive and permanent. Hence it should not surprise us that the free flow of formation powers and energies is repeatedly halted. We are inclined to invest this energy time and again in dissonant directions. Once these dispositions have been germinated, they remain in us. They keep attracting new investments of energy and interest. They try continuously to reassert themselves. A flexible vigilance in their regard remains necessary if we want to escape their greedy, grasping, and manipulative hold on our life.

Dissonant dispositions are interrelated. Together they constitute a counterfeit form of life with which we must always reckon.

Quasi Autonomy of Stilted Form Dispositions

As we have seen earlier, a stilted form disposition is reduced to its behavioral expression. It is no longer directed and nourished by our distinctively human resources. Hence its character is uninspiring and compulsive. It becomes empty and despiritualized. It reacts as if it were autonomous. In an integrated life, human form dispositions remain in dialogue with their inner center. The disposition is stirred by some event in the formation field. Its response is partly habitual. Still, the deeper dimensions of the personality co-respond in their own way. The spiritual center of the life-form is always appealed to by the formative act, no matter how fleetingly. There is a moment of free inner participation in the act. A subtle centering graces each consonant act with a distinctive human quality, if only by implicit allowance of its execution.

A split-off disposition reacts as if it existed on its own, outside the sphere of one's personal-spiritual presence and freedom. Such dispositions give rise to a chain of reactions that follow one another automatically as soon as the first link is activated. We should realize, however, that one and the same disposition in us may at one time be alive in a distinctively human or spiritual sense, at other times be stilted and reduced to its behavioral component.

Imagine that we have developed a formative disposition for ritual as practiced in a religious form tradition. When stilted, our liturgical form giving and receiving is no longer guided and nourished by spiritual inspiration. When the ritual evokes our customary response, we may go through the required actions meticulously, but our heart is not in it. The ritual act is not graced by its being centered in a prayerful spirit. It occurs at the periphery of human presence. Each successive phase of the ceremony follows the other automatically. It is like a mechanical chain of ritual reactions activated the moment we enter the ceremonial circle of events. In better times we may come to live our ritual disposition once again from within. We then recover the link between ritual behavior and spiritual presence.

In some instances, the mechanistic reactivity of dispositions is rooted in infrafocal feelings and attitudes. They can exert a stereotypic, monotonous influence over some of our dispositions. As children, for instance, we may have been compelled by insecure parents to feign affection we did not really feel. The infrafocal dread of being abandoned by them made us develop a disposition of displaying unfelt affective behavior. We wanted desperately to feel safe and to avoid rejection.

Later in marriage we may be disposed to manifest stereotypic expressions of affection for spouse and children, no matter how we feel about them. We are the victims of a split-off behavioral affective disposition that cannot take away the chill of a heart that never learned to give form freely to loving relationships. As long as such infrafocal determinants are not disclosed and reformed, they keep our dispositions insensible and inflexible. We blindly repeat certain reactions, no matter how ill-adapted they are. Such insensitive reactions block the easy and spontaneous flow of our formative energy. Infrafocal strivings emerge from deep inside us. They compel us to maintain dispositions that make us react rigidly.

Routine dispositions that are dissonant may have been sedimented in our personality early in life. Accustomed to them for a lifetime, it is difficult to reform them. They cannot be altered all at once. The process requires time, perseverance, and patience. It is basically a process of integration. We have to link them with our spiritual center, in whose light they may be gradually reformed. A whole world of associated customs and reactions may have evolved around the dissonant disposition. This will worsen our plight and increase the work of disclosure and reformation of this dispositional counterfeit form of life. The counterfeit form of life is based on the quasi-foundational, autarchic pride-form. The consonant dispositional form of life is rooted in the primordial foundational life-form.

Ground of the Development of Form Dispositions

We may ask ourselves why the human life-form needs form dispositions? The answer lies in an insight developed in Volume One, where we discussed the difference between prehuman and human life-forms and their corresponding formation fields.

Prehuman life-forms are instinctually directed in relation to their formation field. Human life-forms are not; they need to develop directive dispositions to take the place of instincts. Directive dispositions enable us to give human form to life and world in concrete ways. The more we exercise such dispositions, the more powerful they become. The more we keep them in tune with our spiritual life-form, the less danger there is that the dispositions will deteriorate into mere routines.

The more a disposition becomes consonant, the firmer its beneficial power, for it participates in the human form potency at the heart of our existence. A disposition that lacks formative power and consonance cannot be termed a distinctively human disposition. It lacks sufficient firmness. At most, it is only a potentially human disposition.

Effectiveness of Disposition

If sufficient form potency is invested in a disposition, it becomes effective. Its effectiveness implies four qualities: readiness, alertness, facility, and flexibility. Readiness refers to our propensity and preparedness to respond in accordance with the form direction invested in the disposition. Alertness points to our promptness of action when an event in the formation field elicits the response to which we are disposed. Facility is the quality of fluid and tactful execution of the action that flows from the disposition. Flexibility represents the built-in adaptability of the action of a form disposition to variations presented by each unique situation. This flexibility implies an openness to all fluctuations in the actual conditions of the formation field for effective action. This relaxed openness facilitates our astute apprehension of relevant details.

Appreciativeness and Joyousness of Disposition

An effective form disposition enables people to act with appreciation and joyousness. Appreciation points to the fact that a consonant disposition predisposes people to value and cherish the formative meaning of their actions. They cultivate the disposition because their power of appraisal leads them to value these acts as consonant and formative. This original appreciation and motivation is deepened in each action.

Reinforced appreciation gives rise to joyousness. The deeper one's appreciation is rooted in spiritual participation in the mystery of formation, the more profound is the joy one experiences when the consonant disposition is activated. This joy encompasses, yet transcends, satisfaction and pleasure.

Satisfaction, or contentment, is the rewarding experience of one's functional competence and efficiency in performing any act toward which one is well-disposed. Pleasure or gratification is the feeling engendered in the vital dimension of one's effective disposition. This agreeable vital feeling is due to the fact that the disposition enables people to use less vital energy, to experience dexterity, neuromuscular ease of movement, and to suffer less fatigue. In the long run, the action may become almost effortless.

Foundational Features

Every formative act and disposition in human life implies some support by the foundational triad of faith, hope, and consonance, and is inspired by awe and the trust and abandonment to which awe gives rise. (Abandonment has been discussed at length in Volume One.) Similarly, any formation act or disposition has to be congenial with what one is called to be, in tune with one's consonant form traditions, compatible with one's formation field, and compassionate in regard to one's own and others' vulnerabilities.

Form Dispositions and Formation as a Whole

An effective disposition enhances and enriches each one of its acts and corresponding experiences. The actuation of the disposition also advances human formation as a whole due to the rootedness of form dispositions in our spiritual center. Their effective acts, and the heartening experiences they provide, cannot help but affirm the basic human form potency and its striving after consonance. This overall rise in potency-feeling and consonant directedness strengthens in turn the dispositions.

A consonant form disposition is interwoven with the distinctively human powers of formation. They animate the disposition as well as strengthen its increase and continuation. This effect is not only a question of the reiteration of certain acts. Much depends on the depth of the motivation of these acts by the central formation powers. The potency of this motivation is contingent upon three factors: first, the intensity of appreciation by the appraisal power; second, the decisiveness of the will and its accompanying feelings; third, the scope of enlistment of formative imagination, memory, and anticipation. These factors determine the strength and formative quality of the act of the disposition. The higher the formative quality of the act, the more the disposition used by the will for it is strengthened.

Thus it is not reiteration in and by itself that makes for the initiation and increase of a disposition. More important for the higher dispositions is the seriousness and vividness of motivation by the central formation powers. Hence, various form traditions emphasize reflection and imaginative dwelling on the consonant acts and dispositions one wants to form in life.

People remain free to use or not to use a formation disposition with which they have been endowed. They may even act in opposition to its direction. This weakens the disposition. In the end a form disposition may be deactivated by lack of exercise or by repeated acts that militate against its consonant orientation.

A distinctively human form disposition thus has two main aspects: formative presence and the expression of that presence, which together constitute a form disposition. Formative presence is rooted in the distinctively human powers of formation. Expression occurs in part by conditioning through which we learn acceptable modes of expressing our form dispositions in our formation field.

Free and responsible life formation does not exclude conditioning. Rather, it welcomes it as an ally. We are all creatures of conditioning. The skills that make possible the effective expression of our form dispositions are for the most part the deposits with which conditioning has enriched us.

We should add here that we are not only conditioned by our culture and form tradition. We can condition ourselves. We can reform our formation field or enhance aspects of it. We do so by selective apprehension, appraisal, affirmation, imagination, memory, and anticipation. We can choose our own rewards and punishments.

Presence Aspect and Expression Aspect of a Form Disposition

The presence and expression aspects of a form disposition can be separated. When the form disposition loses its dimension of human presence, we can no longer call it a distinctively human disposition. It becomes only a routine disposition. The spontaneity of formation is lost; the prepersonal determination of conditioning prevails.

We may feel called to social work among disadvantaged people. Moved by human concern, we develop a disposition of effective social presence. We express this in concrete acts of care for those entrusted to us. Lack of success, overexertion, administrative indifference of our supervisors, and other factors begin to erode our initial enthusiasm. Our social presence is depleted. Yet the behavior in which we expressed this presence is routinely repeated. The agency that employs us as social workers has conditioned us to act in certain ways. Initially, we invested these customs of care with true social presence, but now we only go through the motions and our heart is not in it. The behavioral dimension of our disposition has been isolated from a social presence that is no longer alive in us.

The routinization of social behavior is a degradation of our human disposition. A mechanical disposition for routinized acts has lost contact with human apprehension, appraisal, affirmation, creative imagination, memory, and anticipation. In the extreme it manifests the rigidity and stereotypic procedure of a computer or robot. Our social behavior starts automatically, simply being triggered by external stimuli provided by an agency or clients. This sets in motion corresponding internal stimuli that get us through the day as social robots without much concern and compassion.

Thanks to our learning by conditioning, we may be disposed to execute meticulously the social procedures demanded by the agency. The stimuli of reward and punishment, of maintenance or loss of job, of increase or decrease in salary and position, of administrative approval and disapproval keep triggering the routine disposition for social comportment. The tendency to replace form dispositions by routine dispositions is fostered by our inclination to prefer inertia of spirit over effort, to be acted upon rather than to act.

A routine disposition is not always the result of a separation of the expression aspects of the form disposition from its presence dimension. Certain routine dispositions are often first directly formed by conditioning. Only later do they become subservient to the spirit.

Conditioning forms and consolidates routine dispositions by repetition, stimulated by reward and punishment. As we have seen already, form dispositions become distinctively human when personal concern enters the picture. Creative apprehension, appraisal, affirmation, imagination, memory, and anticipation are sources of personal presence. The routine aspect affects mainly the expression dimension. A distinctively human form disposition transcends, therefore, the stereotypic expressions of a routine disposition.

All our consonant form dispositions constitute together a basic formation structure of countless variations. They offer us a latent treasure of formation resources. We can rely on them each time we are faced with a new situation in our formation field. The pliability of our social and cultural presence not only affects each singular form disposition; it also applies to the whole subtle gamut of interrelated dispositions accumulated during our formation history. At any moment we can appeal to this treasure. We may find the unique dispositions we need to respond to an event that challenges our formation potency. At times we may be amazed by the resources of latent dispositions suddenly awakened by new challenges in our life.

Initial Formation of a Disposition

Skill is needed to express a form disposition effectively. Such skillfulness is formed by practice in the actual implementation of the disposition.

Here conditioning is important. Without practice in the inner and outer spheres of our formation field, no effective disposition can be established. The presence dimension alone is not sufficient to draw forth an effective disposition. Concrete operational dispositions simply cannot be thought out and willed into existence. Usually, the opposite occurs. We move formatively in our concrete formation field. Routinely we adapt to its demands. We gain skill in this adaption. Constant repetition establishes the skillfulness necessary for a specific compatible interaction with the formation field. Our human spirit begins to apprehend and appraise what is going on in this interaction. It asks itself, at least implicitly, about the congeniality of this interaction with its own unique life call, its consonance with the epiphanies of the formation mystery in its interiority, its compatibility with its formation field and its form tradition.

Out of this intraformative dialogue comes the decision of the will to allow this interaction to go on and to infuse it with the presence of the human spirit. Thus integrated in one's full formation field, the human formation disposition is born. Its development is modulated from now on by both elements: formative presence and its skilled expression.

Take the case in which one has developed the form disposition of fair play in sports and daily life. To be fair in play demands skill. As a child, one learned such skills. One did not think about them but simply took part in sports and games. One had to play by the rules and be fair with fellow players. If they did not play fair, players were penalized by referees or lost confirmation by their peers. Routinely adapting to such demands, one gained the skills of fair play. Slowly one began to apprehend the meaning of fair play in interaction with others. One sought its meaning in one's life. Why should one be fair with others? One may, for example, have related this value implicitly to the endless play of the formation mystery in which all participate. Probably one could not say so in words, but somehow it was possible to fit the disposition of fair play into the wider horizon of distinctively human values and motivations.

The will, thus enlightened, permitted the routine development of a fair-play disposition while complementing it with the spontaneity of the spirit. Human presence, in the disposition of fairness, thus elucidates and animates its vital-functional skills and expressions.

Inclusion of All Dimensions of Formation

By now we surmise that a form disposition includes all dimensions of formation. It flexibly takes into account the sociohistorical nuances of each situation. It involves the well-disposed vital dimension of the form-giving person in each specific realm of embodied presence. The ambition of the functional dimension to implement the direction of the disposition as skillfully as possible is operative in each of its actualizations. The transcendent, distinctively human dimension provides the deepest nourishing ground of the form disposition.

The initially conditioned learning phase of a disposition can be described to some extent as prepersonal. It is not yet distinctively human. The conditioned disposition only becomes personally formative, humanly speaking, when its realm extends to the transcendent dimension.

Experimental psychology is complemented by formative spirituality. The conditioned disposition is elevated to a form disposition that participates in the spiritual life of the person. The disposition is no longer merely a sociohistorically conditioned vital-functional skill. It is inwardly enriched and transformed by a transcendent aspiration to act formatively and creatively in the light of distinctively human ideals.

(In a later volume of this series, we shall consider how the Christian form tradition views the transforming operation of the pneumatic dimension in our conditioned dispositions. This factor leads to the development of a Christian spirituality with its doctrine of infused virtues and transformation in Christ.)

Form Dispositions and the Foundational Life-Form

Form dispositions are facilitators of formation. They have so much become ours that they function spontaneously and almost effortlessly. They become a secondary foundational life-form. In their mutual interaction, when consonant, they should ideally approximate our primary foundational life-form as it has disclosed itself to us at this moment of our formation history. The opposite is possible as well: the constellation of form dispositions that constitute our secondary foundational life-form may be dissonant. This dissonant constellation is rooted in the autarchic pride-form.

In practice, we have both a consonant and a dissonant constellation of form dispositions. Often we waver between them and hope that our consonant constellation may prevail as our secondary foundational form of life. This secondary dispositional form of life becomes so natural to us that it operates by itself. In regard to such dispositions, it is no longer necessary to be engaged in explicit appraising and deciding. Appraisal and willing in relation to their operation have become so facilitated that their operation is usually no more than one of allowing these dispositions to act in tune with their established, spontaneous bent.

Summary and Conclusion

Formation science sees the distinctively human form dispositions as constituted by two mutually complementary elements: the transcendent element of human presence and the functional-vital-sociohistorical element of expressions of this presence in life and world. The transcendent element illumines the direction of the disposition and animates it with spontaneity. Having done that, it distances itself, leaving the form disposition on its own, so to speak, as its trusted delegate.

This communicated spontaneity enables people to be congenial, compatible, and compassionate in the effectuation of their dispositions in regard to the ever changing prevalence of formation poles or spheres in their formation field. Such spontaneity needs to remain attuned to the spirit, at least implicitly. Hence it continuously needs the implicit allowance of the spirit as appraising and willing. Otherwise the disposition could be overwhelmed by vital, functional, and sociohistorical aspects. It would thereby lose spontaneity and succumb to routinization. This would mean a loss of effective spirituality in this specific area of our personal life.

The routine aspects of the form disposition represent the vital-functional reactive side of a disposition that is socially conditioned. These routine aspects are illumined and directed by their compliance with the spirit animating them with the spontaneity of the spiritual life. This spirituality enables them to become congenial, compatible, and compassionate in the execution of their acts. This compliance cannot be the work of the unaided functional-vital form potencies themselves. Only the spiritual form potency can effect such obedience to itself. The vital-functional aspects, when divorced from the transcendent, become routinized and mechanical. They paralyze the spiritual life in the realm concerned.

We all are endowed with transcendent form potency. We can imbue our higher routine dispositions with inspirited spontaneity. By contrast, inertia would lead to neglect of our spiritual life. The potential for inspirited form dispositions would not be activated. Our secondary foundational life-form would then deteriorate into a constellation of only routine dispositions. Instead of being an approximation of the disclosed direction of our primary foundational life-form, it would become a power of paralysis of this ongoing disclosure and manifestation. Each tentative appearance of its nobility and spontaneity, as communicated through the human spirit, would be aborted.

The fossilized life of only routine dispositions is a life of alienation from our human spirit and from the unique foundational life-form it tries to disclose to us over a lifetime of formation. Our autarchic pride-form gives rise to dissonant form dispositions that pose a threat to the consonant spiritual life. Another threat is our bent to spiritual inertia. Because of our penchant for spiritual lethargy, the threat of a routinization of all of life is inscribed in every one of our form dispositions.

The neglect of spiritualization of dispositions abandons them to the power of conditioning. Thoughts and words become stale and insipid. Life becomes platitudinous. Conditioning becomes enslaved to passing pulsations. The despiritualized routine disposition reacts in fixed patterns to the same aspects of the life situation. One wants to fixate on them rigidly, as they have always been in one's memory. As a result, one's formation field shrinks. Any potential change is experienced as a threat to one's routine form of life. The threat is the possibility that one's spirit may be awakened by changes in the environment that disturb the routine dispositions. In that case one's whole secondary, routinized life-form is at stake. The primary foundational life-form may begin to assert itself through the awakened human spirit.

The preformation of human life initiates a polarity between the transcendent and the vital-functional dimensions, between freedom and conditioning, spiritedness and inertia, spiritual openness and the closure of autarchic pride. Formation dispositions are one particular expression of this polarity.

Humanity is called to a consonant form of life that transcends yet includes all polarities in itself and its formation field. In the realm of dispositions, consonance is served by the transformation of at least the higher routine dispositions into inspirited spontaneous form dispositions. They adopt flexibly the skills and routines learned by conditioning, while allowing these skills to grow continuously.

CHAPTER 2

Dispositions, Formation Fields, and Dimensions

T he notion of a formation field refers in this science to the fact that we do not live our lives in relation to the world as such but to the world as relevant to our formative aptitudes, strivings, apprehensions, appraisals, affirmations, and interests. We call this relevant world the inner and outer spheres of our formation field. In what way do our dispositions influence these spheres and how are they influenced by it?

Formation Fields and Dispositions

Formation is not the result of isolated reactions to stimuli unrelated to the rest of our life and surroundings. The way we respond is the effect of a continuous attunement of our life as a whole to the various spheres of our formation field. For example, the way I respond to the announcement of a drop in the stock market depends on my involvement in the market, my understanding of economic issues and the impact they may have on my family here and now, my memories of the past, the place of the national economy in my hierarchy of values, my optimism or pessimism, and countless other factors that play a role in my formation field as a whole.

This attunement to events within our formation field is motivated partly by our striving for consonance in life. We are naturally inclined to keep things together within ourselves and between ourselves and our surroundings. The fact that the stock market dropped may be significant in the special history of our life, its field of action and experience. Therefore, we try to give this event a meaningful place in the total structure of our existence. We try to fit it into our story of formation, thus attuning ourselves to its reality and ramifications. When we engage in this attunement process repeatedly, we may develop certain lasting dispositions. These play a dynamic role in our presence to reality. If we know something about the dispositions of people who receive news of a decline in the stock market, we may be able to predict how they will respond. Dispositions thus account for a vast range of styles and adaptations in populations and cultures.

This example may illustrate the correspondence between dispositions and formation fields. People who have been formed in the disposition that economic gain is the ultimately important factor in life may panic or despair when a depression strikes. Their disposition makes this economic factor meaningful in their formation field in a way that is different from what it means for those who value most highly human relationships, family love, or religious faith. We cannot understand a person's particular formation field without understanding the dispositions that give form to it. Likewise their dispositions can only be understood in relation to that field, to what things mean to them because of their dispositions.

Our example makes clear, too, that no formative event is an isolated occurrence within one's formation field. The impact of a decline in the economy is related to other aspects of the same field, such as one's way of maintaining a sense of form potency, of paying bills, of setting goals, of cultivating friends and acquaintances, of appraising economic values, of belonging to a church or synagogue. Any fact that becomes a formative event in our lives is a special expression of our formation field as a whole. Acts and dispositions respond to events in their interwovenness within that field. Hence we cannot fully explain a disposition without taking into account many facets of the formation field to which it is a response.

Formation theory, presented in Volume One, stressed that the poles or spheres of the field are always in interaction. There is interformation between people themselves and between the outer formative interaction that takes place between them and their situation and world. Here we want to stress that the result of all such interaction is the development of a whole tissue of dispositions that give stability to one's ongoing formation.

Influence of Past, Present, and Future on the Formation of Dispositions

Disposition formation is influenced not only by the conditions of one's present field of action but also by the past and future. Consider the disposition of a mother toward care of husband and children. Her present formation field influences the actual conditions under which she has to care for them. Her care disposition has to take into account such factors as their particular character and temperament, the nature of the neighborhood, the family income, the housing situation. Memories of her past formation at her own parental home have an impact on her care disposition, too. The way in which her mother did things at home and expressed herself to husband and children is certainly influential. She may imitate some of these ways or react against them in the forming of her own dispositions. In both cases she is in some way moved by her former formation field.

Other disposition directives come from the future. A mother may anticipate what her formation field may be like when her children grow up and leave home. In view of that anticipated life situation, she may form her care disposition in such a way that she does not become overdependent on her children. She allows some reasonable time for her own growth and development and for the cultivation of friends of her own generation. She protects and deepens her personal, intimate relationship with her husband. All this will enable her to continue her life meaningfully when her children have their own families and cannot pay as much attention to their parents.

Each formative act and disposition is coformed by those that preceded them and they anticipate those that will follow. In this sense, all formation is interaction not only with our present formation field but also with that of the past and future. This is true not only of dispositions in individuals but also of sociohistorical dispositions in populations.

A convincing illustration can be found in James Michener's book on South Africa, *The Covenant*. The deformative disposition of the white Afrikaners toward the black population is made clear in a penetrating description of the past formation field of the Boers, the present formation field of the Afrikaners who are now in power, and the Afrikaners' anxious anticipation of their formation field in the future when and if the blacks rise up against them. All fields together constitute their present dispositions. They can only be understood fully and dealt with effectively if one grasps how past, present, and anticipated future give form to these dispositions. Thus every act and disposition takes something from those that have gone before and preforms in some way the content and structure of those that will come after.

From our examples, it is evident that the formation of dispositions is not totally determined in advance. The disposition of the Boers toward the blacks coformed the disposition of the Afrikaners but did not totally determine it. Their new situation of political power and the change from an agricultural to an industrialized nation created nuances in this disposition and its execution that could not have been foreseen and predicted in detail.

If our dispositions were totally determined, we could only develop routine ones. While we have many useful patterns of doing things that do not change, we have other dispositions that are flexible and open to reformation. The routine disposition of tying one's shoelaces is different from that of music appreciation. The former is mechanical, the latter is amenable to refinement, amplification, and deepening. If all dispositions were routine, they could only be the result of automatic conditioning. There would be no room for free spiritual formation. Distinctively human or spiritual life would not exist.

Because spiritual dispositions are possible and a fact of life, we have to complement the important findings of experimental psychology with those of the science of formation. Our dispositions in lower dimensions can be subordinated to our transcendent dispositions without losing their own character. For example, the disposition to vital-sexual interaction in marriage can be intimately directed by a spirit of deeply human love, respect, and tenderness. In that case, it is neither a routinized nor a routine disposition. The disposition is transformed in its core by the spirit. It is adventurous and open, flexible and adaptable to inspiration, mood, need, and human situation.

Disposition Memory and Project

It may sound strange to speak about the memory of a disposition, possibly because the word memory connotes the memorizing of multiplication tables and other exercises. However, memory in the widest sense means any capacity to retain things learned. For this reason we can speak of some kind of memory included in our dispositions, insofar as they retain something of what we have imbibed.

For instance, the disposition of riding a bicycle implies a retention of vital and functional adaptations learned in the past. These antecedent actions made the formation of this disposition possible. We learned to ride by a specific sequence of acts: getting on the bike, adjusting the pedals, keeping our balance. A detailed sequence of external and internal acts combined to effect a coherent response to the demands of bicycling. This sequence is preserved in what we may call the formative memory of a disposition. When similar demands emerge, this memory is activated and we are able to ride immediately. This riding disposition, without any reflection on our part, projects a similar sequence of effective acts that enable us to pedal smoothly. It is for this reason that we can speak of a disposition project.

The word project connotes at first a plan made up in our mind. However, any formative sequence of effective acts that is in some way anticipated can be called a project. A project in this sense refers to a scheme, strategy, or action that is ready-at-hand. In addition to the formative memory of effective bicycling, this disposition also includes a project of bicycling that is activated the moment we begin our ride and that continues throughout this exercise. We do not have to think about what we are doing or try it out laboriously, as when we rode for the first time.

The project inherent in any disposition does not necessarily give form to each particular of our subsequent response. Bicycling obliges us to adapt to changes in the situation. During a race we ride differently from how we ride when we are alone on a country road. The less routinized a disposition is, the more room it leaves for the adaptation of its standard sequence of actions to new situations.

A case in point would be doctors in emergency wards who specialize in cardiac-arrest cases. Over the years they have developed a disposition to diagnose and treat patients by a sequence of acts that respond to immediate danger. They engage almost routinely in the right steps, yet their disposition to treat patients in the best possible way keeps them attentive to complications. It readies them to modify the usual sequence, if necessary. Their disposition explains the ease, skill, speed, and alertness with which medical specialists handle emergencies. The creative appraisal or diagnostic element of their disposition explains the varied and flexible approach, if and when complications arise.

Deformative Dispositions

The same memory and project power operates in deformative dispositions. Past dissonant interactions with our formation field inscribe their sequence of acts in the disposition memory. For example, a person may have grown skillful in stealing various items from supermarkets and stores. He enjoyed the thrill of the risk involved, the easy acquisition of objects that attracted him. He developed a sequence of acts that enabled him to escape detection. He smuggled the stolen goods outside under his coat or in other ways that proved successful. He relished the suspense, the feeling of secret potency. He gave in to the temptation to try shoplifting over and over again to test his skill of execution and perhaps to defy authority.

Deformative dispositions become as much a part of our secondary foundational life-form as formative ones. This explains their hold over our life. It demands more effort to resist or reform them than to learn them. The steady reiteration of the standard sequence inscribes such dispositions more indelibly in our life. The moment we find ourselves in a similar situation, the deformative disposition urges us to repeat the usual sequence. When the shoplifter browses through a store, he feels tempted to take something the moment his disposition strategy tells him the situation is favorable, that he can get away with it without much danger of detection.

In this way deformative dispositions, like their formative counterparts, become interwoven with our secondary foundational life-form, thus sharing in its foundational power and stability and in the continuation it gives to our emergent life.

It is difficult to dislodge or reform any well-established disposition. It affects and is affected by other dispositions. For instance, stealing from stores affects the dispositions of honesty and justice and of respect and compassion for owners, salespersons, or customers who pay for the deficits stores suffer as a result of such actions. It affects also the dispositions of self-respect and effective maintenance of a sense of consonant form potency and self-esteem.

Because a reformation in depth of this one disposition touches so many others, no disposition can be reformed in isolation. It always implies some modification of our secondary foundational life-form as a whole. Many other correlated deformative dispositions come into question. So does our formation history. What made us inclined in the first place to engage in this kind of stealing? Does it go back to incidents during initial formation? Do we try to get even with past authorities whom we experience as oppressive by defying the authority and the regulations that govern a store and thus secretly exercising our form potency and power over them? The latter is only one of many possible explanations to account for the initiation of this deformative disposition.

Because of its interwovenness with our basic secondary form of life and its genesis, it is difficult to resist the urge of a strong disposition. Its hold over us is powerful. It may override our finest apprehensions, appraisals and affirmations, despite the best sermons we receive regarding its pernicious nature. Often, the only way to escape this deeply rooted power is to turn our attention away from the occasion that stimulates us to indulge in the familiar sequence.

Dissonant dispositions have often been acquired by interformation with others. Thus we may change them more effectively in interformation with persons who are similarly afflicted. For example, we may have indulged with others in regular "bitching sessions." As a result we developed a negative, depreciative disposition. We may profit from appreciative sessions with persons who suffer from the same dissonance and who want to become more positive. We may help each other in this way to reform a negative outlook.

Even deformative dispositions acquired by ourselves are easier to overcome when we feel supported by others who attempt a similar reformation. This is one of the principles behind a reform movement like Alcoholics Anonymous. It also explains the support we find in well-assimilated form traditions that foster opposite dispositions.

Affective Affinity of Dispositions

Dispositions not only have memory and project power; they betray a certain affective affinity. Sculptors disposed to work mainly with marble have a certain affinity to this material. They may even feel an affection for it. People disposed to appreciate classical music feel an affinity with that music. Such affection and affinity become invested in corresponding dispositions. The special quality of such affinity and affection, inherent in our dispositions, has been engendered by previous interaction with people, events, or things to which we are well-disposed. The stronger the affinity, the more intense the need to live the disposition out when the occasion presents itself again. A man and a woman who have formed a disposition of intimate love for one another feel an intense desire to experience and express their love each time they meet.

This affective affinity is of great value in the realm of consonant dispositions. Nature intended this strong affinity of our dispositions and of the secondary foundational life-form they coform. This bonding enables us to give form to our life and world with increasing facility and satisfaction in a consonant direction. For instance, if people have been drawing and painting for many years in fulfillment of their talents, they enjoy more and more ease and pleasure in the exercise of this artistic disposition. The same disposition affinity applies to swimming, playing baseball, basketball, or other athletic games.

This ease and attraction turn against us in the case of dissonant dispositions. Years of rigidity make it difficult for us to become more gentle and relaxed. We often try to reform such undesirable dispositions by means of abstract appraisals, logical reasonings, and strong decisions. This may be a helpful beginning but in and by itself it is not enough. The problem is that such abstractions are not yet invested with the affective affinity of our imagination and of concrete recurrent life experience. Such logical insights and choices are initially not as compelling as the living dispositions they try to reform. These alive dispositions constitute our actual basic form of life with its typical attractions and aversions. To reform that basis, even in one of its dispositions, we need to complement logical thought with active situational imagination and recurrent practice that is sufficiently realistic and limited to give us some experience of accomplishment.

Form Dimensions and Dispositions

In Volume One of this series, we developed the theory of the transcendent, vital, functional, and sociohistorical dimensions of human life. These are the main form potencies of the human life-form. The strivings connected with these dimensions were classified as inspirations and aspirations, ambitions, impulses, (or pulsions), and pulsations. There is always a mutual interaction between the form dimensions themselves and the strivings proper to them. What is the relation of dispositions to these dimensions and their strivings?

A certain hierarchy applies to the form dimensions. The highest potential of human life is the transcendent dimension. Only the human spirit or power of transcendence sets people apart from infrahuman forms of life. It makes people distinctively human or spiritual. The other dimensions participate in this humanness or spirituality in the measure that they allow themselves to be formed by it. The same applies also to dispositions. They may be primarily related to one or the other of our life dimensions. Yet at the same time they can be subordinated or attuned to the transcendent dimension.

Cooking and cleaning, for instance, are first of all practical activities related to the functional dimension of our life. So are the cooking and baking dispositions we may develop over the years. We may cook and bake well because we feel moved also by a transcendent motivation to really care for those for whom we prepare a meal. We may appreciate them as maintained by the same formation mystery that makes us be. We may cook and bake in such a way that we do not unnecessarily disturb others with our activities. This concern, too, may be motivated by a transcendent respect for others and their unique calling in the great scheme of things. If this is so, a transcendent motivation enters into the core of our specific functional approach to cooking and baking. In that case we may say that the functional disposition is simultaneously a spiritual disposition. In some measure it is coformed by our transcendent apprehension, appraisal, and affirmation.

All dispositions, including those not influenced by our transcendent dimension, are somehow formative. They help us in some way to give form to our life and world. We may weed the garden and feel quite disposed to do so without any transcendent motivation whatsoever. Yet we cannot deny that such weeding gives a certain form to the garden and indirectly to our own muscle tone and manual dexterity. It is formative without being necessarily *spiritually* formative: in this case, it does not contribute directly to our distinctively human formation.

Briefly, spiritual form dispositions are to varying extents under the direction of the transcendent dimension of our life. Other dispositions are not directed that way. This does not necessarily mean that they are at odds with the formation of our life. They may be coformative to the degree that they fit into the consonant formation scheme of our life as a whole. For instance, the routine way in which we tie our shoes may not be influenced in the least by any transcendent appraisal or motivation. It may be merely a remnant of childhood training. Yet this routine disposition happens to be in conformity with the customs of the population to which we belong. It facilitates the consonance of our life within this population. By the same token, spiritual people may include all they do, even tying their shoelaces, in the overall spiritual meaning of their life as symbolized in the form tradition to which they are committed.

Such differences make it clear that the word disposition, as used in the science of formation, is an analogous term. This means that some of its meaning is the same for all kinds of dispositions, yet other aspects have a different meaning, depending on the different kinds of dispositions involved. For instance, the dispositions of weeding the garden and of religious contemplation are the same insofar as any disposition implies a certain inclination, proficiency, memory, project, and affinity power. They are different in their object and motivation and in the life dimension they primarily involve.

Distinctions between Dispositions

The science of formative spirituality looks at all dispositions in relation to the transcendent dimension. In the light of this relationship, we can make a general distinction between dispositions that are influenced by our spirit and those that are not. Only the former can be called *spiritual* form dispositions. They are in some measure affiliated with the transcendent dimension of our life. Because of this affiliation with the human spirit, they contribute to distinctively human formation. It does not matter by what higher or lower dimension of our life this disposition is formed initially. It can be functional, vital, or sociohistorical. As long as it is affiliated with our spirit, it serves our spiritual formation.

Various form dispositions may be more or less intimately connected with the spiritual life. In regard to the intimacy of this relationship, we can distinguish two main types of spiritual form dispositions. Those having a *primary* affiliation with the transcendent dimension constitute the first type. Those having only a *secondary* affiliation with our spirit belong to the second.

The disposition of prayerful contemplation is intimately affiliated with our power of transcendent appraisal, with our spirit as such. We cannot imagine its possibility without the human spirit. The disposition of athletic sportsmanship, by contrast, may or may not become affiliated with our spiritual life. If it does, it is a spiritual disposition, but it could exist without this affiliation, which spiritualizes it in a secondary sense. This transcendency is not inherent in the primordial structure of the disposition of sportsmanship as such. This differentiation between primary and secondary affiliation is the basis for other distinctions regarding the dispositions pertaining to the transcendent, functional, vital, and sociohistorical form dimensions.

Transcendent and Functional Form Dispositions

A transcendent form disposition has a primordial or essential affiliation with our spiritual life. It is impossible for such a disposition to survive if it is separated from our spiritual powers. An example is the disposition of aspiration for union with the transcendent mystery of formation. The potency for this aspiration is always in us as a kind of predisposition. It becomes an actual disposition when we cultivate it by reiteration of corresponding acts of aspiration.

A functional form disposition can also be affiliated with our spirit. This connection, however, is not necessary for the survival of the disposition. It is only a secondary connection. The link can be strong or tenuous; it can be cultivated or neglected, maintained or lost. The disposition of a functional ambition to be a diligent housewife can be inspired by transcendent motives. This spiritual motivation can be total or partial, continuous or intermittent. The same disposition could as well be motivated by mainly functional concerns. Functional mind and will are then almost totally in control.

The functional dimension may maintain a vague and tenuous connection with one's spiritual life and thus still in some measure be a spiritual form dimension. We may even venture to say that a total absence of any spiritual influence on functional mind and will, no matter how slight, may be rare. Some people, for example, seem to live only out of an ambitious disposition for political power. Their life appears to be without any spiritual influence. Yet their striving to go on living, even when they lose any chance for political power, may rest on a vague spiritual awareness that life has to be meaningful in a more basic sense. On occasions such as illness, death in the family, loss of position or possessions, a glimmer of this spiritual awareness may surface.

An exclusively functional disposition would not be *distinctively* human. It could not be called a spiritual disposition. The functional mind and will would in no way be sparked by the spirit, not even implicitly.

Routinizing Dispositions

A mere functional disposition would be either a *routinizing* or a routine disposition. The verb *routinize* is used here to indicate an ongoing, active, alert direction by the functional mind and will. This direction is not an inspiring but a routinizing one. The functional dimension of our life-form selects past routines that promise to be useful in the present situation. It may imitate successful routines of others. It may as well initiate new routines, if this seems desirable. Because the routinizing disposition disposes people to *actual* routinizing, it is essentially different from a mere routine disposition.

An example would be the disposition to routinize ritual. One goes through the ritual customs and rubrics routinely without inspiration or spiritual presence. Yet one is disposed to maintain a functional alertness to any adaptation that may be demanded by the type and number of attendants or by the special occasion to be celebrated. This is an example of a routinizing disposition that is dissonant and deformative. Participation in religious ritual should be formative. To be consonant with its meaning, there should be some spiritual involvement or interest, at least in intention, if not in feeling.

Not all routinizing dispositions are dissonant and deformative. Consonant routinizing dispositions are possible. Driving our car efficiently is based on a routinizing disposition. We drive almost automatically. The word *almost* is crucial here: our functional mind must be alert for any adjustment to be made in view of traffic signals, other drivers, pedestrians, and emergencies. We adapt our driving routine continuously to changes in our field of action. Skillful adaptation is built into our driving disposition. Yet we try to routinize our driving as much as possible. The disposition of driving a car is in some measure consonant with our life formation as a whole. For one thing, the routinized disposition helps us not to use up our energy unnecessarily. Still, a deeper consonance can be attained when the routinized disposition is also done in the light of the formation mystery. It remains the same routinized disposition, mainly directed by functional mind and will, yet it is linked to our spiritual presence by simple intention.

During the routinizing exercise of the disposition, there may be no explicit attention to its position in the spiritual scheme of things. This direction and motivation can be renewed, however, at other moments in which one deliberately reaffirms this transcendent orientation. In the long run, a steady renewal of orientation may begin implicitly to influence one's routinizing driving disposition. While remaining the same in its main source and execution, an implicit spiritual motivation may deepen preconsciously our caring involvement in safe and courteous driving.

Routine Dispositions

A routine disposition is one in which the active direction and alertness of functional mind and will is absent for all intents and purposes. The functional mind in this case would not be at all vigilant. It would abstain from any active direction in principle, which is to say that it would stay out of the routine operation for the sake of fostering efficiency. A routine could not operate perfectly if the functional mind were in any way to watch or interfere with it.

An example of a functional routine disposition would be the way a man puts on his tie. He does not have to routinize that action because it is totally routinized already. If he begins to think about it, how to do it precisely, or if he starts to watch each detail of the sequence, he interferes with the routine and disturbs its smooth operation.

Like routinizing dispositions, so also routine dispositions can be taken up in one's spiritual life orientation. One can explicitly ennoble and enrich them with this meaning at moments of overall life orientation outside the routine action itself. A routine disposition, which is already functionally consonant, then becomes also spiritually consonant. It becomes simultaneously a transcendent form disposition. It is still a routine disposition, but no longer a *merely* routine disposition.

Functional routinizing and routine dispositions are not *distinctively* human. This is not to say that they are not human at all. Evidently they are human in some way. For one thing, infrahuman life does not develop the more intricate routines humans do. However, these routines are not *distinctively* human if they are not in any way enlightened by the spiritual orientation and presence of the human person. Routinizing functional intelligence can be easily incorporated and expanded in computers and robots. The same could be said a priori of mere routines, because none of them are distinctively human. The science of formation for this reason feels indebted to the development of robots and computers. One could not imagine a more compelling demonstration of the difference between what is distinctively human or spiritual and what is merely functional intelligence.

Vital and Sociohistorical Dispositions

Vital form dispositions differ from functional ones. They have their origin in needs and acts that stem from vital pulsions. For instance, purely physical-sexual dispositions originate in the vital-sexual drive in reaction to stimulation in the vital formation field. Such repeated stimulation and corresponding reaction can give rise to routine sexual dispositions. These begin to give form to sexual behavior easily, consistently, and pleasurably. Hence they become vital-sexual form dispositions. Ideally they should be related to both the functional and transcendent life dimensions. When this happens, a slow and gradual process of intelligent functionalization and elevating spiritualization is initiated. These processes may progressively reform, elevate, and deepen the vital-sexual form disposition without necessarily paralyzing its consonant carnal knowledge and passion.

Our sociohistorical dispositions originate in the cultural pulsations we share with our society. They may become ours by what we call *situational osmosis*. Mere sociohistorical dispositions give rise to the routine performance of acts that are in accordance with such pulsations. It was the pleasurable reiteration of such acts confirmed by others, that led in the first place to the formation of this kind of disposition. The subsequent acts were executed with increasing ease, consistency, pleasure, and satisfaction. This strengthened the disposition. Such dispositions take into account the vital pulsions embedded in and excited by the sociohistorical pulsations.

Many Germans, for instance, initially followed Adolf Hitler without any functional-intelligent or spiritual reflection. They assimilated by situational osmosis the pulsations moving the excited masses in the stadiums and public squares filled with symbols of a new source of vital power and passion. For many this event marked the birth of corresponding sociohistorical dispositions in their somewhat drab and unexciting lives. Another example is the unquestioning investment of one's dispositions in new fads that may stir a religious or secular population at a certain moment of its formation history.

An interiorized pulsation that has become a routine sociohistorical disposition can still be rejected or purified by its carrier. It can be elevated to the level of intelligent appraisal and control by the functional-critical mind, or it can be spiritualized by the transcendent mind. In that case it becomes a secondary spiritual form disposition without losing any consonant contribution that may have been inherent in certain sociohistorical pulsations.

Overview of Different Form Dispositions

Before discussing some implications of these various dispositions for formation, it might be helpful to summarize briefly what we have discovered thus far.

All dispositions having to do with our spirit are in some degree spiritual dispositions. They can be spiritual either in a primary or a secondary sense. If their affiliation with the spirit is necessary, we classify them as primary. Otherwise they are secondary because their affiliation with the spirit is not necessary for their survival.

As for dispositions in our functional, vital and sociohistorical dimensions, each has to be appraised individually in terms of its relationship to the spiritual life. To the degree that there is some affiliation with the spiritual life, albeit not a necessary one, they can be classified as secondary spiritual form dispositions.

We distinguished also merely functional dispositions. They are not spiritualized in the secondary sense. They may or may not be in dialogue with the functional mind and will. Depending on this relationship, they are either routinizing or routine dispositions. They are routinizing if some dialogical relationship is maintained between the functional disposition and the functional mind. They remain in potential or actual contact with functional mind and will. If there is no connection between the functional disposition and the functional mind and will, they are functional routine dispositions.

The same applies to vital and sociohistorical dispositions. They are merely routine, or they can become routinized or spiritualized. The latter happens when we initiate a dialogical relationship between them and the functional and transcendent mind and will.

One of the many auxiliary sciences we draw upon is experimental psychology, which has focused its attention mainly on routinizing and especially on routine dispositions (which psychologists usually call *habits*). This limited specialization in only one kind of disposition is advantageous for our integrational science of formation. Such specialized attention to one aspect of human formation can provide formation science with detailed insights and findings that otherwise would not be available. The only danger is that people may assume that the partial findings of one important auxiliary science cover all there is to know about their formation. Already the term habit has been so exclusively applied to routinized and routine dispositions by experimental psychology that we cannot use it any longer without running the risk of misunderstanding, mainly because of its mechanistic connotations; hence the use of the term *disposition* in formation science.

Disposition Formation

At this juncture it may be proper to suggest some principles regarding disposition formation. As a general rule, all dispositions are initiated and developed by their corresponding acts. The disposition of typing is initiated by the act of typing. Something similar can be said of spiritual dispositions. We learn to pray by praying, to love by loving, to be appreciative by appreciating. There is, however, a difference between the effective ways of initiating various dispositions. It depends on what kind of dispositions we are considering.

There are three main sources of disposition formation: motivation, reiteration, participation. These factors do not have the same effectiveness for the formation of every kind of disposition.

Motivation and Reiteration

All spiritual dispositions, whether primordial or secondary, require a *motivation* that has a certain spiritual depth. To establish a prayerful disposition, a disposition of loving respect for people, or an appreciation for fine art requires a motivation deeper than that pertaining, say, to being the life of the party. If such a spiritual motivation is not ours, no matter how often we reiterate the act, the disposition will not be rooted in our life. If we cultivate this deeper motivation, accompanied by *reiteration* and increasingly wholehearted *participation*, the spiritual form-disposition after which we aspire will gradually be established.

Routinizing dispositions require motivation, too. This motivation is not necessarily as deep as that needed for spiritual acts. Functional motivation will suffice. To develop an athletic disposition, for instance, it may be sufficient to be attracted by such functional gains as dexterity, fitness, a feeling of well-being, or perhaps some social or economic advantage. Such motivations engage us in the reiteration of athletic acts until the disposition is established.

The initiation of a spiritual disposition must be supported by a motivation for things not immediately seen and experienced, not tangible and instantaneous. Attraction in this case must come from a deeper center of the personality. This attraction is easily overwhelmed by the demands of everyday life, at least in the beginning. If our spiritual motivation loses its strength and is not renewed, it will soon be impossible to persevere in the reiteration of spiritual acts. Hence, we affirm the necessity of reflection and meditation on the meaning and content of spiritual aspirations that invite us to seek the transcendent formation of life.

Finally, routine dispositions are almost exclusively the fruit of reiteration alone. Dressing, talking, sleeping, eating, and so on, result from reiteration of actions partly or totally rooted in our preformation and early environment. It would be a mistake to try to form in the same way a spiritual disposition. Imposed reiteration, without sufficient attention to building spiritual motivation, is not an effective means of fostering transcendent dispositions.

Participation

Participation as a condition for disposition formation covers four areas, namely, participation in the source of all form dispositions, in one's foundational life-form, formation field, and form tradition.

The higher and more demanding the form disposition to be initiated, the more we become aware of the insufficiency of our own limited form potency. Feelings of discouragement and failure could prevail unless we abandon ourselves to a higher power. The faith and hope that we can effectively participate in the mystery of formation that indwells in our own tenuous form potency enables us to develop dispositions in spite of our weakness. Alcoholics Anonymous, for example, utilizes this principle of disposition formation in an exemplary way.

Participation in one's foundational life-form immensely strengthens disposition formation if this formation is congenial. The initiation of form dispositions should be interwoven, if possible, with dispositions we have already developed in congeniality with the unique image we are called to realize in life. Similarly, new disclosures of this hidden form should support the unfolding of the new disposition.

The formation of a disposition will be appropriately enhanced and fortified if we develop it in flexible consonance with the formation field. Dispositions are responses to this field and the arena in which one lives them out.

Finally, participation in form tradition is necessary for the initiation, maintenance, and unfolding of dispositions. Dispositions and traditions are intimately interwoven. One cannot be fully understood without the other. Form traditions are alive in the dispositions they foster and exemplify in their adherents. All major dispositions familiar to us can be traced back to religious, ideological, familiar, form-segmental, phasic, and professional form traditions. These traditions provide not only descriptions and exemplars of such dispositions but also motivations toward them. They create an environment and atmosphere of similarly disposed people that facilitate the development of dispositions in consonance with the formation field. Traditions sustain the motivations they suggest by apt symbols and rituals. Wholehearted participation in such traditions is an effective way of being initiated in their favored dispositions and of persevering in them.

Deactivation or Reformation of Dissonant Dispositions

The deactivation or reformation of dissonant dispositions is difficult because of their emotional hold over us. Simply trying to eliminate a personal disposition without its replacement by an opposite does not seem to be the most effective approach. The replacing disposition has to exclude coexistence with the dissonant one. For instance, the disposition to depreciation can best be overcome by the opposite disposition of appreciation. Simple reiteration of a few isolated acts of appreciation would be insufficient. One should motivate oneself to grow in appreciation as such. Participation in a consonant form tradition can be of great help. This presupposes, however, that one personally reflect and meditate on what the form tradition has to offer in regard to motivating the desired disposition.

It may be possible to undo dispositions by omission of corresponding acts. After a certain period of time the undesirable routine may drop out. It is no longer a customary part of our repertoire of routines. In some cases it may be helpful to substitute temporarily a somewhat similar but innocuous routine for the harmful one. I remember a person who discovered that his smoking disposition was partly bound to the routine of holding something in his mouth while he worked. He substituted the routine of taking a toothpick between his lips at any time the urge for a cigarette emerged. In his case it worked. After a few months and countless toothpicks, he overcame his smoking disposition. A while later he was no longer interested in the toothpicks either.

The science of formative spirituality wants to assist people in the exercise of their limited freedom via transcendent and functional mind and will. It fosters the initiation and development of flexible dispositions in the service of one's spiritual formation and growth. Formation science tries to overcome what it calls formation ignorance. It promotes reflective awareness and attention as necessary conditions for the initiation or reformation of dispositions. The longer the pertinent formation of questions regarding one's dispositions are delayed or denied, the more any emergent awareness of them evokes irritation, anxiety, and guilt. People may return to ignorance in order to escape such anxiety. They may fear the possible discovery that they are lacking in some basic dispositions. For instance, they may defensively exalt functionality in and by itself as the main or only meaning of life. This saves them from the necessity of appraising the absence of transcendent form dispositions. An escape like this is in the end counterproductive. It leads to deformation, not formation.

Spiritualization of Dispositions

In considering dispositions in relation to the various life dimensions, we reflected on the intraformative movement of spiritualization. Dispositions should be illumined and mellowed by the spirit. Otherwise they are obstacles to the full and free unfolding of our spiritual life. They block our foundational life-form as a unique epiphany of the formation mystery in which it is rooted. We cannot awaken to our deepest being without awakening to the mystery from which it continuously emerges in its beauty and nobility, its joy and serenity. In and through the gift of this hidden form, we are present to the Holy, the unspeakable One who fills the universe. United with the mystery, we are open to its direction as manifested in our formation field. This field is pervaded and transformed by the same mystery that makes us be.

The routinizing and routine aspects of dispositions tend to hamper this openness and flexibility, this flow with the mystery, if they are harsh and unyielding. Hence, full spiritualization implies a softening of traces of rigidity in the routine aspects of our dispositions. Mere routinizing and routine, if idolized, constitute basic obstacles to liberation. This is especially true of routine dispositions of the mind.

Spiritual formation aims at a gradual shattering of the rigidity of inflexible routines of appraisal. This does not mean that routines as such are rejected as useless. What is changed is their meaning, function, and position in our life. Instead of dominating our appraisal, they become like tools at hand, ready to be taken up when the spirit signals that they can be used proficiently in service of its aspirations. We become detached from them. We no longer identify with our dispositions as if the secondary foundational life-form they provide is our real self.

Once we discover our truest and most primordial form of life as embedded in the mystery, our dispositional life-form becomes relativized. Our transition to the fullness of the spiritual life means a release from the hold which rigidified routines of apprehension, appraisal, affirmation, and action exercise over us. It is not so much a change from one routine to another as a liberation from our attachment to the routine process itself. We may secretly fear that we would fall apart without the rigor of these routines. This bond is slowly lifted and finally dissolved. We are no longer the slave of our mental and emotional dispositions. The patterns are still there, available when useful. They are activated in consonance with the rhythms of the epiphanies of the formation mystery. These rhythms are intensely creative and far from repetitive. They cannot be encapsulated in any exhaustive conception or prediction. Nevertheless, we may be tempted to capture these rhythmic flows in our appraisal dispositions. This cripples our capacity to transcend such dispositions when the flow of the mystery carries us beyond past appraisals and appreciations.

The mystery of formation is a mystery of renewal, creativity, and change. The consonant use of repetition and routine is not in itself opposed to this creative presence in our life. What hampers the creativity of the mystery is the ossification of dispositions, the idolization of them as life directives that would override the inspirations and aspirations of the spirit. Idolized routines are the synonym of the death of the spirit. The inertia of routines weighs us down. The spirit cannot soar upward. The dynamism of our form potency is stilted or curtailed. The gift of our primordial life-form becomes barely discernible under the straitjacket of secondary patterns of life. Their grip becomes all powerful, their encapsulation absolute.

Release from the Dominance of Unappraised Pulsations

This condition is aggravated if it mirrors historical pulsations that have not been appraised personally and spiritually. When the spirit illumines the functional mind, we become aware of our blind servility to slogans and catchwords, fads and fancies, in-people and movements. We discover how much they dominate our routinizing and routine movements. The prison of unappraised routines begins to open. Our formation ignorance begins to be illumined by glimpses of our call to transcendent formation. Initially, however, our response is still mainly on the level of the now liberated functional mind and will. This dimension, when not directed by the consonant spirit, is easily dominated by the autarchic pride-form deep within us. One becomes excited by one's own daring reaction against historical pulsations that overpowered one's potency of appraisal.

The autarchic pride-form of the soul is always ready to parade as the true foundational form of life. It grasps this occasion to seduce the newly released functional appraisal power. It attempts to initiate new appraisal dispositions that will value everything now in terms of autonomous self-actualization and fulfillment. This is the final and perhaps most dangerous illusion. It gives rise to countless illusions in regard to one's formation field. This field is seen through the distorting glasses of one's excessive self-assertion. These illusions of autarchy must be purged and transcended. Then the road will be open to spiritual unfolding beyond idolized dispositions. We may be lifted into the heart of the mystery itself, the supreme source, that eludes the grasp of any disposition of the human mind.

Illumination of Dispositions

When the spirit is illumined in its encounter with the mystery, it mirrors this light into all dimensions and articulations of our formation. The same light shines into our dispositions. Having lost their rigidity, they are not only "disposing for" but "at the disposal of" the mystery. Dispositions will always be necessary as extensions of our human form potencies into the formation field. The mystery of formation is not only to be contemplated. It intends to form the world with and through us.

Hence, we see the necessity of adaptative dispositions as bridges between inspirations and the concrete formation fields we are called to cultivate. These dispositions should be available to the mystery. The disposition that is mellowed by the mystery is no longer deterministic, deformative, or dissonant. It performs its functions fluently in harmony with its deepest source.

Enlightened dispositions imply both regularity and spontaneity. Regularity contains the perpetual danger of stifling spontaneity. Spontaneity, on the other hand, threatens life with dissolution and arbitrariness. There is no cure for this polarity of the disposition. It is up to us to keep both elements in balance in the light of the spirit. When spontaneity is silent the consonant disposition will still carry us forward by its pattern of regularity. It enables us to remain faithful in actions that give consonant form to life and world at moments when spontaneous feelings do not move us in that direction. This aspect of regularity is essential.

We are not formative people because we act sometimes in consonant ways. We have only become consonant when we are disposed to act this way on a regular basis. The absence of spontaneous feeling and alertness at the moment of the realization of a form disposition does not impair its formative power. People extending kindness and courtesy to fellow human beings are a benediction regardless of whether they steadily feel a spontaneous warmth toward others. The initial decision to be confirmative of others, embedded in the disposition, is carried out in the apparent life-form regardless of one's changeable mood and feeling. There is no deception in this appearance if it incarnates one's honest will and intention. In this way our dispositions are liberated from the capriciousness of moods and feelings.

CHAPTER 3

Spontaneous and Deliberate Disposition Formation

D isposition formation implies two poles: spontaneous and deliberate. If one of these falls away, the formation of our dispositions may be either hampered or falsified.

To speak of specifically human or spiritual formation does not mean that only the transcendent dimension of our life unfolds. This dimension is not isolated from the sociohistorical, the vital, and the functional. Human or spiritual formation means that our dispositional life unfolds in all of these dimensions in the light of the human spirit. In the measure that this unfolding happens freely and harmoniously under the impetus of a person's transcendent inspirations and aspirations, we call it *spiritual* formation. To foster such unfolding, formative reflection and guidance are necessary, together with two interrelated processes: differentiation and integration.

Differentiation of Form Dispositions

When we look more closely at the unfolding and formation of human life, we become aware of both the differentiation of dispositions and their integration. These two movements form a polarity in our spiritual life.

The movement of differentiation of general form dispositions is one of disclosure of their implicit specific nuances and of the implementation of such nuances in new specific dispositions. In the case of spiritual formation, such specific nuances are disclosed in the light of the inspirations and aspirations of human life. To be in spiritual formation is to be present to the formation mystery and, in its light, to self, people, events, and things as they manifest themselves in our formation field. This disposition of presence in general becomes increasingly differentiated in special dispositions. For example, a person may be present to art in transcendent admiration, to the suffering of others in inspired care, to nature in respectful curiosity. The human spirit is operative in all of these dispositions. They are examples of the differentiation and articulation of the disposition of human presence as such.

This differentiation is not only a movement to disclose new life directives; it also attempts to assimilate and incorporate the subsequently affirmed and deepened modes of presence in corresponding dispositions.

Integration of Form Dispositions

If formation were only a differentiation of mutually unrelated dispositions, life would become disorganized and lose its centeredness. Therefore, another movement has to complement this necessary differentiation. This balancing movement is that of integration.

Differentiation divides; integration unifies human presence. For example, people may experience the formation mystery in a new light by discovering a different mode of being present to it. They may be so absorbed in this experience that they temporarily lose the integration of their empirical life-form. They may neglect other areas of living, for instance, letting their studies slide, losing sight of the demands of their health, being less attentive to their family or friends. The newly emerging disposition almost seems to exclude others. One needs the movement of integration to restore wholeness and consonance. Integration enables them to reactivate these dispositions and to harmonize them with newly discovered modes of presence.

Another example would be that of people who take on a new field of study. They may become so involved in this area of differentiation that they fail temporarily to be attentive to the mystery of formation. The formation of life by differentiation gives rise to the disclosure of a new task or study. Integrative formation in this case does not necessarily mean the denial of these new experiences and ambitions nor a rejection of the subsequent new dispositions. Integration is to take place within the totality of the person's empirical form of life. Formative appraisal and reflection guide this natural movement of integration, which is potentially operative in all human formation.

Spiritual formation entails both movements. It wisely takes into account and guides both the differentiation and integration of dispositions as they are found in one's spontaneous unfolding. Growth always implies ongoing differentiation and integration of the dispositions of apprehension, appraisal, affirmation, memory, imagination, and anticipation. This differentiation may lead to a temporary loss of balance at moments when a person feels overly anxious or excited about a new experience or field of interest. This temporary loss of balance will not be detrimental if the person allows room for the inner movement of integration and guides the latter by wise formative appraisal. Then the discovered life directives and subsequent dispositions may be accorded their rightful place in the emergent empirical form of life.

Tension Evoked by the Polar Movement of Disposition Formation

People may at times fear the tensions that result from the polarity of the formation movement. They may want to escape the intervals of creative discontinuity. They are tempted to say: "I have reached a moment of peace and integration in my life; please let me stop differentiation. Don't get me involved in the new projects of people, their ideals, problems, and directions. Such differentiation will make me lose again the form of life I have currently attained; it takes so much time and energy to integrate new concerns by initiation of appropriate dispositions. Please don't distress me with disposition change. Don't expose me to another environment, to other readings, to the needs of people, to new insights in my own deficiencies. Preserve me from new inspirations. Don't interrupt my routine. Don't demand other activities that will diminish my peace of mind. Let me alone, at least for the time being."

Such laments are understandable. We momentarily lose peace of mind. It takes time to integrate new modes of prayer, of social action, or of study by initiation of corresponding dispositions. Integration may demand a restructuring of what one has done for many years, of one's apprehension, appreciation, affirmation, memory, imagination, and anticipation. It may affect our other dispositions and their structural hierarchy. It is the price we have to pay for growth. The alternative is to become fixated in one stage of life, or one set of stilted dispositions. If one's life is no longer differentiating, one will die as a person before dying physically. Yet if one is to differentiate and integrate one's life wisely in such a way that it fosters spiritual growth, one cannot leave this developmental task to spontaneous movements alone. One has to be guided by formative appraisal, at least implicitly.

The result of integration, by reordering or reforming dispositions and initiating new ones, should never be seen as a frozen thinglike state. Nor does it mean putting our dispositions in a deep freeze after ordering them. Integration is not a state but a movement. This movement will go on as long as we are keenly and humbly aware that there are always dispositions to initiate, reform, and integrate. In other words, integration is possible only when our life of dispositions keeps dynamically differentiating. Differentiation and integration depend on one another. One process cannot take place without the other.

Principle of Spiritual Integration of Dispositions

From our discussion and the examples given thus far, we may have gained some insight into the relation between the spontaneous and deliberate formation of dispositions. The formation of dispositions implies reflection on our spontaneous unfolding and its movements of differentiation and integration.

The moment we begin to reflect on formation, we can critically appraise our subsequent reflections and compare them with the reflections of others. We can also search for more information that will enrich our thoughts. During this process, certain reflections may reveal universal principles that are foundational to any attempt to give form to our spontaneous unfolding. We may then try to integrate such principles systematically into a theory of formation.

Thus we begin to sense the possibility of the emergence of a science of formation. To deepen our awareness of both the possibility and the desirability of such a science, let us reflect further on the nature of formative integration. We need to integrate our differentiated dispositions in the light of our deepest, transcendent presence to our formation field. This presence is communal and unique. We are invited to disclose and live a life direction that is congenial with the unique demands of our foundational form of life and compatible with the life situations and formative communities in which we are inserted by the formation mystery in its historical epiphanies. Hence our personal integration should be guided by a unifying spiritual life direction, insofar as it has become manifest to us at this moment of our life.

In the light of this emergent direction, we discover that we cannot live all of our differentiating dispositions at the same time and with the same intensity. We cannot simultaneously meditate, assist the poor, study, enjoy music, and play baseball. In short, the activation of certain form dispositions must be preferred to others, according to the demands of our life situation. For example, at one time we should meditate and not worry about our studies; at another time we should study and not be concerned about meditation.

Integration presupposes, therefore, a certain order of preference in our dispositions. To put this another way: true integration implies a hierarchy of dispositions. According to this hierarchy some dispositions will be central in our lives and others will be subordinated to such primary dispositions. The integral direction of our life will imply similar, but not identical directives in other dispositions that are less central. This hierarchy, in turn, will be in tune with the present manifestation of our foundational life direction.

To guide us wisely in the unfolding of this harmonization of our human presence, we can benefit again from a universal science of formative spirituality. This spirituality should draw its wisdom from consonant form traditions in dialogue with the findings of the arts and sciences. This wisdom should enlighten and deepen our communal and personal reflections in service of the hierarchical formation of our dispositional life.

For adherents of religious form traditions, the disposition of presence to the mystery of formation and to its communal and unique direction of their life will be most central. They foster other dispositions and their directives, insofar as they do not oppose but rather deepen their transcendent commitment. Transcendent presence does not exclude other dispositions, like those for friendship, social presence, study, technique, appreciation of aesthetic surroundings, pleasant entertainment. All of these dispositions and their directives can participate in one's transcendent and inspired presence, provided they are in harmony with one's foundational life direction.

Spontaneous and Deliberate Formation of Dispositions

Experience and observation make it clear that there is a spontaneous movement of unfolding in every human life. Our deliberate formation of dispositions should always be in dialogue with this movement. Therefore, formation cannot be understood in its foundational reality without an understanding of the spontaneous movements of life's unfolding within the human person. We could describe spiritual formation as an ongoing dialogue or a creative tension between the human spirit as formative and life's spontaneous unfolding.

Deliberate formation does not mean the imposition of a predetermined set of dispositions on our own spontaneous formation or on that of others. A deliberate formation of dispositions should be consonant. This implies, among other things, that people who subject their disposition formation to the deliberate direction of other people or of form traditions should do so in dialogue with their own unique form potency as it manifests itself in one's spontaneous disposition unfolding.

The idea of consonant formation presupposes that there are certain universal form directives in accordance with which the formation of our dispositions can take place. Here, however, we have to make an important distinction. While we may know which distinctively human form directives should direct the formation of our dispositions, we cannot foresee precisely how we ourselves or others should realize these directives concretely in our dispositions and actions. We do not know in advance how these directives will give form to our life or in what communal and unique way we should make them concrete. We cannot anticipate which distinctively human directives will play the most decisive role in our disposition formation or in the formation of others. Nor can we immediately be sure about the path people should follow in order to realize in their dispositions the form directives that are congenial and compatible in their life formation. While certain formative dispositions may be known to us in a general way as desirable, the concrete form these dispositions will assume and the way to develop them are not immediately known.

Spiritual or distinctively human formation implies, in fact, two principles: the principles of respect for the calling and life direction of the person and the principle of giving form to his or her spontaneous life formation by means of dispositions that are congenial, compatible, and compassionate. Formation becomes deficient or even deformative if one of these two principles is either denied or onesidedly emphasized.

Formation versus Molding

Formation may be misunderstood as a matter of molding people's dispositions in accordance with one's own idea or with sociohistorical pulsations. Some formation counselors think and act as if disposition formation is exclusively or mainly dependent on their own opinions and actions. They are overly sure of their own wisdom, excessively critical, and openly or implicitly patronizing. The natural and graced powers of formation, which reside within each human life they try to direct, are not appreciated, and perhaps are even distrusted. Such distrust is manifest, for example, in the puritanical view of formation.

Inexperienced formation directors and counselors may be so convinced of the worthwhileness of one concrete form or specific embodiment of a form disposition that they feel compelled to impose it upon their own spontaneous life formation or that of their directees. They look at a form disposition proposed by a form tradition as if it were a "thing." They limit its potential manifold expressions within human life to the special manifestation they have in mind, convinced that they know the one exclusive way in which this disposition should be implemented in their own life or that of others.

In this view, formation means, in fact, the molding of our constellation of dispositions until it is in conformity with a special model. The formative director is active; the directee is passive. The director is the subject, the directee the object of this molding process. Moreover, molding is mainly understood in a negative way. It consists principally in the removal of dispositions that are incompatible with the collective or personal model that is proposed. Hence, the mistaken notion emerges that formation of dispositions means first of all to correct or prevent any deviations from the collective or personal model. This notion implies the idea that formation directors have the essential right to engage in such arbitrary corrections.

Another principle of molding people is that reward and punishment are the best means of disposition formation. This view of formation was practiced by certain formation institutes in the past when formation was often equated with molding.

If disposition formation meant merely molding life in accordance with a collective or personal model, and if this molding were merely a matter of correction and prevention, the question would arise: What is it that has to be molded? What makes correction and prevention possible in the first place? The answer seems to be: the spontaneous formation of human life with which the formation director is confronted. The spontaneous formation of life is in reality a condition to be taken into account critically and creatively in all consonant later correction. Therefore, the deliberate formation of dispositions ought to take into account spontaneous preformation.

We know that a human life to be formed must be able to unfold itself out of its own spontaneous form potency. One must remain active and able to unfold as a subject with one's own initiatives. What people cannot know in advance is the empirical form their life ought to assume. They cannot be sure about which directives and dispositions will make their congenial and compatible formation possible. Nor do they know the succession of life situations in and through which they will have to disclose such directives while implementing them in dispositions and actions.

Our reflection on the structure of formation thus reveals an element of initiative or originality in the life-to-be-formed. Each human life must be in some measure the author, or perhaps better still the coauthor of its own disposition formation. It is true that people cannot know in advance what their empirical life-form ultimately will be or which path they should take to disclose and implement the directives that seem to point to the life-form disposed for them by the mystery of formation. Yet this process of trying out tentative directives of human formation implies a certain initiative on their part. Human life cannot be a sponge that indiscriminately soaks up all the directives that come its way.

Relative Autonomy of Human Formation

This element of originality in disposition formation should not be seen in isolation from the whole process of formation as if other elements were not equally important. Fidelity to one's originality should not be totalized as if it were the whole of formation. Such a onesided emphasis would lead to the misunderstanding that people should be exclusively autonomous in choosing their life direction and in devising the subsequent constellation of dispositions this direction implies.

Many today may fall into a mistaken view of disposition formation. The inclination to exclusive autonomy can be understood if we look at its development historically. In the past, one's life direction and dispositional life-form were more or less fixed and familiar. Medieval society, for example, was much more homogeneous than our present-day culture is. When that society broke down, it was succeeded by relatively isolated subcultures formed exclusively around their own form traditions. Each subculture tended to determine for its people what their position and dispositional life-form should be. Within such a community, the life-form one should strive after seemed as familiar as the air everyone breathed. The style of life, dispositions, customs, and exercises that were needed to realize the approved cultural forms of life were carefully outlined by one's social status and particular form tradition. Certain modest variations of these traditional patterns were acceptable; however, they were far from revolutionary. In such a climate, not many would be tempted to choose or construe in exclusive autonomy their own dispositional form of life.

Today, however, the various subcultures have broken open. The rigorously delineated forms of life have fallen to pieces. People are faced with a variety of possible life-forms in a pluralistic society. It is in this highly diversified concrete world that people are called to give form to their existence. In personal dialogue with the foundations of their form traditions, they begin to disclose their own possibilities for living a consonant life. They realize also that their own life-form should be developed in personal interaction with the situations in which they find themselves.

As a result of daily dialogue with a pluralistic society and a bewildering array of suggestions from the media and from the arts and sciences, people become more than ever a question for themselves. It is not surprising that they may fall victim to the illusion that they alone, in exclusive automony, must disclose and implement a consonant constellation of form dispositions. Irritated by the fixations of the past still lingering on today, and preoccupied with effective adaptation to the present, they may feel unreasonably adverse to the wisdom of any form tradition in regard to disposition formation. This prejudice may prevent their interformative interaction with such traditions. They reject or neglect the traditions that reveal *foundational* lasting truths that should inspire any dispositional form of life. The more we seek new adaptations, the more we need to be rooted in founding form traditions.

Another negative aspect of the search for a contemporary spiritual formation is an increasing vulnerability to the excessive claims of certain self-styled gurus, prophets, spiritual masters, metapsychological therapists, encounter movements, and spiritualities inside and outside religious and ideological form traditions. Representatives of these movements and groups may be convinced that they can satisfy the need for a new contemporary way of spiritual life by means of original styles of disposition formation. They try to supply an answer to the inner need for novel formation directives. Often their mistake is that they imagine they know in precise detail what the exclusive style of life should be for their followers. Nobody can know exhaustively the mysterious life direction that awaits its awakening in each human journey. All people must conform in their disposition formation to certain basic truths; yet they are also called to be a *unique* expression of these truths.

There are universal foundational directives that should be basic for any disposition formation. Hence, formation can never be totally autonomous. We have to extract such universals from consonant form traditions. This extraction should be accompanied by dialogue with the formative and deformative experiences in one's own life and that of others and with the basic insights provided by the arts and sciences. But the assimilation of such necessary foundational insights is not enough to predict in precise detail what each human life will be like. No philosophy of nature, political ideology, ontology or theology of the person, anthropology or personality theory, psychology, or system of spirituality justifies an absolute prediction of the concrete future of a human life.

As noted earlier, disposition formation should always take into account the spontaneous unfolding of human life. This "taking into account" is an expression of our respect for the mystery of each person's life direction and preformation. It remains equally true that our spontaneous life formation needs to be balanced continuously by wise deliberate formation. The latter should be guided by critical reflection on and appraisal of our situated experiences. Both reflection and appraisal should be illumined by the universal foundational principles of formation that apply to all human life.

We conclude that spontaneous life formation needs the complement of deliberate disposition formation. Similarly deliberate disposition formation should be nourished constantly by spontaneous life formation. This deliberate formation can then become spontaneous and prereflective again. Disposition formation evokes a creative tension. One pole of this tension is spontaneous life formation; the other is deliberate formation. If either of the two poles disappears, the situation can no longer be called one of human formation. The ideal formative situation aims at a wise balance between the dynamic forces that emanate from both poles.

CHAPTER 4

Disposition Formation in Childhood

W e may not be inclined to think of spiritual formation as beginning in infancy. How can activities like feeding, cleaning, dressing, playing, and experiencing affective mothering have implications for the spiritual unfolding of a child? Are they not merely external? How can they affect the dispositions of an infant?

It is difficult for us to believe that spiritual formation can happen in infancy through bodily care. Most of us are haunted by a dualistic view of human life. We tend to split the transcendent from the vital-functional dimensions of life as if they were separate entities. This dualistic view may be the result of a Platonic or Neoplatonic model of human life. The Platonic model depicts the transcendent spirit as captivated and bound by a physical body. Similarly, we may have been influenced by Cartesian thinking, which posits a human consciousness segregated from what is called a "body thing." The only relation between the two is one of mutual causality; there is no mutually permeating unity.

Formation science holds that the human life-form is a substantial unity. It can be described as "spiritualized bodiliness" or "embodied spirit." In principle there is no dichotomy between body and spirit. This view is corroborated by modern sciences of human life. They, too, make clear that bodily influences can have implications for a person's spiritual formation.

Elementary occurrences in early childhood influence the formation of the dispositional life-form. Such influences may be regular or irregular patterns of feeding, the gradual or sudden weaning of the infant, harsh or gentle toilet training, the consistency or inconsistency of reward or punishment. If the first interformative interaction with the mother is satisfactory, it gives rise to an elementary dispositional triad of faith, hope, and love. This fundamental triad, awakened in the early mother-child relationship, is significant for the wholesome formation of the child's distinctively human or spiritual life.

The foundational formation theory, elaborated in Volume One, indicated that the primordial option and subsequent fundamental disposition of the consonant life entailed abandonment to the formation mystery. The triad of faith, hope, and love gives rise to this abandonment and the trust that flows from it. Hence the significance of this triad in infancy is unquestionable. The fundamental dispositions of human faith, hope, and love are communicated to children in bodily, interformative interaction with the mother or her substitute. She grants her children the basic experience of someone being there without whom they cannot *believe* that it is good to be alive, without whom they cannot *hope* that they will be able to do things well, without whom they cannot be in sympathy or *love* with themselves or others, and with whom everything will be fine in the end.

The three dispositions that constitute this original triad are intimately interwoven. Each of them is enhanced and deepened by the other. In the infant these dispositions are evoked in an elementary, implicit, and germinal way. The potentiality for them is inherent in the child's humanity. They can be awakened only by the mother or her substitute. The seminal faith, hope, and love experience of the child is a spontaneous reaction to her own manifested faith, hope, and love.

This spiritual disposition formation reaches the child via bodily manifestations. Between mother and child an interplay develops of mutual manifestations of the three foundational spiritual dispositions. This mutuality strengthens each of them. In this play of primordial spiritual sympathy, facial expressions, smiles, caresses, and other signs of reciprocal recognition are important. In fact, the manifested recognition of the child by the mother as a potentially believing, hoping, and loving form of life is the first confirmation of the child as a distinctively human subject. Such recognition confirms for children in prereflective ways that their mothers *believe* that they are worthwhile and unique, *hope* that they may make good in life by finding their right direction, and *love* them unconditionally.

This earliest meeting in mutual faith, hope, and love, no matter how vaguely and implicitly it is experienced, no matter how elementary its level, is the beginning of the child's spiritual formation. A child's later appreciative abandonment to the formation mystery is linked to this primordial event. Formative memory preserves traces of the awakening of the first seeds of the natural dispositions of faith, hope, and love that lie dormant in the spiritual core of each human life.

One could say the same of the influences of the sociohistorical situation of children on their formation. Poverty or riches, attitudes of family and neighbors, racial or cultural discrimination, the emotional climate created by the formation segment of the population to which one's family belongs —these along with other vital, functional, and transcendent influences are crucial: the infant's initial dispositional form of life emerges in bodily-spiritual interaction with its formation field.

Transcendent Life Dimension and Disposition Formation

Experience teaches us that human life is spiritual through and through. Certain acts of the human person are in some measure free and conscious. This means that they transcend the immediate sociohistorical and vital-functional determinations of human life. Something transcendent or spiritual is manifested in them. This dimension of human life can be distinguished essentially from other dimensions of the same life-form. In other words, the transcendent dimension cannot be explained as an outgrowth of its sociohistorical or vital-functional dimensions. However, this distinguishable transcendent dimension manifests itself constantly as a quality of our life as a whole. It is not possible to indicate a concrete line of division by saying, for example, that human life is transcendent from the neck up and vital-functional from the neck down.

It is impossible to identify *concrete* human acts that are purely transcendent. Overtly spiritual activities, such as praying, meditating or thinking, are sometimes thought of as purely transcendent. Even though these acts are primarily transcendent, they always have some vital-functional component. To exemplify this fact, we only need to look at an artistic representation of a meditating person. The posture and facial expression of the person-in-meditation express absorption in the sacred and detachment from daily involvement in the world. The artist paints the praying person in a bodily expression of prayerfulness. This manifestation is spontaneously experienced as belonging not only to the transcendent, but to the vital-functional dimensions as well.

Without this posture and facial expression, we would not recogize meditating as meditating. If the artist had painted the person as a ferocious soldier hacking down an enemy, he could not have spontaneously evoked in us the sense of a meditative stance. In other words, we recognize the transcendent dimension in the functional-vital manifestations of life. This dimension manifests itself both in vitally functioning human persons and in vitally functioning human communities.

This insight has consequences for our understanding of the spiritual disposition formation of each person. If the transcendent dimension is part of human life as a whole, then the operation and manifestation of this dimension will follow those channels and pathways of disposition formation already developed in the other prespiritual dimensions of the same personality.

Innate and Adopted Dispositions

We could posit life dimensions as primarily composed of "innate dispositions." In fact, our given life-form is preformed by certain innate dispositions; they give rise to the primary formation of life. However, all of the life dimensions are also composed of "adopted dispositions." Above and beyond their innate dispositions, people adopt new ones during interformation with others and in interaction with successive life situations. In and through these processes, human life discloses and unfolds its empirical form. Such adopted dispositions express themselves in the attitudes, gestures, and customs of people. Sociohistorical pulsations, which are at work in every life situation, play an important role in the selection and absorption of such adopted dispositions.

Adoption by Assimilation

The process of adoption can take place either through interactive assimilation or through assimilation by osmosis. In the case of interactive assimilation, people play an active role. They are selective and decisive in the process of adopting new dispositions. Their power of appraisal is activated. In the case of assimilation by osmosis, human life is more passive. It tends to adopt in an implicit way the dispositions valued in its formation field. Assimilation by osmosis is clearly prevalent in infancy whereas interactive assimilation marks later phases of life.

For example, Christian children in prayer within a Christian family or community will assume a different posture from that of Muslim children. From infancy, children in a Muslim prayer situation bow repeatedly toward Mecca with their forehead touching the ground. By contrast, Christian children in communal prayer at home and in church learn to kneel or sit while praying with their eyes closed. The adopted directives are clearly different in each situation.

This adopted life-form emerges in childhood as children take up by osmosis communal form dispositions that are implicit in the style of life they share spontaneously with the people they meet daily in their formation field. In this way, life in formation adopts certain dispositions in regard to speaking, sleeping, playing, praying, eating, or meeting people. Similarly it adopts spontaneously by osmosis certain approved gestures and facial expressions to show displeasure or impatience, to gain attention, or to manifest contentment. Children learn all of this without explicit instruction. They simply grow into certain dispositions by implicit interformation.

Spiritual Formation Potential of Prespiritual Dispositions

All of the above constitute formative influences on the spontaneously unfolding dispositions of human life. Such customs, no matter how prosaic, ultimately have a spiritual impact. To be sure, the dispositions that result are not explicitly or immediately spiritual. They are potential receptacles of spiritual expressions. They become available as dispositions in which the transcendent dimension of life may sooner or later express itself. As potential vehicles of the spirit, they may later give a specific form to such spiritual expressions. In this way, prespiritual dispositions may eventually participate in the spirituality of people who are able to express their spiritual stances more fully in and through them.

Reflect for a moment on the attempts of small children to share in family prayer before or after meals. They do so spontaneously. Because the adults pray like this and because this is one of the forms of life in the children's sociohistorical situation, they adopt it as their own. At the same time, they begin to feel a vague awareness that it is not right to eat one's food without a moment of prayer. Later, they may be surprised and feel disapproval when other children begin their meal without praying.

The custom of praying before meals is due to sociohistorical pulsations springing from certain religious form traditions. The form of prayer in which this pulsation is expressed is determined historically and culturally. This does not mean, however, that this formal spiritual expression of the deeper meaning of nourishment is nothing more than an historical accident. This custom is characteristic of the spirituality of a form tradition. It expresses a distinctively human appraisal of the act of eating in the light of transcendent aspirations and inspirations. The fact that this custom in this form entered at some time in the formation history of a people does not explain anything ultimately. The real question is how such a spiritual idea, the bond between the act of eating and the transcendent, could enter into the history of formation in the first place.

The deepest explanation is that the dynamics of spiritual formation were always operative, at least implicitly, in human history, manifesting themselves in the cultural emergence of certain forms of behavior. These express, evoke, and reinforce certain inner dispositions conducive to a specific kind of spiritual formation. Clearly, the form traditions into which children are born initiate in them certain dispositions while closing off others.

Formation as Evocation

Spiritual formation is the disclosure and implementation of a communal and unique dispositional form of life. Ideally, this formation should be congenial with one's foundational life-form, in tune with the consonant foundations of one's form traditions, and compatible with one's successive life situations.

The mystery of our foundational life direction is ontologically prior to both spontaneous and deliberate disposition formation; it situates both uniquely in time and space. Spiritual disposition formation takes place from the very beginning of life. It happens implicitly by the initiation of children into the formative aspects of their sociohistorical ambience. This initiation unfolds through everyday acts and customs that express the spiritual dispositions of the form traditions to which their families and communities are committed.

Formation is not an imposition but an evocation. The word *evocation* literally means a calling out or a drawing forth. It brings to birth the direction that lies dormant in the innate dispositions of one's unfolding life and of the formative communities and situations to which one is exposed. This is in no way a ready-made identity, already present like a seed that must sprout into this or that empirical life-form. Realistically, we can posit a certain directedness implied in initial elementary dispositions that points in turn to a limited variety of possible dispositional life-forms. These suggest more evolved and manifold dispositions that offer reasonable possibilities of emergence for this uniquely situated life. By the same token, this directedness points out negatively what types of dispositional life-forms will never be possible for this unique person as situated in time and space. Some people, for instance, can never become musicians or engineers, mechanics, good athletes, or mystics.

In the course of one's personal and spiritual development, the life direction becomes increasingly articulated. As a result of decisions, often made after various crises and their consequent dispositions, the number and kinds of possible life directions will decrease. Each basic decision moves the person in the direction of certain life-form disclosures while excluding others. The implementation of such basic decisions tends to articulate and strengthen one's potential for further development in the chosen direction while diminishing concrete potentialities for the development of other directions.

The first evocation of the life-form happens in the vital dimension. Children are born with a set of direction potentials or potential dispositions that distinguish them from other children. How this vital dimension develops depends in part on the form traditions into which a child is born. To be sure, it is still uncertain in childhood what life direction children may choose in the future. Yet more immediate directives are already present, not only in the children themselves but also in their early life situations.

These latter directives exercise a formative influence on the child's emergent life. It makes a difference, for instance, whether the child spends his early years in a black ghetto in New York or in a country estate in Connecticut. Different situational directives are at work in each of these environments.

Initial Formation of the Dispositions of Sensibility and Responsibility

In the second part of this volume, to be published soon, we will consider the formation of what we call the core dispositions of the human heart. Here we shall discuss only the initial formation of two dispositions that begin to develop early in the core form of the child's life. These two dispositions are sensibility and responsibility, which refer to the ability to sense vitally or to feel, and to the ability to respond. Responsibility could also be called felt-conscientiousness. Sensibility refers to the vital excitability of human life. Responsibility in childhood is a primordial, elementary, affective capacity to experience some responsibility for certain acts or omissions. It also implies some pristine ability to act upon that germinal feeling of responsibility.

This fundamental sensibility and responsibility is the subtle fruit of a first implicit spiritual formation. These germinal dispositions influence the later choice of a spiritual life-form, the nature of this choice, and its further articulation and refinement. It is implicitly influenced by the unique nucleus of the core form. This nucleus resides in the natural affiliation of the core form with the foundational life-form of the child. This affiliation, inherent in the unfolding core form, colors deeply the formation of its dispositions of sensibility and responsibility.

This basic sensibility-responsibility structure, its potential depth and intensity, and its unique image-affiliation with the foundational form are all qualities of the core form, which is the continuous or relatively enduring form of life. This quality is not only a result of innate dispositions, but also of the early formative influence of the environment upon them. Initial sensibility and responsibility are a mixture of innate and adopted dispositions, assimilated mainly by what we have called earlier situational osmosis. For example, neglected children may manifest little or no vital excitability. For them it may be difficult, if not impossible, to come to a vital experience and expression of affection in their lives.

This emergent sensibility, and the capacity for vital affection linked with it, is of crucial importance for the development of a spiritual life that is not only inwardly consonant but attractive and harmonious in its outward appearance in this world. A full, harmonious spiritual life implies a transcendent love and compassion that can express itself effectively, vitally, and graciously in human society. The disposition of love in its deepest core is not a question of exuberant feeling but of a transcendent willing of the good in self and others as well as in all the other aspects of one's formation field.

Transcendent "good will" is evoked by a certain delight in the goodness of the formation mystery as manifested in our formation field and in the actual or potential goodness we believe to be present in ourselves and in our neighbors. When vital sensibility has been well-developed in early childhood, it will facilitate the birth and expression of this appreciation. Such positive approval enables the will to strive lovingly after the good in self and others.

Formation of the Disposition of Vital Sensibility in Children

How do children develop the disposition of vital sensibility? How do they learn to love vitally? The answer is by being loved. How does that formative love express itself? It is again by the loving presence of the mother or her substitute as expressed in the primordial triad of faith, hope, and love, manifesting itself in her consistent appreciation and confirmation.

Parents or their substitutes inwardly and outwardly express their faith, hope, and love toward the child. They do so by inner and outer blessing or benediction. The word *benediction* literally means a speaking or wishing well of someone. Traditionally it means an inner wishing well that is manifested outwardly by word and/or gesture and at the same time implies and expresses an invocation of the mysterious power of formation that directs humanity and the universe.

The main dispositions of the benediction that expresses faith, hope, and love are attention, affection, appreciation, and confirmation. These are also vitally expressed and incarnated. Children need the full and loving attention of those around them. This attention makes them be, it gives them back to themselves, and it enables them to see and esteem themselves through the loving eyes of the attentive other. Attention sustains a child's initially awkward attempts to learn and grow. Loving attention, vitally expressed, is truly formative. Affection is communicated in the warmth of word, embrace, and caring gesture. It is deeply formative to feel the vital expression of true love without conditions or strings attached. Appreciation gives children the necessary feeling that they are truly worthwhile, that they carry within themselves reasons why others show faith, hope, and love, and why children themselves should have faith, hope, and love in relation to their own emerging life. Confirmation makes children feel that their parents or their substitutes say yes to their being and unfolding, that they bless and encourage vitally the basically good persons they are and are trying to become. Confirmation implies at the same time a "being-firm-with," an appeal to the form potency or firmness rooted in the children themselves.

These four dispositions of a parental life of love and benediction are the greatest formative gifts that can be granted to children during their crucial early development. If the basic vital sensibility of the child is neglected, later spiritual direction and formation must try to make up for the lack of evocation of this potential. Worse than this, the vital sensibility of the child may have been deformed already in infancy. Children may be unfortunate enough to have been born into an unhappy family situation where they are initiated into hate instead of love, competition not compassion, envy not appreciation, diminishment of others not confirmation.

Early neglect or deformation of the vital sensibility of life may affect a person's feelings toward the formation mystery and toward self and others for a lifetime. Only direction in depth may heal the wounds of childhood. The quality and depth of the sensitivity dispositions of children are one of the basic constituents of the spiritual life-form they will gradually develop.

Formation of the Disposition of Responsibility

Conscientiousness or responsibility feeling is a second core disposition. It should be firm, free, and flexible. This happens if the responsibility feeling is complemented and permeated by the vital sensibility disposition described above. Faith, hope, and love for the formation mystery, for oneself and for all people, with a concomitant expression in inner and outer attention, affection, appreciation, and confirmation, give rise to a gracious conscientiousness. This loving responsibility adapts itself easily to the demands of human and transhuman love.

An early stern environment with a high sense of duty and a low sense of love usually fosters a cool responsibility feeling. It tends to develop a mood which is harsh, demanding, obsessive, and compulsive. A dissonant disposition like this may lead to a basic deformation of the spiritual life. By contrast, an early environment that tries to foster vital feelings of affection without demanding conscientious implementation of such affection in concrete acts of loving care would also be deformative.

Emergent vital sensibility and transcendent responsibility, with their moods and feelings, are thus at the heart of our spiritual life. These dispositions are formed largely by the early life situations. Such situations can evoke our true life direction by calling forth the vital sensibility and responsibility feelings to which each child is uniquely predisposed by virtue of his or her heart's affiliation with the foundational life-form. Even if the life situation evokes in some measure a child's potential unique sensibility and responsibility, it may not do so sufficiently to enable one to develop these germinal dispositions to their fullest potential.

Initial Spiritual Disposition Formation of the Functional Life

The spiritual disposition formation of children thus begins on the vital level of life. It takes place in bodily expressions of faith, hope, and love, of benediction, acceptance, attention, affection, appreciation, and confirmation. The bodily expressions of these dispositions are more directly oriented toward the vital needs of the child, but these same influences play a role also in the higher, specifically human, functions of life.

We can now move from the vital to the functional dimension. To reach this level, four modes or four main dispositions of functionality are necessary: the individual, the technical, the social, and the functional-aesthetic. All four have to be evoked in the child. The child has innate potentials to implement these four basic articulations in more refined dispositions. But while spontaneous self-unfolding surely plays a role in the development of these dispositions, it is not enough.

Consider language development, which is one of the many dispositional articulations of the technical mode of the functional dimension. We know from experience and observation that the technique of speaking does not develop automatically and autonomously as the leaves or flowers of a plant unfold. Nor is the development of this linguistic disposition due merely to active formation by people who surround the child. It is not enough that adults teach the child intellectually how to verbalize ideas or how to relate socially to others. Linguistic formation presupposes a spontaneous identification of children with the speaking people around them. In this identification they open themselves to their formative influence. They assimilate the language and the dispositions implicit in it.

Spiritual formation of others requires that we offer ourselves to them as a good subject for imitation and identification. Not what we teach but who we are counts here. Our life-form affects others more than our words. Spiritual disposition formation is not only a question of verbalizing well. If there is a noticeable gap between our life-form and our words, our presence may be disappointing and deformative.

How does language formation take place in children? They do not learn to speak by means of an introductory course with a set of practical exercises. It is precisely in their imitation of and identification with the people around them that children assimilate spontaneously, by situational osmosis, the emotional and functional meaning of the sounds adults express to them and to each other. These sounds convey how they feel, what they want to be done, what things mean to them. Since children are spontaneously sensitive to this expression of what moves the people with whom they identify, they begin to feel and speak as they do. They interiorize the emotional and functional power of their words. These words begin to speak, as it were, within them, they exercise a continual formative influence on their emergent dispositional life.

If the people who coform the formation field with the child live a spiritual life, their spiritual dispositions will somehow color the choice of their words, the timbre of their voice, the meaning and function of the things and feelings they express, their hierarchy of dispositions, interests, concerns and convictions, and the faith, hope, and love that animates their life. Children whose language formation takes place by identification with such people, will imbibe a spiritual disposition formation interwoven with the technical language customs they spontaneously assimilate. Similar influences will characterize the assimilation of all the modes of functional selfhood that emerge in its individual, technical, social, and functional-aesthetic articulation.

Our example has described technical language formation and its deeper implications. It illustrates that the formation of a mode, articulation, or disposition is not isolated from a person's spiritual formation. The formation of every consonant human disposition prepares a pathway or channel for the expression of the overall spiritual formation of people.

Initial Formation of the Dispositions of the Transcendent Dimension

Like the dispositions of the vital and functional dimensions of life, those of the transcendent dimension are initiated by the combined influence of spontaneous unfolding and deliberate formation This dimension aspires toward what is *more than* the object poles of historical pulsations, vital impulses, and functional ambitions. The transcendent dimension of life is also the arena of spontaneous interest in the Sacred, toward which the child is innately directed or predisposed.

Because of this seminal orientation, children vaguely sense the meaning of sacred gestures and words in the traditions of their family and community. They surmise the mystery toward which they point. Their aspiration for the Holy is awakened. Before focal instruction and direction, children sense something of the Transcendent, whose presence is reflected in the devout dispositions of adults who surround them during their moments of prayer and religious ritual.

This prefocal formation of our transcendent disposition goes on from infancy to old age, most of the time without our focal knowledge. Already as children we assimilate transcendent experiences and aspirations. Our "lived" aspirations come first of all from our formation field, from the way our family prayed at table, the way our mother lit a candle before a statue, the way the parish priest said Mass, the way the minister or rabbi led their congregations in prayer; the way a teacher spoke about the Sacred. These and other expressions of their religious dispositions affected us not on the level of reasoning but prefocally through our spontaneous, interformative identification with such significant people.

The prefocal formation of transcendent dispositions implies that we open ourselves continually to formative spiritual influences. Such spontaneous, interformative identification flows from a receptive attitude, a relaxed docility that allows formation to affect what is already unfolding in our emergent life. This prefocal process of disposition formation should be corrected, complemented, and deepened, but not replaced, by intellectual processes. For example, courses in systematic theology become proximately formative in the measure that we assimilate their content also in an inspirational-practical way.

We can thus see that spiritually formative influences depend partly on the quality of the transcendent dispositions manifested in the persons and surroundings that influence the child. These dispositions are spontaneously formative. They evoke similar dispositions in others via a formation that is mostly one of wordless witnessing. This power of transcendent evocation is proper to the human person as spiritual. Being human means that we also bear the responsibility of being spiritually formative to ourselves and others and of being receptive to spiritual formation by others. This is a possibility, a responsibility we did not choose or devise ourselves; it is a call we cannot escape. It is our inherent possibility of and responsibility for transcendent formation.

This call points to a mysterious context that goes beyond our special group, culture, or life situation, even beyond ourselves. Therefore, the ground of our spiritual formation must be the Ground of the human lifeform itself. In other words, the basic orientation toward spiritual disposition formation is always already present in every human being. The only thing we can do is awaken and evoke this slumbering direction. We cannot force its emergence. We can only promote or hinder it, take care of favorable conditions or allow unfavorable ones to obstruct it.

By ourselves alone we can never be the sufficient cause of any spiritual formation. It is ultimately a mystery, a gift from a transcendent source. It is unique, not in the sense that it is autonomous, insulated, or absolutely independent, but in the sense that it is a unique epiphany of an ultimate reality.

Transcendent Form Ability

Spiritual form ability accounts for the form ability of human life as a whole. This transcendent form ability refers to our innate capacity to receive and promote a natural spiritual form for our unfolding life. Transcendent form ability is the human capacity, due to the natural makeup of human life as human, to receive and promote a unique formation of one's life in accordance with innate and adopted transcendent dispositions.

The human transcendent ability for spiritual formation is not a potentality that people themselves have acquired, thought out, or even chosen. It is their inescapable fate, their lot, their being, their destiny. All of human life is an attempt to take the right stand toward this fate of having to receive and foster the spiritual formation of one's unfolding life. Our whole life can be seen as a demand to disclose and implement our call to ongoing, distinctively human formation within the cultural communities whose destinies we shape while being shaped by them in turn.

Form ability has a transcendent character; it aims at a spiritual life-form that goes beyond mere conformity; it invites us to rise above the immediacy of our daily surroundings, of our vital-functional determinations. Spiritual disposition formation aspires after a life-form that opens one to the mystery of the "more than." Restlessness remains in the human heart as long as the form given to the emergent spiritual life is not in communion with its mysterious ground. This ground transcends the functional context of our lives. Jewish, Christian, Muslim, Hindu, Buddhist, and other spiritualities point in symbol, myth, ritual, and doctrine to this openness of the life-form to the transcendent.

Form ability precedes formation. Form ability is a potentiality, formation is an act. The potentiality for an act always precedes that act; it is presupposed by the act. In other words, an act is the actualization of an already existing potentiality. All formative acts and dispositions are thus actualizations of form potency. We cannot observe a potentiality directly; we know it in our experience of its various actualizations. We know it implicitly. An experience of our form ability is, therefore, implicit in all our experiences of actual formation.

This ability is rooted in the fundamental structure of our life as spiritual. It is precisely our spirituality that makes us distinctively human. People would not be human if they were unable to foster uniquely the spiritual formation of their life—a formation that includes yet transcends and transforms its vital-functional determinants in time and space.

In daily life we are usually not aware of our form ability or form potency. Yet at privileged moments we may experience the invitation to transcend the material and social determinations of our lives. We may hear the call of our deepest nature to bring forth a spiritual formation, one which is much more than mere conformity to the pulsations and functional demands of our immediate surroundings or to the pulsions of our vital form potencies.

CHAPTER 5

Formative Mind, Will, and Disposition Formation

W hat is the role of mind and will in disposition formation? Our mind must appraise the dispositions that should be fostered. For example, people who aspire to be writers must choose dispositons that are conducive to the writer's life. Their dispositions have to be more compatible with the life of an author than with the life of a salesperson, football player, or actor. The future author will have to cultivate dispositions for solitude, thoughtful reading, quiet reflection, empathic observation, and sensitivity to good phrasing. To decide if one should commit one's life to the nurturing of such dispositions, appraisal is necessary.

Formative Appraisal and Disposition Formation

Formative appraisal is the work of our mind as formative. Its appraisal potency is twofold: it is both transcendent and functional. Transcendent appraisal is the fruit of our power of appraisal as illumined by the spirit whereas functional appraisal is the act of our appraisal potency as informed by functional awareness of the concrete conditions within our formation field.

For example, when one tries to appraise the desirability of developing dispositions for a writer's life, both appraisal powers should be engaged. In functional appraisal, we ask such questions as: Am I vitally able to sustain this kind of solitary exertion behind a typewriter? Am I functionally equipped with skills, aptitudes, and language abilities to develop these dispositions effectively in my life? Do my social position, family ties, and economic prospects make such a choice feasible?

The kinds of questions posed by transcendent appraisal would be: How does professional writing fit into the overall unique calling of my life? Is it really what the formation mystery intends for me? How can my choice be enlightened by the transcendent form tradition to which I am committed?

Does my answer to these deeper questions affect the way in which I give form to the dispositions necessary to become an effective writer?

Guidelines for Appraisal

What guidelines for appraisal help us to answer such inquiries? Formation science has developed eight main criteria: openness, appreciation, congeniality, compatibility, compassion, joyousness, competence, and effectiveness. Furthermore, in regard to the social dimension of human life, congeniality leads to the criterion of formative justice; compatibility gives rise to formative peace; compassion generates formative mercy; concern for personal effectiveness is complemented by concern for social effectiveness; and personal joyousness usually promotes a joyful atmosphere for others. These are not merely abstract criteria. They are living dispositions to be cultivated assiduously in the consonant life.

For instance, if we aspire to become professional writers, we must appraise whether we are *open* to all pertinent aspects of this life and its demands. Is this dispositional life *congenial* with our primordial life-form, our transcendent call, and our functional-vital makeup? Is it *compatible* with our life story, our familial and other obligations, our present life situation? We must appraise in *compassion* our own vulnerability and that of our dependents. Will the development of such dispositions be too much for us to tolerate? Will it put an undue strain on those with whom we have to live daily? Does this kind of life agree with us so well that we find a certain *joyousness* in it? Can we become *competent* in this area? Can we really be *effective* in life as writers? Do we serve social justice best by writing? Is our effectiveness as writers so limited that we ought to spend our lives in other ways to serve society? Can we foster peace and harmony in society most effectively by writing because of the type of persons we basically are? Will we be able to refine our dispositions in such a way that they lead to the kind of writing that promotes attitudes and acts of justice and mercy in our readers?

These are only a few examples of the numerous questions that can be raised in each unique case of disposition appraisal. They will differ from setting to setting and from person to person.

Appraisal and Volition

Appraisal by the transcendent and functional mind is not sufficient to bring us to a final decision. It needs the assistance of another power: the transcendent and functional will. The mind forms the will in some respects and the will forms the mind in others. Our formative will is moved by the appraisal powers of our formative mind. Our mind radiates its appraisals, as it were, into the will. The formative will in turn moves the formative mind. This movement issues from the effective or dynamic nature of our will. No matter how clearly we see with our appraising mind that we should begin to develop the dispositions for a life of writing, nothing will happen if our will does not give the final push by its affirmation or decision to do so.

We know of this need for effective willing from other experiences. Many of us may have appraised in our mind the importance of deactivating our dispositions for smoking or for overindulgence in eating and drinking. We discover, however, that first we have to form our will gently and firmly. We-as-willing have to make this choice and execute it by well-motivated, reiterated acts that implement the affirmation of our will in daily life.

Gentleness and Firmness of Will

Two conditions or general dispositions developed by the science of formation relate to formative willing: gentleness and firmness. Without gentleness, willing deteriorates into willfulness. Willfulness tries to force dispositions into existence without sufficient appraisal of all adverse and favorable conditions, such as our vulnerability, the impact of the affirmation by our will on others, our vital energy as available at this moment, and so on. The willful person lacks patience, relaxation, and a flexible flow with the epiphanies of the formation mystery in his or her life and formation field. This flow tends to mellow the will, making it pliable in its implementation of one's affirmation of the mind's appraisal.

Firmness, by the same token, prevents flexibility from becoming flabbiness. It enables us to persevere quietly in the necessary reiteration of well-motivated acts that form the desired dispositions over a period of time. Firmness of will sustains our courage in the face of repeated relapses in opposite acts and dispositions. It also keeps our appraisal potency in a stance of dwelling appreciation of the desirability of the disposition formation to which we have committed ourselves.

An act of will is thus necessary for effective formation. Appraisal only becomes actual in a final and decisive way because our formative will affirms that this or that should be done.

Constitution of the Act of Disposition Formation

What constitutes the act of formation of a consonant disposition? First, we exercise formative appraisal and volition: Is this directive consonant in regard to fostering the disposition? This appraisal and volition ought to be illuminated by transcendent insights and directives as well as by the information that our appraisal and volition potency has gained by means of our functional-vital formation powers.

For example, we may ponder the pros and cons of initiating or strengthening a disposition for an artistic profession. Our appraisal and voluntary affirmation of a life of art depends partly on our transcendent view of life and partly on our awareness of our unique call by the formation mystery. Yet we also try to gain insight into our functional aptitudes for such a life, our talent or lack of it. We engage our mind in comparative appraisal and appreciation. How did others manage in similar situations? How does my painting compare with theirs? Am I a budding artist or only a dreamer?

Limitations of Dispositions and Freedom of Volition

Anything I can do and enjoy, no matter how attractive, is always finite. So, too, are dispositions. We can focus on the limitations of any disposition, on what it is not, as well as appreciate its attractive aspects.

To return to our example, even if we feel increasingly that a life of painting is really for us, we can always look at the other side, at the things we will miss in life by being a painter as opposed to what we could enjoy by being a fine athlete, a business person, or an administrator. Therefore, the appraising mind needs at a certain moment the affirming power of the will to make its appraisal final and binding. There comes a moment when we must say, "I have pondered enough, I must decide now: I will or will not become a painter and form my dispositions accordingly."

Our affirming or negating will is unable in and by itself to appraise the situation about which it has to decide. It is a blind formation power. By itself it cannot appraise whether it is advisable to become a painter. Our willing is dependent on the information and inspiration it receives from our appraising mind. It can then follow or refuse the directives that are proposed by the mind. Of course, the will is not a separate thing that decides; it is the whole me-as-wiling.

Deformation of Appraisal

From experience, we know that the formative appraisal of our mind can be mistaken. It can be deformed partially or totally by ignorance. For instance, I may not know what the life of a painter concretely entails, though I decide to dispose myself for that kind of life anyway. Later I may discover that I underestimated the economic hardships it entailed and that I overestimated my ability to tolerate them.

Appraisal may be distorted by other kinds of deformation. What if I have a disposition to overdependency? By associating with a quasi-artistic crowd, I may have identified my life with theirs in my need for acceptance. I no longer saw that I was not really destined for the artistic life. This lack of self-insight made me try to develop a disposition that was not right for me, that was, in fact, uncongenial. The appraisal power is often deformed by the quasi-foundational pride-form in all of us. In the circle in which I move, artistic sensitivity and production may be exalted as a sign of superiority. The pride-form may seduce me to opt for a disposition that promises such applauded eminence.

There is no end to the sources of appraisal deformation in regard to the dispositions we want to cultivate in life. To list only a few: deformative dispositions; dissonant form tradition accretions; dissonant pulsations, pulsions, ambitions, aspirations, and inspirations; deformed fulfillment and exertion strivings; malice; demonic obsession. In the case of appraisal deformation, dissonant dispositions may be chosen over their consonant counterparts.

Progressive Approach to the Fully Consonant Life-Form in Limited Forms of Life

The ultimate aim of formation is the fully consonant life-form. This alone promises fulfillment of our human aspirations. The object pole of this ultimate aspiration is the attainment of the fullness of peace and joy in a transcendent participation with others in the formation mystery. To be sure, few people would formulate the aim of life in this way. They want to be happy, healthy, rich, famous, successful, relaxed, strong, loved, and popular.

There is no end to the possible expressions of what people consider to be evocative of peace and joy. All strive, consciously or unconsciously, after an ultimate meaning for their life. They may be mistaken in countless ways about what that meaning should be, but, somehow, no matter how deformed and distorted it is, this fundamental striving comes to the fore. People want a life-form that guarantees happiness and fulfillment. Their actual life will be constituted by the dispositions they opt for and try to maintain in view of some project they believe will assure this fulfillment.

In other words, the ultimate aim of disposition formation is given and cannot be changed. What is relatively free and changeable are the empirical core, current, apparent, and actual life-forms chosen in view of that paramount purpose. The same applies to the formative acts and dispositions of these chosen life-forms. However, none of these is the ultimate formation pole itself. All are effective or ineffective finite means to that aim. They help us to approximate the fully consonant life-form in the hope that our choice of life will bring us peace and joy.

Primordial Act of the Formation Will

In this light, we may point to the primordial act of the will to formation. This act is prior to the option for any specific form disposition. It is not free. It is elicited of necessity because of the inescapably attractive power of the ultimate object pole of formation.

The final aim of all human formation may not be clearly known to us. In most instances, it is only implicitly apprehended. This vague apprehension or basic intuition is proper to our embodied transcendent mind. It is the veiled intuition that we should try to attain a fully consonant form of life. It follows that we should ratify or initiate and develop only dispositions that will help us to realize that consonant form. It is impossible for our formative will in its primordial act not to will this fully consonant life-form. There is an intrinsic connection between the ultimate aim of formation—to attain full peace and joy—and the necessary means of a fully consonant life-form that leads to that fulfillment.

A fully consonant form of life is the ultimate necessary means to this fullness of peace and joy. Without it, the maximal peace and joy attainable for us will not come to be. The fullness of peace and joy is the universal and absolute good necessarily striven after by the will. Hence the will must seek the life formation that enables us to approximate that good. Therefore, this primordial, necessary act of the will to formation is the hidden force at work in any disposition formation and any actualization of these dispositions. It is not the choice of any particular disposition or deed of formation; rather it is this general will to formation that makes any one of these particular choices possible.

This primordial, general formation act of mind and will is followed by a wide variety of particular secondary acts and dispositions. These latter, unlike the primordial one, are relatively free. Our mind-as-formative is only secondarily concerned with the apprehension and appraisal of particular formation acts and dispositions. Their purpose is to bring about the disclosure and implementation, or maintenance and unfolding, of core, current, apparent, and actual forms of life as constituted by their respective dispositions. Our purpose and hope is that these may be such that they increasingly approximate the fully consonant form of life. This should ideally become a path to the fullness of peace and joy by participation with others in the formation mystery and its epiphanies.

An understanding of this foundational process of the will to formation is basic among the assumptions held by formation science. For this reason, we would like to reiterate our explanation of this process in a slightly different way.

Our will to formation responds to the apprehension of the desirable goal of formation by our appraising mind. The mind as formative apprehends, first of all implicitly and intuitively, the ultimate object pole of any human formation, which is the fullness of peace and joy. The will responds to this apprehension by a spontaneous willing of this ultimate end of formation. However, this absolute will to formation of life in service of that aim cannot itself directly realize the ultimate formation goal. It can will concretely only intermediate forms of life. Hence, the appraising mind in turn looks for intermediate forms that may progressively approach the ultimate formation goal, this again being the fully consonant life-form, opening us to the fullness of peace and joy by participation.

None of these intermediate, tentative life-forms in and by themselves can be the absolute and ultimate goal of formation. None of these is the final, totally consonant life-form that opens us to that fullness. They are all finite and limited; they do not force the will to comply with them, for our will is only compelled to comply with the basic ideal of full joy and happiness and the consonant final form of life that leads to it.

The will is free to accept or reject such limited, relative, intermediate, tentative forms and dispositions of life. This limitation is the basis of the relative freedom of the will in the choice of concrete formation dispositions. None of them is as yet the fullness of the final consonant life-form. The basic absolute formation-will keeps willing the ultimate, fully consonant life-form by necessity. Without this fundamental striving of the will for formation of life in service of that ultimate fulfillment, there would be no will to formation at all. Why should the will want any formation without that promise?

The basic will to formation is, therefore, the lasting source, ground, and principle of any voluntary formation movement, including that of disposition formation. It moves all the powers of formation in human life to formative acts and dispositions.

Necessity of Willing Particular Formative Acts and Dispositions

We have see that the human will foundationally wills the end of formation. In this willing, it moves itself to will other formative acts that seem to lead to that end. It wills all dispositions, which, rightly or wrongly, are appraised by the formative mind to lead progressively to this absolutely aspired and affirmed end of human formation.

Why can we choose only particular means of formation, only particular dispositions? Why can we not at once choose the fully consonant life-form? Our human condition is such that our inherent aspiration for the fullness of peace and joy cannot be fulfilled at once. It can only be realized if our life becomes fully open, transcendent, and transparent. As we know from experience, our life is by no means a final expression of this ideal form. Such spiritualization demands the progressive disclosure and realization of successive dispositions that help to liberate us from our encapsulation in aspirations, ambitions, pulsions, and pulsations, and in their corresponding images, memories, and anticipations.

This disclosure and realization can only be attained gradually and imperfectly. We thus need to foster progressively the intermediate, imperfect forms of life and the dispositions they entail. These forms and their constituent dispositions are meant to approach the final, fully open and transcendent form of life. This consonant form is the necessary ultimate condition for fulfillment of the inherent human aspiration for peace and joy.

These considerations grant us a better insight into the intraformative interaction of mind and will discussed earlier. Our basic will to formation strives by necessity after the fully consonant life-form as a final and necesary means to the fullness of peace and joy. It moves the formation mind to engage in the act of appraisal of potential formation means, such as effective and consonant dispositions. The formative mind, after appraising potential dispositions as consonant, signals to the will that such dispositions promise the possible emergence of empirical forms of life that may progressively approximate the fully consonant life-form after which the will strives by necessity.

Provisional Appraisal of Form Dispositions

Mature final appraisal of a consonant form disposition is usually preceded by provisional appraisal. This appraisal gives rise to a plurality of possible consonant dispositions. Observe a girl who is courted by an attractive young man. She can allow a disposition of love to develop, a unique, special love for him, or she can initiate a disposition of refusal toward his advances. Then she may evolve the disposition for the single life of a career woman. The awareness of many other possible dispositions can be triggered by this formative event in her life, such as, for example, the disposition to become more warm and outgoing or more cool and distant, to appreciate the other sex or to reject advances, to become a homemaker or a career woman.

Initially the directives for such different dispositions may be considered equally attractive. Out of many directives suggested by the appraising mind for various dispositions, a number are selected as *potential* directives for one's actual disposition formation. They are kept equally under consideration. There is not yet a decision as to which one of them may finally win out as most consonant with one's initial and ongoing formation. One is still at the stage of provisional appraisal and selection of equal possibilities of disposition formation.

Such provisional appraisal includes four stages. First, we engage in a preliminary scanning of the formation situation in which we find ourselves. What formation directives, means, meanings, and opportunities does it offer? Imagine being in a situation at the end of college in which one can choose between equally developing dispositions for life as a business person, a politician, or a journalist. If one is wise, one scans the economic, political, and social situation before deciding. One scrutinizes one's assets and limits, one's plans for marriage or the single life, one's financial needs, and so forth.

Second, one translates the opportunities and limits discovered in each field into imaginary and anticipatory formation dispositions. One asks oneself what would they mean in terms of what one has to do practically if one wants to begin to develop dispositions for an effective career in these fields of human endeavor?

Third, one usually makes, implicitly and informally, a kind of tentative inventory of all such potential directives to see whether they seem promising in view of one's consonant disposition formation.

Last, one may look over this inventory, again usually implicitly and prefocally. One is engaged in a general appraisal that is conditional. One does not decide definitely on any directives to be implemented in one's disposition formation. One appraises only whether this or that should remain on the list of potential dispositions, some of which may eventually be chosen for actual implementation.

Ideally, of course, this general, provisional appraisal should take place in the light of the ultimate aim of formation. If so, the process promises to be a preliminary preparation for a disposition formation that may be truly consonant.

Formative Will and Provisional Formation Appraisal

The will acts toward this provisional formation appraisal by accepting these potential dispositions provisionally. They are presented by the appraising mind only as *provisional* dispositions. Provisional means that the will does not yet affirm any one of them as its final choice. One has not yet decided to initiate dispositions for becoming either a business person, a politician, or a journalist. We remember that the will as formative is directed by necessity toward the final formation end. As of yet, it has not learned from the appraising mind which choice would be most in consonance with the end. At this moment, the will accepts provisionally that any of these possibilities may be conducive to progressive attainment of the final aim of human formation.

At this stage of preparatory disposition selection, the formative will does not exclusively favor any one of these possibilities. It extends itself equally to all of them as promising, potential form dispositions. It does not affirm any of them in particular. These provisional dispositions please us, at least up to a certain point. Their affirmation by our formation will is only conditional, qualified, tentative, and not yet conclusive. A final choice of form disposition should follow full and mature appraisal. The stage of provisional appraisal is thus only a phase of preparation.

Duration and Degree of Attention
in the Process of Appraisal and Volition

Such exercises in provisional appraisal and volition can be done with more or less attention. Their duration differs from situation to situation. Much depends on the importance of the formation issue at stake. Evidently I need less deliberation about forming a disposition for fishing than for forming a special love disposition that will lead to marriage.

Another factor is the quality and intensity of the vital-functional condition of the person involved in a choice. To decide for a disposition regarding what one should eat daily is less complex for an average, healthy young adult than for an aging person who suffers from diabetes, has had a series of heart attacks, and is plagued by ulcers.

The same applies to the influence of transcendent factors on one's appraisal and volition, such as the special illuminations described in certain form traditions. Such an experience of being called to something extraordinary may demand prolonged deliberation and consultation about all the conditions involved. One should not lightly develop the disposition to follow such a calling as trustworthy.

Usually the processes of provisional appraisal remain prefocal. They may be performed effectively with lightning speed. Conscious focusing and reflection is desirable when the decision is of paramount importance for one's life formation or when it is difficult to reach. In some cases people may be inclined to short-circuit such processes, with unfortunate consequences for their consonant disposition formation.

Another reason to replace the usual prefocal process by focal reflection is the deformative impact of other powers, such as sociohistorical pulsations. These may influence one's disposition formation before one's personal formative appraisal and will have exercised sufficient control.

For most people, it may not be necessary to know intellectually this natural process of preparatory disposition formation. Formation counselors, however, should be familiar with it. They may be consulted by people who have made serious mistakes in this preparatory phase. During formation sessions, it may be helpful critically to review how this process went wrong, or why it was insufficiently engaged in, how it led to the establishment of dissonant dispositions, and so on. A person may need assistance to come to the right decision. Formation counselors cannot make decisions for such people. They should be able, however, to illumine them about the right preparatory process of disposition choice and formation or reformation. They may do so by explaining the various stages of the process in a focused and reflective way.

Phase of Final Formation Decision

The preparatory phase of disposition choice is now over. The moment has come for the final decision. One has to choose a disposition. This choice must go beyond the earlier provisional appraisal, which resulted in a selection of a plurality of potential dispositions. The provisional appraisal made available a selection of possible dispositions from which to choose. Now one has to engage in a final practical appraisal. One asks, "Shall I or shall I not develop a special amorous disposition for this person?" "Shall I initiate and unfold in my life dispositions for the profession of business, politics, or journalism?"

At this advanced stage of formative appraisal, the mind must appraise which form dispositions should be affirmed in preference to other potential dispositions. The formative mind should ideally exercise this appraisal in light of the probable degree of consonance of the dispositions to be chosen with one's foundational life-form as disclosed at this moment of one's history. This disclosure is the fruit of collaboration by the transcendent, functional, vital, and sociohistorical dimensions of one's formative appraisal power. The formation mind is sustained in this appraisal by the powers of both transcendent and functional memory, of imagination, and of anticipation.

Formative final appraisal by the mind alone is not enough to move people to the implementation of this appraisal in their disposition formation. The formative mind by itself alone cannot make a final appraisal of formation dispositions that become practically directive for one's dispositional life. It can only do so if the formation will moves the mind to this decisive final act of appraisal. The final appraisal of the formation mind only becomes functionally final and effective because the will affirms this functional or incarnational finality.

Formation Appraisal and Definite Disposition Affirmation

What does this final affirmation in regard to our dispositional life imply on the part of the mind? It means, first of all, a definite and final appraisal and appreciation of the affirmed disposition. Our power of appraisal values the disposition as consonant both *ultimately* and *proximately*.

The disposition is ultimately consonant insofar as it is in tune with one's foundational life-form according to transcendent appraisal. The disposition is proximately consonant because the same disposition is in functional congruence with one's concrete life situation, according to functional appraisal. One disposition is clearly and definitely preferred to others. They were all present in the provisional collection of potential dispositions to be affirmed. Yet one has gained preference. It implies a choice to channel formation energy along specific lines of concrete formation of one's dispositional life. The energy is channeled in such a way that the preferred disposition or disposition reformation may be realized.

The formative affirmation is not the work of the isolated mind or will. The enlightened person as a whole prefers this form disposition or its reformation, with all the consequences involved. It is clear, therefore, that people are responsible for their dispositional life. They are able to direct their formation powers in relative freedom. They can do so in the light of personally affirmed formation directives for their disposition formation.

What is the essence of one's decisive affirmation in regard to disposition formation? It consists in an affirmed preference for one form disposition over other alternatives. The affirmed disposition is appraised as more consonant at this moment of one's formation history. The preferential affirmation implies an elimination or deactivation of competing form dispositions that were made equally available in the provisional stage of appraisal.

Formation Volition and Definite Disposition Affirmation

The preferred form disposition is presented by the appraising mind to the will for its definite affirmation. In this final affirmation resides the exercise of the human freedom of formation. The will affirms the final election of a consonant form disposition and its implementation. It affirms this disposition as more consonant than those previously affirmed by the will as potentially consonant during the provisional phase of formative appraisal.

Is our will really free in this final decision? As we have seen earlier, the will strives by necessity after the fully consonant life-form. It is not free in this primordial striving, for the fully consonant life-form is the only final and necessary means for the attainment of the fullness of peace and joy by participation. The aspiration after this fulfillment and its necessary means is implanted in human life itself. In this foundational striving, the will is not free.

The person-as-willing is free, however, in regard to the formation of particular dispositions and their formative consequences. Such dispositions are the necessary means for the attainment of the fully consonant life-form. Dispositions are chosen rightly or wrongly. They have been initiated in the hope of attaining progressively the fully consonant life-form. Such mediating formation dispositions and the resulting life-forms are necessarily limited and imperfect. Their relation to the final, fully consonant life-form, and the fullness of peace and joy it implies, is not entirely clear. Hence they do not exercise the irresistible attraction that the final, fully consonant life-form does. They do not manifest the undeniable link with the fullness of peace and joy the human will necessarily strives after.

People discover that they can refuse, deny, or exclude any particular disposition or act proposed to them. They feel free to give or withhold their consent. They experience, at least implicitly, that neither the affirmation of a form disposition nor the implied affirmation of its consequences is an act of their isolated will. They experience their will not as an isolated power of formation but as an expression of the whole person in formation, the formative person as willing. They themselves determine their own formation, through the use of the power of their will, by the formation of the dispositions they consider to be conducive to a consonant form of life.

This freedom of the formation will expresses most strikingly the transcendent core of human formation. To choose one's life-form freely through the choice of one's acts and dispositions is the hallmark of human formation. It marks our formation as transcending the absolute form determination typical of plant and animal formation. These life-forms cannot freely initiate formation dispositions but must follow instincts and their evolution. Formation freedom of dispositions and acts makes people worthy of praise or blame, reward or punishment, in regard to what they have freely chosen. To be sure, this freedom is relative and vulnerable. It has to overcome many appraisal and decision obstacles that make it impossible for people to attain the fully consonant life-form by means of their own powers of formation alone.

The quasi-foundational pride-form obscures and weakens formative mind and will. It distorts appraisal by deformative exaltation or totalization of finite formation dispositions and life-forms. This pride-form has its ramifications in all our dispositions. Hence, consonant form traditions propose means of overcoming the encapsulation by the pride-form and of receiving healing formation powers from the formation mystery in its manifold epiphanies.

Finally, there comes a moment in which active transcendent acts cannot further purify, illumine, and make consonant our appraisal and volition. The formation mystery itself has to complete this process by emptying us of all remnants of the obstinate pride-form. We can only be truly receptive in this regard at the moment in our formation journey when the formation mystery announces a new form, leaving our active appraisal and volition powerless and in darkness.

CHAPTER 6

Appraisal and Formative Strivings for Fulfillment and Exertion

Formation science distinguishes between two main types of formative striving: one for receptive need fulfillment, another for potency exertion that satisfies performance needs. In principle these two types do not exclude but complement each other. Ideally they should approximate mutual consonance; in fact they are often dissonant. Frequently one excludes the other or does not sufficiently take into account the contribution of the complementary striving.

Fulfillment Striving

The striving for fulfillment refers to our innate predisposition to fulfill our receptive needs. These needs may be vital or transcendent. We call the vital needs *pulsions*. They comprise vital passions, inclinations, impulses, vital compulsions, and interiorized vital-sociohistorical pulsations. We call the transcendent receptive needs *receptive aspirations*. For example, quiet contemplation may take care of our need to fulfill our receptive aspiration for consonance with the sacred. On the other hand, enjoying food and drink, body massage, or physical relaxation may satisfy our striving for the fulfillment of vital-receptive needs for nourishment and for bodily rest and restoration.

Exertion Striving

The striving for exertion refers to our innate predispositions to exert our potencies of form donation. They satisfy our needs for performance. They may be functional form potencies residing in our aptitudes and ambitions in the functional life dimensions. Or they may be transcendent potencies of form donation residing in the transcendent dimension of our life-form. We call the latter performance aspirations, or aspirations for form donation. For example, writing a song, a love poem, or a prayer is primarily an exertion of an aspirational form potency. Because of the unity of the human form of life, such aspirational exertion usually involves some activation of functional form potencies. To write a love poem, no matter how inspirational it may be, we have to move our pen, pencil, or typewriter keys.

Examples of exertion of our functional form potencies are: categorical construing of a theoretical system of concepts, programming a computer, administering a school or organizing a labor union, doing practical household chores.

Dissonance between Corresponding Appraisals

How are such strivings for fulfillment and exertion related to appraisal? To fulfill a receptive need or to exert one's potency in satisfaction of one's performance needs, appraisal of the anticipated acts of reception or performance is desirable. A similar appraisal is mandatory for the formation of dispositions to act regularly in accordance with a certain style of either receptive need fulfillment or potency exertion. Any dissonance between such appraisals will be mirrored in the corresponding acts and dispositions.

Various types of dissonance are possible. The main types are: dissonances between exertion strivings that are functional and receptive fulfillment strivings that are either vital or transcendent; dissonances between a potency exertion that is functional and one that is transcendent; and dissonances between a receptive need fulfillment that is vital and a fulfillment that is transcendent. Any of these dissonances in striving will reflect dissonances between the corresponding appraisals and dispositions. For example, a person may mistakenly seek fulfillment by developing a disposition for promiscuous sexual experiences or for excessive eating and drinking. The more we allow such vital dispositions to develop in isolation from aspirations for consonant fulfillment, the more we obscure disposition appraisal. Vitalism of this sort weakens the will to consonant formation and reformation. It becomes increasingly difficult to subordinate our vital fulfillment pulsions to our transcendent fulfillment aspirations. The same applies to the replacement of transcendent by exclusively functional dispositions. Moreover, vital and functional strivings are both strongly affected by interiorized sociohistorical pulsations that have not been spiritually appraised, purified, and enlightened.

Transcendent Fulfillment and Exertion Strivings

The formative mind as transcendent aspires to fulfill its need for peace and joy by participation with others in the formation mystery and its epiphanies. It appraises dispositions that may lead to a fully consonant life-form conducive to this participation. Correspondingly, the formative will as transcendent aspires to exert itself in implementing such dispositions. The primordial dispositions or aspirations for fulfillment and exertion are not mere sublimations of vital fulfillment impulses and functional exertion ambitions, as some theories of personality may suggest. These dispositions are original manifestations of the foundational embodied human life-form as a whole. For this reason, vital-fulfillment dispositions and impulses, as well as the functional-exertion dispositions and ambitions, are in principle intrinsically susceptible to the directives of transcendent fulfillment and exertion dispositions and aspirations.

Integration of Higher and Lower Fulfillment and Exertion Dispositions

This susceptibility of our functional, vital, and sociohistorical life for transcendent fulfillment and exertion dispositions exists initially only as a potentiality. This susceptibility has to be activated. Such activation happens through the mediation of appraisal by the formative mind. Both transcendent and functional appraisal are necessary to guide this integration of the lower fulfillment and exertion dispositions into the higher ones. This appraisal, if consonant, enables us to integrate both levels of dispositions. It leads to the intraformative consonance of pulsations, pulsions, ambitions, and aspirations. Indeed the transcendent fulfillment and exertion aspirations and dispositions should ideally avail themselves of the power of the corresponding vital and functional dispositions. They need the latter to incarnate one's chosen transcendent dispositions in the everyday formation of life and world.

This formative integration of the sociohistorical, impulsive, and ambitious dispositions must start from an acceptance of their existence as somehow meaningful. Vital fulfillment and functional exertion strivings and subsequent dispositions within a sociohistorical context are a necessary and integral part of our human formation. We must be receptive toward them. This implies as well a receptivity to their dynamics and communications. We should be open to the formation messages these pulsating, impulsive, and ambitious dispositions convey. Receptivity does not mean that we follow these dispositions blindly, but that we take them into account wisely in the process of formative appraisal.

Consider, for example, the functional ambition to exert ourselves relentlessly in order to find fulfillment by achievement. This disposition begins to wear us out. We may feel that in spite of performance we are not really finding the happiness and contentment for which we long. We may discover that a higher exertion, that of the spirit, can open us to a wider horizon of meaning. Gradually, we initiate a more spiritual disposition of self-exertion. We engage in the kind of asceticism that opens us to the transcendent meaning of things. The work we have to do appears in a new light. This does not mean that our former functional disposition for performance has become superfluous. It actually contains many kinds of subtle approaches to our task that remain useful or necessary for our effectiveness. However, the excessive functional disposition of relentless self-exertion is eased by the transcendent meaning of both our exertion and the task at hand.

Motivated and nourished by this deeper meaning, the lower exertion disposition becomes the flexible servant of the higher one of distinctively human exertion. The lower no longer dominates life exclusively and immoderately. All the functional information, dexterity, and vital strivings crystallized in this achievement disposition are now at the disposal of the corresponding transcendent disposition. Consonance begins to reign in a more relaxed life that becomes wiser and hence more effective, competent, congenial, compatible, and compassionate. Once our spirit has actively gained as much consonance of life as it may attain, the formation mystery itself may complete this integration. For it alone can grant us a consonance that surpasses our own formative potential.

Reverence for the Potentially Formative Messages of All Dispositions

In the consonant life, this relaxed and realistic receptivity for the message of all the dispositions will be accompanied by reverence. We should believe that the formation mystery may speak in every vital and functional disposition. We should listen in reverence to any potential message that such vital and functional dispositions may convey. Because of the presence of the mystery in them, we search for the potential contribution these dispositions may make in subordination to those that are transcendent. Finally, the formation mystery itself may enlighten this search in a delicate and ineffable way that transcends our own lights and powers.

Receptivity and reverence should give rise to a well-informed appraisal and appreciation of our dispositions toward *vital* fulfillment and *functional* exertion. Such respectful appraisal and appreciation serves many aspects of our formation. For instance, it helps us to idenify dissonant expressions of these dispositions, distinguishing them from actual or potential consonant expressions. A vital-sexual disposition for physical fulfillment may contain seminal elements and expressions of real love, tenderness, and affective care. How can we highlight and foster them? How might the formation mystery itself elevate them to a striving for loving consonance with itself and with its epiphanies in people who are profoundly lovable because of its mysterious presence in the depth of their life.

The same patient and respectful appraisal enables us to recognize increasingly how dissonant expressions and directives obscure and deform the foundational thrust of these pulsations, pulsions, and ambitions themselves. They point to the deeper capacity in us to move toward distinctively human dispositions. This hidden thrust accounts for our natural receptivity to the corresponding *transcendent* fulfillment and exertion aspirations. In and through their integration into these aspirations, lower strivings become ready for the gentle invasion of the formation mystery. In our example, we may recognize in vital-sexual dispositions the need for the other, for an intimacy that goes beyond mere physical involvement, that hungers for the other as a unique expression of the formation mystery that loves and embraces us.

Exaltation of Merely Functional, Vital, and Historical Dispositions

Our dispositions remain merely functional, vital, and sociohistorical if they are not penetrated and elevated by transcendent appraisal and volition. They tend to become exalted in their isolated promise of mere vital fulfillment and functional exertion. As a result of this isolation and exaltation, they are mistaken as total expressions of the foundational strivings of human life formation in its transcendent orientation. This prefocal, deceptive identification of vitalistic and functionalistic dispositions with foundational formation strivings for exertion and fulfillment leads to their totalization. This usually infrafocal or prefocal absolutizing withdraws these disposition from gentle transcendent appraisal and volition. Totalized in this way, they become deformative, dissonant, and even destructive.

Appreciation of Vital and Functional Dispositions
and Purification of Their Dissonant Directives

Respectful appraisal and appreciation generates growing insight into the art of gently mitigating, purifying, and mortifying *not* the vital and functional dispositions themselves, but those of their felt directives and expressions that are formatively dissonant. Frantic functional overachievers, for instance, do not have to destroy their disposition for achievement, only its excessive expression; its lack of congeniality, compatibility, and compassion; its motivation by pride, insecurity, anger, and immoderate self-assertion. Once purified, it might serve the loving concern of the transcendent disposition that wants to exert itself in effective performance. We must cultivate appreciative appraisal for any aspect of these dispositions that are potentially in harmony with the corresponding higher dispositions. In this way, they may merge progressively with the consonant formation of our life.

Respectful appraisal and appreciation foster an integration of higher and lower dispositions that tempers the unbridled explosive force of blind pulsations, pulsions, and ambitions. The lower dispositions are often unable to contain this force. Yet respect for what is valuable in them enables us not to paralyze the vitality of these dispositions into rigid, stilted, and compulsive patterns that are only routine. Well-integrated, these dispositions gradually begin to operate with that spontaneous lively consonance characteristic of spiritually enlightened dispositions. Yet this purification, illumination, and integration of our dispositions will remain insufficient as long as it is dependent on our own formation potential alone. At the highest point on our journey, our attempts have to be silenced. The formation mystery has to enter to effect the deepest purification and illumination, and the highest consonance in union with itself.

Deformation of the Dispositional Life in Childhood

Our dispositions can be exposed to the grave danger of lasting deformation already in childhood. This happens when the initial interformation between parents and children does not foster in the children realistic receptivity to the potentially formative directives implied in their lower dispositions. Initially, the dispositions in children may be strongly colored by their needs for vital fulfillment; later on, by those for successful exertion of their functional form potency. Parents may communicate to them, in focal or prefocal ways, that the vital and functional strivings embedded in these dispositions are appalling and shameful, that they cannot be integrated in higher beneficial dispositions. Such intimations prevent the gradual formation of respect for the dignity and form potency of vital and functional dispositions as gifts of the formation mystery.

The strivings for fulfillment and exertion are basic in the human lifeform. They manifest themselves in all its dimensions and consonant dispositions. These will be consonant to the degree that all our dispositions are integrated under and within the transcendent ones. It is difficult to persevere on the path of gentle integration if one has been taught in childhood to distrust and despise the first dispositional manifestations of these strivings. What is distrusted and rejected cannot be integrated.

The dispositions we develop in life are of great variety. Yet they embody fulfillment and exertion strivings, touched by the transcendent if they are consonant. If they are not consonant, our dispositions may be either dominated by pretranscendent manifestations of these strivings, or they may be onesidedly dominated by either the fulfillment or the exertion striving.

Prevalence of Functional Exertion Tendencies
in Western Form Traditions

In Western culture, we often find people whose lives are dominated by functional exertion dispositions of a religious or secular nature. Their repudiation of fulfillment strivings in their dispositions may lead to severe formation problems. Observe, for example, a child in a rigid, routinized, religious family. The family may exemplify and foster only functional exertion dispositions in the realm of religious living. The child knows religion only as a system of dos and don'ts under the threat of eternal punishment. The need for human and spiritual fulfillment is suppressed. Every manifestation of this need is frowned upon. The deformation of this child's life may be horrendous. Later on, the blessing of good formation counseling may help to restore the balance between fulfillment and exertion strivings as incarnated in their various dispositions.

The deepest fulfillment and exertion of human life can only be a gift of the formation mystery itself. It is an undeserved participation in the fullness of the all-embracing formation power of this mystery. This experience is usually only granted to those who first generously foster integration and balance in active transcendent presence and abandonment to this mystery.

Interdeformative Sources of the Repression
of Vital and Functional Strivings

Children may learn to depreciate the formative role of vital and functional manifestations of human fulfillment and exertion strivings. They may be encouraged to favor onesidedly one of them at the expense of the other in the forming of dispositions. Two main sources of such disposition deformation are overdirection and overprotection.

Both overdirection and overprotection result from indiscriminate anxiety, fear, and distrust in parents or their substitutes in regard to the vital and functional manifestations of the human strivings for fulfillment and exertion. Another source of overdirection and overprotection is an excessive need to dominate and control all details of disposition formation. Such a need may be typical of a formation community, such as a family, subculture, or ethnic or religious group. The need may also be fostered by the dissonant accretions of a form tradition to which the parents or other representatives are committed.

Potential Deformative Consequences of Overdirection and Overprotection

Overdirection and overprotection may lead to the formation of ambivalent appraisals, decisions, and subsequent deformative dispositions in regard to sociohistorical pulsations, vital pulsions, functional ambitions, and their felt directives. Another consequence can be found in ambivalent appraisals and dispositions in regard to people who have prevented in their life the development of a relaxed and realistic receptivity in regard to the potential formative message and power of their historical, vital, and functional dimensions.

The subsequent neglect of the ascetical dispositions of purification, illumination, and integration of one's vital and functional dispositions leads to a weak and inwardly dissonant life-form. This weakness is accompanied by a gnawing sense of deficient formation or deformation. This sense is usually prefocal or infrafocal. Often one feels that one has missed out on something vibrant in one's life. The cause of this feeling is the focal or infrafocal repudiation of the vital and functional manifestations of the fulfillment and exertion strivings in one's emergent dispositional life.

Other consequences may be overdependency and lack of resiliency, trust and confidence in life. One is inclined to withhold the emotional or passionate manifestations of fulfillment and exertion strivings from transcendent appraisal. One cannot believe that the lower manifestations of these strivings can in any way coexist with the transcendent manifestations of the same basic human strivings. The result may be that the vital fulfillment strivings and passions become dominated by the functional exertion strivings instead of by the human spirit.

Such domination by functional religious or secular ambition may lead to a life-destructive disposition of perfectionism. The disposition of religious or secular perfectionism tends to subdue and disclaim vital fulfillment dispositions that do not coincide with the emotional directives issued by this functional disposition. Perfectionism may affect the appraisal capacity of the mind, bending its appraisals in favor of the directives suggested by this functionalistic disposition. It tends forcefully to exclude the message of vital fulfillment needs and directives still vaguely emitted by weakened and repudiated vital dispositions. The ignored dispositions begin to fester in deformative ways, unappraised by the spirit.

Deformative Reactions and Responses to Overdirection and Overprotection

To compensate for the sense of underformation, due to early overdirection by others, people may develop excessively ambitious dispositions. Their excess is rooted in the exalted pride-form of life. Such dispositions are nourished by exalted and exalting emotional form directives. The latter emerge from functional dispositions that are not enlightened and tempered by the spirit. The exalted, ambitious directives of such dispositions tend to inhibit conflicting directives that may emerge from the vital fulfillment dispositions.

Consider the case of a young woman who has been made to believe from infancy on that only masculine functional performance is valuable. She imagines that her feminine, vital sensitivities are foolish and sentimental. An excessive masculine style of life and appraisal has both overdirected and overprotected her life. She feels unappreciated and underformed. To prove herself in this masculine world, she cultivates excessively ambitious dispositions. She does not balance them with either vital fulfillment dispositions or transcendent aspirations for spiritual fulfillment and exertion. Functional ambitions dominate her whole life. They make her repudiate both her vital, and her transcendent dispositions.

Such overreaction can result in a crippling alienation. Because these dispositions in their exaltation are uncongenial, they alienate persons from their foundational life-form. For the same reason, they are often incompatible with one's life situation, and they lack compassion for the vulnerability of self and others. Exalted dispositions estrange people from their own foundational life call and potentialities, from daily reality, and from others.

In reaction to overdirected and overprotected formation, people may develop other dissonant dispositions, such as excessive fearfulness, paranoid feelings, distrust, anger, hatred, hostility, enduring depreciation, and compulsiveness. The potential directives and warnings implied in the vital dispositions are ignored and dismissed by the functional overexertion of ambitious dispositions. Thus bottled up, the pulsions and interiorized vital-social pulsations represented by these vital dispositions may manifest themselves in sudden explosive outbursts. These in turn could evoke excessive feelings of guilt and shame.

It is also possible that ignored and dismissed emotional aspects of one's vital dispositions give rise to compulsive patterns of thought, imagination, memory, anticipation, and behavior. In that case, the vital dispositions become routinelike and obsessive. Their compulsive patterns are veiled manifestations of the ignored and unappraised vital dispositions, with their consequent pulsions and pulsations.

Foundational Dispositional Triad and Deformative Depreciation

How is the foundational dispositional triad of faith, hope, and love or its absence related to the depreciation of the initial vital and functional dispositions in childhood?

Appreciation of emergent dispositions is based on an implicit openness to the unique foundational life-form of the child. Such appreciation implies respect for the initially awkward vital and functional manifestations of the child's basic strivings for fulfillment and exertion of form potency. Parents affirm this emergence by their expression of faith, hope, and love. In the case of overdirection and overprotection, we see paradoxically an expression of a lack of faith, hope, and love, and of the trust and abandonment that are its fruits.

This lack manifests itself early in life in an unwillingness or an inability on the part of parents or significant others to manifest genuine faith, hope, and love in children by means of parental vital and functional acts and gestures. Such expressions on the part of loving parents should warmly and effectively respond to the vital expressions of the child's need for this parental manifestation of faith, hope, and love. Children crave such tangible blessings of their abilities, their worthwhileness, their vulnerability. They hunger for the confirmation of their attempts to functional exertion of their awakening form potency. Encouragement and appreciation should promote this emergence of the vital-functional dimension in the life of children. Withholding verbal and physical expression of the foundational triad paralyzes their consonant disposition formation.

Causes of Withholding of the Foundational Formative Triad

A withholding of vital and effective expressions of faith, hope, and love may stem from various sources. The formative community or collectivity to which one belongs may lack faith, hope, and love in regard to the transcendent dignity and mystery of the foundational life-form in self and others. No matter how limited, imperfect, or unattractive the secondary dispositonal life-form may be, the foundational life-form, the splendor of this hidden image, is a gift of the formation mystery to be revered.

Lack of verbal and physical communication of the triad may be due to lack of ability, willingness, empathy, or sensitivity. Because of this lack, parents or their substitutes may be incapable of expressing warmly and genuinely the basic formative triad in response to the hidden dignity in the child. They do not know how to radiate their faith, hope, and love concretely, vitally, and effectively at the beginning of a child's formation history.

Last but not least, they may have insufficient faith, hope, and love in regard to the transcendent source of formation itself. The formation mystery preformed with infinite love and care the foundational life-form of each child. This life-form was then entrusted to the faith, hope, and love of the parents or their substitutes.

Later in life, this preformed treasure in the child may be hidden under a secondary dispositional form that is dissonant, even repulsive. Without abandonment to the formation mystery, it is difficult for others to maintain their belief in its hidden presence in such an ill-disposed personality. Hence, such deformed children tend to evoke depreciative dispositions toward themselves. These confirm and intensify their disposition to depreciation of their life-form.

Deformative Consequences of Withholding the Foundational Formative Triad

Parents or their substitutes may thus withhold the gift of the foundational formative triad from those entrusted to their care. This withholding may lead to the formation of dissonant dispositions. Children may develop dispositions of depreciation and rejection of their life. They may feel angry and resentful against those who later in life do not fulfill their immature, excessive need for vital manifestations of faith, hope, and love.

Another consequence is the underformation of consonant dispositions that are related to the fulfillment striving, such as love, joyousness, peace, dedication, and appreciation. This underformation begets an excessive, childish, usually prefocal or infrafocal craving for affection, recognition, praise, and approval, and their open or hidden manifestation.

Lack of faith, hope, and love in regard to one's form potency as a gift of the formation mystery is also deficient. One is unable to relate to the formation mystery and to others in one's formation field with mature faith, hope, and love. One does not foster the penetration and transformation of vital and effective expressions by transcendent appraisal and appreciation in light of the formation mystery.

By means of active transcendent acts, perhaps supported by formation direction and counseling, a person may overcome for a great part these dissonant dispositions. Yet their self-centered remnants will remain in some measure. Only the formation mystery itself can purify the dispositional life-form from such residues. Active transcendent acts must then be replaced by receptive transcendent dispositions and a readiness for the path of illumination. Initially, the purely receptive articulation of one's transcendent form dimension will be experienced in darkness and aridity. The reason is that one has become so accustomed to directing one's own formation that one feels lost when the formation mystery takes over and begins a painful purification and illumination of these vital-functional residues of excessive neediness on the way to the consonance of union with itself.

Deformative Reactions and Responses to the Withholding of the Foundational Formative Triad

To compensate for emotional underformation by early withholding in life, people may form dissonant dispositions of perfectionism, subservience, rebelliousness, greed, and so on. They hope that these will fulfill their excessive need for vital-effective affection, approval, encouragement, and acceptance. They may form dispositions of withdrawal, fear, and hiddenness to escape any disapproval, rejection, blame, or discouragement. The formation directives of such dispositions may begin to dominate their formation, meaning that deformation may occur in their empirical life-form as a whole.

Such craving, grasping, complaining, and fearful dispositions and directives are deeply rooted. Their soil is the unfulfilled need for vital and effective manifestations of faith, hope, and love in regard to one's foundational life-form and its tentative expressions. Since this triad was sorely missed in childhood, its absence may darken a person's entire formation journey.

Such overly demanding, hypersensitive dispositions generate life-forms that are dissonant. This means they are uncongenial with the foundational life-form, incompatible with the demands of later interformative life situations, and incapable of genuine compassion for the vulnerability of one's own life and that of others. Dissonant dispositions tend to alienate people from their own foundational life call. They inhibit or pervert one's relaxed, wholehearted participation in the interformative processes of the human community.

Often formative direction may be necessary to help people to reform their dispositional life. Such direction should be permeated by the triad of faith, hope, and love they have been missing since childhood. Finally, only the formation mystery itself can grant the purification and illumination that would remove all residues of this deformation.

Conditions for Reformation of Deformed Dispositions

We considered initial dissonant disposition formation in childhood and its consequences. How do we cope with such dispositions later in life. How do we reform them? Evidently a necessary condition for any reformation is our awareness of dissonance, combined with a sense of personal responsibility for our own life formation. We must stop blaming the past. We only become aware of dissonance in the light of consonance. Dispositions should be in consonance not only with our formation field but also, and foremost, with the mystery of formation. Our appraisal power as transcendent discloses to us that participation in this mystery is the true aim of formation. Unfortunately, we tend to live in formation ignorance. To overcome that ignorance we need the assistance of others; we need to benefit from an interformation that removes our blinders. In the end we need the purifying impact of the formation mystery itself to burn out the last blind spots that obscure our appraisals.

Horizontal interformation may happen in encounter with truly enlightened people in our times or surroundings. They are less ignorant of the true nature nature of disposition formation than we are. We may or may not find such people. In any event, we should also profit from vertical interformation with those who lived before us. Their wisdom is preserved in consonant form traditions. To commit oneself wholeheartedly to such a tradition is to open oneself to enlightenment. When we overcome ignorance, we begin to appraise the presence of the formation mystery in our lives. Such appraisal can become prolonged in moments of silent appreciation or contemplation.

In contemplative presence, we realize that we are more than our dispositions. We no longer identify with our secondary dispositional life-form as if it were the foundational life-form itself. Neither do we evade personal responsibility here and now by transposing all responsibility to our parents or educators. In the light of transcendent appreciation, we are able to distance ourselves from our dispositions. This distancing enables us to take a stand toward them. We are no longer their prisoners. Instead we live in the peaceful awareness that we belong to the mystery of formation. To focus excessively on the past, on the how and when of dissonant dispositions, on the affection and affirmation we felt was missing, is to become more and more encapsulated in them. Our heart and mind become enslaved to our problems and to the tactics of evasion of personal responsibility.

To open to the mystery of formation is to gain a standpoint outside of these dispositions. From that standpoint we can see them for what they are. This is half the battle. The rest is a question of patience and gentle waiting while quietly reforming dissonant dispositions, first through appraisal and volition in our imagination, memory, and anticipation, then in their manifestations in daily life. The most we may often hope for initially is a just-noticeable improvement. In the meantime, we gain immensely in insight, humility, and presence to the formation mystery. Finally, this mystery itself may take over the whole process if we are ready for its transhuman purification and illumination. We manifest this readiness by years of generous exertion of our transcendent human dimension.

Actual Reformation of Dissonant Dispositions

In this light, let us reflect on the reformation or the deactivation of a dissonant disposition. We say deactivation because a dissonant disposition can never be totally eliminated, except when the formation mystery itself burns it away. Otherwise, it remains somehow in our infra- or prefocal memory. At a time of crisis, disappointment, or defeat, it may suddenly flare up again. Hence, we should always be vigilant, albeit in a relaxed fashion.

Let us say that I have formed over the years a disposition of anger. Suddenly I become aware that anger in subtle, indirect ways is influencing my appraisals, decisions, and daily interactions with others. It is affecting my bodily posture, speech, and facial expression. I feel perturbed by this disclosure. I am ashamed about the many moments anger seems to poison my appraisals and feelings. I reproach myself for negative expressions, subtle condemnations, righteous judgments. I keep asking myself how I could have become such a hostile person, why I failed so badly in my disposition formation. I try to recall all the occasions in which I expressed my anger in gossip, belittling the success of others, planting seeds of distrust in the minds of my listeners, or engaging in the subtle art of back-handed compliments. I ask myself over and over again how I could have been so mean without even realizing what I was doing. I feel compelled to explore my past. Was it perhaps the same when I was younger? Does my angry disposition go back to things that happened at home when I was a child, an infant? How can I remedy my hostility, deactivate my angry disposition? I begin frantically to analyze every detail of my dealings with others.

This whole process could be described as one of anxious focusing on my dissonant disposition in merely functional appraisal. I make a willful attempt to figure out the angry disposition, to dig up its roots, to analyze piecemeal its slightest ramifications in my feelings, deeds, and expressions. While this approach may be helpful for the reformation of dispositions, I should also be present to the dissonant disposition in a different way, by acknowledging frankly that I am an angry person. While I feel guilt and shame in regard to the many times I've hurt people and their feelings, I distance myself from my anger, knowing I am more than that disposition alone. My foundational life-form is different. I abandon myself, along with my hostility, sadness, guilt, shame, and failure, to the formation mystery that is the ground of my hidden nobility. My main appraisal in this case is transcendent. My attention is not totally absorbed in functional dwelling on the dissonant disposition. It is centered in the mystery that makes me be. I surrender to the fact that this mystery allowed my life to unfold under conditions that tempted me to develop an angry disposition.

In transcendent appraisal, faith, hope, and love are renewed. I believe that all things will work out for the best. My dissonant disposition is still there, but I am no longer paralyzed by it. It has lost its fascination. Enlightenment in regard to this disposition helps me to become aware of my limitations. This awareness diminishes the power of the pride-form in my life, even if my anger itself is not yet diminished. I humble myself before the formation mystery. It grants me the purifying awareness of how impotent I really am in my encapsulation in functionalistic attempts to reform my dispositions by my own isolated powers. I feel more at home than ever with suffering humanity, whose proclivity to a dissonant dispositional life I compassionately share.

Peaceful and relaxed, I now allow my angry disposition to emerge against the background of this transcendent presence. The power of relaxed appraisal enables me to ponder quietly and gradually possible ways to deactivate the hostile disposition. Without tension I abandon myself to the higher power of the formation mystery. It will enable my form potency to reform this disposition in its own good time. This gentle way of enlightened presence to a dissonant disposition is the way of transcendent appraisal.

Mere functional appraisal of our dispositions tends to be analytical and aggressive. In the long run, it is counterproductive, when it is not complemented by transcendent appraisal. Transcendent appraisal tends to be integrative and gentle. In mere functional appraisal, we isolate what is appraised, such as an angry disposition, from the formation field as a whole. Functional appraisal dissects what is appraised in its inner wholeness.

In our example, we did not put the dissonant disposition in the perspective of our formation field as flowing forth from the formation mystery. We engaged exclusively in a fragmenting analysis of the disposition, its structure, manifestation, and genesis. As a result, we felt more and more its victim, less free, more determined.

Disposition Reformation and Transcendent Appraisal

Exclusive functional appraisal is an appraisal that excludes any insight that may come from transcendent appraisal. Aggressively we try to force functional insight alone. For instance, we appraise the desirability of starting a family of our own merely on basis of practical considerations, such as tax deduction or the advantage of having a double income while sharing the expense of our apartment and meals for two.

In certain situations the aggressiveness of functional appraisal can be beneficial. It enables us to be precise in our practical evaluation of concrete situations. This decisiveness enhances our effectiveness. It is an excellent approach for our functional assessment of the concrete implications of our acts and dispositions. Functional appraisal becomes destructive, however, if it excludes a priori any transcendent appraisal. For it implies that we do not acknowledge the primary importance of the transcendent meanings, life directives, and dispositions that may have something to tell us in regard to our decisions.

Take the example of a merely functional appraisal of a hostile disposition. We felt isolated in our guilt and shame about our impotence in the face of an overwhelming inclination to animosity. We felt cut off from our formation field and its healing source. Transcendent appraisal completes and directs our functional appraisal in this case. In its light, we relativize our dispositions. We see ourselves as having a source in an eternal origin, an all-pervading presence. Dissonant dispositions like guilt, shame, and failure are acknowledged but relativized.

Transcendent appraisal is not divisive but unitive. It makes whole again what functional appraisal divides. It attunes us to a mysterious totality that is already there. Far from being dissective and aggressive, transcendent appraisal is meditative and restorative, a gentle preservation of the deeper unity of life and world below all dissonant dispositions.

Our culture sets great store by utility, efficiency, and success. It fosters aggressive, analytical, functional appraisal, which rightly helps to build science, technique, and efficient organization. Because we are so efficiency-minded, we are inclined to examine all our dispositions only in an aggressive analytical way. Functional appraisal prevails. But we cannot rest in this predilection for the analytical. It is only one side of the story of disposition formation. Mere functional appraisal without enlightenment by transcendent appreciation leads to self-centered isolation. It enslaves us to self-preoccupation and the anxious urge to force at once a constellation of perfect functional dispositions.

Appraisal is transcendent when it enables us to go beyond the manifold dispositions that rise from our pulsations, pulsions, and ambitions. It pushes us beyond the limited meanings of the childhood traumas, sensitivities, faults, and projects that gave rise to dissonant dispositions. In and beyond all of these, it integrates our lives contextually in the whole of the formation field and its all pervading source. It brings us in touch with our primordial form of life, which as such is always open to realization in consonant dispositions. It unites us with the primordial movement of our transcendent will, which strives spontaneously after the fully consonant life-form. It is this life-form that leads to the fullness of peace and joy in participation with others in the mystery.

In transcendent appraisal and appreciation, we do not center on our dispositions as isolated masters of our destiny. Nor do we tighten our hearts to scrutinize endlessly all manifestations of our dissonant dispositions. In both cases we would lose the fruit of transcendent appraisal and appreciation. We would become disquieted instead of patiently forming our dispositional life in an atmosphere of equanimity. A gentle avoidance of any return to an appraisal of dispositions outside the light of the formation mystery is an essential condition for transcendent appraisal and appreciation.

Both kinds of appraisal—functional and transcendent—have their own purpose, time, and place in disposition reformation. Our vision of ourselves as a part of the mysterious whole of reality should be primary and functional appraisal should be secondary. Both kinds of disposition appraisal are necessary, but one cannot replace the other. They are mutually complementary, as are the subsequent movements of transcendent and functional volition and their resulting dispositions.

Historical Development of a Prevalent Functional
Appraisal of Dispositions

The art and discipline of transcendent appraisal and appreciation has been neglected in late accretions of Western form traditions. An overemphasis on functional appraisal and appreciation has seriously hindered the wholesome disposition formation of people inside and outside ideological and religious form traditions. This has harmed not only their spiritual but also their psychosomatic wellness. It has diminished their long-term efficiency in spite of short-term advantages in the realms of production, distribution, consumption, and ethical perfectionism.

At a certain period in the Western history of formation, between the fifteenth and seventeenth centuries, the art of transcendent appraisal and appreciation was in some measure eclipsed by its subordinated functional counterpart. Many people, to be sure, kept longing for a life of dispositions illumined by transcendent appraisal, but society as a whole lost touch with this dimension as a central concern. The Renaissance and the Enlightenment, with a growing emphasis on individualism, science, and technology, made the initiation and perfection of functional dispositions the focus of attention. The medieval vision of reality collapsed and a functionalistic view took over. Living appreciation of the transcendent dimension of human formation was lost. People were no longer disposed to experience their deeper interwovenness with one another—and with nature, history, and the cosmos—as constantly emerging from the formation mystery in its manifold epiphanies.

The efficiently disposed functionary, vying for success within a competitive society, became the model of life. This model generated an exclusively functional style of appraisal and appreciation of dispositions. It heightened the fascination with efficiency dispositions, held together by a functional ego. The emphasis on functional appraisal and appreciation led in turn to an obsession with merely ethical and psychological self-actualization by means of efficient dispositions. Many became more enthralled with self-perfection than with intimacy with the Sacred in a life of transcendent appreciation. In many cases this meant the neglect of the transcendent aspect of dispositions, no matter how many people actualized themselves ethically or psychologically as functionally impeccable members of different churches or humanistic organizations.

Toward the end of the nineteenth century, the scientific world view extended itself to human life and its disposition formation as such. Psychology, psychiatry, anthropology, sociology, education, and the political sciences began to study disposition formation in isolation from the eternal presence that transfigures cosmos and humanity. To be sure, these sciences gave us a wealth of insights that can eventually be integrated into a deeper and richer understanding of disposition formation in the light of transcendent appraisal. They render this understanding more practical and realistic. Functional appraisal of our dispositions will be refined and enriched as a result. This is all for the good, provided functional attention does not outstrip transcendent attention.

In line with humanity's already changing vision of itself, the psychological disciplines began to perfect methods of functional disposition appraisal. They stimulated people even more to look functionally at what was happening in their dispositional life, without relating these dispositions to a horizon of meaning beyond themselves. They began to look at dispositions primarily to assess how they might affect their private efficiency and salvation inside and outside of their religious or ideological form traditions. The deepest meaning of human dispositions within the whole of things began to elude them. Functional appraisal methods mushroomed in many forms. They could be utilized by the individual alone or under the guidance or stimulation of an analyst, a modern spiritual director, therapist, counselor or sensitivity group.

A climate of introspection and functionalism pervaded the culture. All sorts of functional appraisal experts—educational, psychological, psychiatric, sociological, anthropological, psychologistic-spiritual— began to usurp the place of the masters of transcendent appraisal of the great formation traditions. Under this kind of guidance, many people were inclined to center their disposition formation around the ideal of efficient functionality. This ideal integrated as well as possible within the demands of functionality their vital and historical dispositions. It tended to neglect their transcendent aspirations and inspirations. If conflicts were solved, it was usually those between unintegrated vital strivings and functional dispositions. Slumbering conflicts between transcendent aspiration and functional-vital disposition were rarely recognized.

We do not contend, of course, that functional appraisals are useless.

They can be highly advantageous, a definite gain in the realm of disposition formation. Our loss is only that many may no longer find it necessary to integrate functional disposition appraisal into a primary and deeper transcendent appraisal of the same dispositions when the situation demands such integration.

Effects of the Decline of Transcendent Disposition Appraisal

The decline of the practical art and discipline of transcendent appraisal and appreciation led various experts in religious and human formation to borrow functional appraisal methods blindly from the prestigious sciences of human and social life. Some of these experts had lost touch with the treasures of spiritual wisdom in their own traditions. They were unable to recast these new ways of functional appraisal of disposition formation in the light of an all-embracing spiritual vision. These insights remained foreign and therefore harmful elements within the body of traditional formative wisdom and spiritual knowledge about human dispositions.

As a result of the neglect of transcendent appraisal, the dispositional life became precariously onesided. If people foster long enough such onesided or dissonant dispositions, this tendency will show up in their minds and bodies. Inner dissonance affects their mental and physical health. People find themselves increasingly disposed to function as lonely fighters for self-actualization in a hostile or competitive formation field in which they no longer feel embedded. Their dispositions lead them to follow the fast beat of time, to outdo competitors, to live and work in a hurry, to become filled with hidden hostilities toward those who threaten to outshine them by more efficient dispositions and actions.

Our life may be imprisoned in functional dispositions. They dim the vision of the spirit. Most harmful in this regard are those of ascendancy over others. To prove our functional potency, we may strive vigorously to outshine other people. This competitive attitude engenders inordinate strife and self-exertion. As a result our bloodstream may be polluted with overdoses of glandular chemicals. Arteries, brain, heart, and other organs may suffer from such surfeit. Disorder results. Problems like these multiply in functionalistic cultures because they are dominated by social form traditions that neglect the unfolding of transcendent dispositions.

Beyond Functionalism

To rise beyond functionalism, we must regain the awareness of our interwovenness with the mystery of formation. In its light, dispositions for ascendancy and competition are revealed in their relativity. We experience a rebirth of higher aspirations and inspirations, a longing for pathways to the life of the spirit. Initially we may be tempted by strange forms of mysticism, astrology, witchcraft, and exotic cults. Gradually we may realize that the horizon of the whole and the Holy is disclosed in simple everydayness. The hidden and ordinary life is the birthplace of transcendent dispositions.

Abandonment in faith, hope, and consonance liberates us from the tyranny of functional self-actualization. We gain distance from the anxious dispositions it engenders. We are no longer embroiled in a futile battle against time. Our mind is not filled with fights with real or imagined rivals and opponents.

Transcendent dispositions cannot be based on the illusion of an isolated self. This self is imaged as a lonely rock arrogantly and defiantly rising from the sea of reality. It is an illusory self, out of touch with its formation field and its transcendent source. We should center ourselves instead in our hidden form of life, emerging as it does from the mystery within, generating dispositions of presence to its epiphanies in the mundaneness of daily duties.

Functional appraisal, we repeat, should not be neglected. It informs us of the concrete details of our temperament, dispositions, assets, and deficiencies. It keeps us in touch with the conditions of our formation field. The task of functional appraisal is never finished. Its observations should be submitted, however, to transcendent appraisal, for they are signposts to be deciphered in the light of the mystery. Functional appraisal should no longer be the exclusive measure of all things. It has to be wisely guided by transcendent appraisal and appreciation.

Isolated vital dispositions should not dominate us either. They wall us up within ourselves, making us overly sensitive, trapped in our own feelings. We lose the disposition to be wholly present where we are, willing to get our hands dirty in the muddle of life, to share silently the everyday grind of humanity, to labor for justice, peace, and mercy in the midst of oppression.

In mere functional appraisal, we become mesmerized by the limiting dimensions of our formation field. To widen them forcefully, the exaltation of the pride-form supplants the aspiration and inspiration of the spirit. Exalted dispositions lead to disappointment and defeat. The deceptive image of self-perfection changes into its opposite. Frustrated by failure, we may experience ourselves as a miserable collection of countless limitations. This disposition to self-rejection is as false as the disposition to self-exaltation. In neither case do we walk humbly in the light of the truth of who we are.

Functional and Transcendent Volition

At the end of this chapter, we would like to clarify the two kinds of willing mentioned in passing. Transcendent willing is primary; functional willing is secondary. Both are necessary for the formation of concrete spiritual dispositions. At times we refer to the first kind as receptive or appreciative volition: receptive, because it is an answer to inspirations and aspirations that the will receives from the power of transcendent appraisal; appreciative, because it is an affirmation by the will in appreciation of a spiritual form directive and the dispositions it implies. Such form directives and dispositions are disclosed by the appreciative spirit to us as willing persons.

Functional volition is sometimes called executive, or managing, willing by formation science: executive, because we will the execution of concrete acts that engender in our life the dispositions disclosed to us by the appraising mind and the transcendent appreciative will; managing, because the functional will manages concretely the acts and dispositions that form our daily life in the unique and communal image of the mystery we are called to be.

Unfortunately, Western social form traditions may incline us to substitute managing volition for receptive willing. To highlight the difference between the two, let us take the example of a painter. Functionally, she can will to paint a landscape. She can go to a quiet place in a meadow overlooking a stream or in the woods surrounding the water and daydream under a lovely sky. She can put her canvas before her, open her paint box, and take her brushes in hand. She can will to distance herself from other concerns and distractions. She can focus on the sights before her. But she cannot will in the same way the creative painting itself, or the inspirations, aspirations, feelings, and visions that it may symbolize in striking beauty. The more she encapsulates herself in mere functional volition, the more the inspiration seems to recede. We may have had similar experiences when trying to produce an inspiring letter, poem, or paper. This may be one cause of the writer's block we may have experienced at times.

Managing willing takes care of the preliminary acts described above. When the inspiration comes, other acts of the managing will are necessary, such as choosing the paints, making the brush strokes, correcting them in the light of one's inspiration. Over and above these executive acts, however, the painter's transcendent receptive volition is submissive and open to the guiding inspiration itself. It directs functional willing in its obedient execution of the inspiration.

Likewise, I can organize the right conditions for the initiation or reformation of a transcendent disposition. But I cannot will myself functionally into the inspiring dimension of such a disposition. This is a gift to be received and affirmed in appreciation by my transcendent will. This will is one of receptive openness to spiritual form directives as disclosed to my power of transcendent appraisal by the formation mystery.

Consider the disposition of inspiring social presence. Functionally, I can will to act socially in behalf of underprivileged people. I can will all the motions that express social concern, but I cannot will in the same way true love, warm care, and felt reverence for these people as unique suffering images of the mystery of formation in which we all share.

To foster that dimension of my disposition, I must cultivate a receptive attitude, open to any inspiration that may come my way while functionally involving myself. Inspiration may arise in the pauses between the hours of management. Both this waiting upon the disclosure of the inspiration and our affirmation of it are acts of transcendent-receptive volition. Managing willing remains necessary for the formation of concrete dispositions. It should be enlightened, however, by this receptive willing and by an appreciation of the epiphanies of the formation mystery.

Receptive willing reaches its zenith in the imageless and wordless loving surrender to the formation mystery itself when it transfers our striving from the vital-affective, functional, and actively transcendent dimensions to the purely receptive articulation of the transcendent dimension. This subtle presence of the mystery in its new epiphany in pure receptivity leaves the active transcendent and functional will in utter emptiness and powerlessness. The will no longer moves itself but is gratuitously moved by the mystery in its own good time. Only the mystery decides the moment and the duration of this undeserved gift of light and darkness, of fullness and emptiness, of power and powerlessness. We are receivers. We can only accept or refuse the gift, flow with it or resist it. Our will is a will of pure receptivity.

Blind surrender to dispositions that prevail in a community to which we belong does not necessarily mean that we grow from mere functional to transcendent willing. I may bind myself along with other "functional willers" into a group of executive do-gooders. Within this group we may mutually reinforce a functionalistic willfulness. An absence of the transcendent dimension in our shared dispositions may lead to quasi inspirations and false totalizations. We may have silenced our aspirations for a fulfillment of life and an exertion of form potency that are transcendent. We may have cultivated a disposition of silent refusal of inspirations and aspirations.

Repudiation and Refusal

It is possible for us not only to deny the impulses of our infrafocal consciousness; we can do likewise with the aspirations of the transfocal consciousness. In this case, what we do is an act of refusal, for, by way of contrast to infrafocal repudiation, some focal free act is initially involved in refusal. Refusal is not the infrafocal repudiation of a pulsion that threatens us before we know it focally and linguistically. Refusal is the initially free rejection of an invitation by the formation mystery that appeals to us from the deeper regions of our intrasphere. Soon this disposition of refusal may become prefocal.

In spite of refusal, our innate longing for the fulfilling mystery may seep into our functional and vital life. Because of our prefocal refusal, we no longer know the transcendent mystery that evokes and gives sufficient grounds for this striving for the infinite. Hence the longing that lost its source seeks its object mainly in passing people, events, and things. It is attached by the functional will to some finite disposition in search of exalted projects to be executed in one's formation field. A finite disposition and its object pole become totalized, as if they were the path to fulfillment of life's meaning. Such totalization can render dispositions compulsive-obsessive, hysterical, or fanatical both in their exalted striving for fulfillment and in their excessive power exertion.

Fanaticized Dispositions of Collectivities Called Communities

Striking historical examples of such fanaticized dispositions can be found in many followers of Fascism, Nazism, Communism, and certain exotic cults. In many instances, as in these examples, fanaticized dispositions happen to be collective. They pulsate through a so-called community and contaminate the dispositions of many members through shared enthusiastic exaltation. This is often reinforced by exciting symbols, such as marches, banners, slogans, and martial music. This explains the reluctance of many refined and distinctively humanized individuals to participate in mass demonstrations: they are wary of the vital-functional excitation that may silence the spirit and its quiet power of subtle transcendent appraisal; they fear the birth of exalted dispositions that have been the cause of war and social injustice. Christians, for example, could never have persecuted so many thousands of Jews over the centuries or burned so many "witches" without such temporarily fanaticized collective dispositions.

The absolutizing of a disposition for a finite holy cause always leads to the absolutizing of hate against those who we imagine stand in the way of its fulfillment. This disposition is heightened and inflamed by a similarly disposed group of people, like certain cults or collectivities, a street mob or a march of demonstrators that runs out of control. To be saved from vital-functional idealists of any persuasion is the fervent hope of a humanity in search of justice, peace, and mercy.

Formative Communal Dispositions

Formative communal dispositions, on the contrary, are marked by the primacy of the spirit. They counteract lower dispositions that tend to total-ize any missionary or social enthusiasm of a community or of any pressure group within its midst. When such transcendent dispositions prevail, vulgar injustice toward outsiders and toward the uniqueness of community members tends to diminish. These distinctively human dispositions dispose the community also to unmask communal ideals that are mainly vital reactions to the momentary moodiness of the group. They dispose the community to defend the human rights of each of its unique members. This disposition counteracts the absolutizing of any finite cause, no matter how holy and humane it may seem.

History has taught us this lesson in blood and tears. Such dispositions always end up in the subtle or open persecution of nonconforming persons. Indeed, exalted communal dispositions for finite holy and humane causes plant the seeds of social injustice and its consequent cruelty. Any spirituality that disposes people to social injustice is a false spirituality, no matter how virtuous and high sounding its principles and ideals may be.

Mere Functional Dispositions Dull the Formation Field

Transcendent dispositions disclose the beauty and truth of our formation field. They open us to horizons of meaning that lift us beyond pedestrian preoccupations. Without them our formation field may become boring and lifeless. Some people live lives of mere routinization. They may develop an exalted fantasy life to break the tediousness of an existence that is not uplifted by transcendent presence. This fantasy life is fed by unappraised pulsions, flamboyant ambitions, and popular pulsations. To escape meaningless routines, people develop a deformative disposition for the novel, the grandiose, the latest, the newest, for fads that emerge within and without their religious or ideological form traditions. This disposition makes them babble excitedly about their illusionary projects and make-believe accomplishments. The silent beauty of the hidden life is abhorrent to them. Such a deformative disposition affects the appraisal potency of people. It feeds into a deluded self-appreciation.

Transcendent Dispositions and the Richness of Everyday Formation

Transcendent dispositions open us to the richness hidden in the concrete people, events, and things we meet humbly in our everyday formation field. They make us realize how everydayness is carried by the mystery that shines forth in all things. Our dispositional life is trustworthy to the degree that it is faithful to the everydayness of the common life. It enables us to live everydayness as the manifestation of a deeper mystery. It keeps us in touch with the ordinariness of daily existence and its inconspicuous routines. It acknowledges and controls these supportive lower dispositions, elevating them by spiritual appraisal and appreciation. Lived transcendent dispositions diminish the need for exalting dispositions of a deceptive fantasy life. One can be task-oriented when this disposition is called for and relaxed when it is not.

Any disposition that alienates people from their concrete formation field is suspect. Such dispositions tend to close people off from others. They become proud or depressed or easily enticed victims of exalted spurts of the imagination. They are isolated from the consonant form traditions out of which their life emerges and by which it is sustained. Uprooted, they no longer share vigorously the task of humanity to give form to life and world in the image of the mystery.

Dispositions of Mindfulness and Forgetfulness

Abandonment to the mystery of everydayness is fostered by a wise balance between the dispositions of mindfulness and forgetfulness. The disposition of focal appraisal, vigilance, and reflection is beneficial when it is balanced by a disposition of spontaneity and focal forgetfulness. We need periods of quiet in which the disposition of mindful appraisal and appreciation restores us to the deeper meaning of life. In between these moments of letting go, we need dispositions of spontaneous involvement, forgetful of focal appraisal and appreciation. Such dispositions reimmerse us in the natural flow of our formation field.

There should be a dialogue between the dispositions of appraisal and those of spontaneous immersion in daily life. Focal appraisal should never quell the spontaneity of dispositions of daily living. Without this forgetfulness of focal appraisal, we could become alienated from the epiphanies of the mystery of formation in everydayness. Reimmersion in daily life in forgetfulness is as much a homecoming to the mystery as focal appraisal and appreciation. Finally, if an undeserved invasion of the mystery invites us to total emptiness and receptivity, forgetfulness is mandatory. Without it we cannot rest in pure, silent receptivity to an ineffable, delicate form of presence.

Transcendent Appraisal and Appreciation

Transcendent appraisal and appreciation flourish in a climate of stillness and repose. They foster consonance with all dimensions of one's formation field and with its source, the mystery of formation. Transcendent appraisal evaluates and purifies our secondary foundational life-form of dispositions. It makes it consonant with our primordial life-form as well as with our formation field.

Transcendent appraisal and appreciation awaken us from illusions embedded in dissonant dispositions. Mirages are no longer the object poles of our disposition formation. Dissonant dispositions are divisive. They lead to a loss of inner wholeness. This loss obscures the splendor of the presence of the forming mystery. It veils its image in the depth of our being. Concealment of the inner source leaves us victims of a multitude of illusions that distort our disposition formation. Enchanted by unappraised pulsations, pulsions, ambitions, aspirations, and inspirations, we become forgetful of the image within. Separated from our center, identified with our dispositional life-form, we live in illusion.

Transcendent appraisal and appreciation imply a certain detachment from functional and vital involvement. This distance helps us to appraise the illusionary dissonant dispositions that rule our relations with people, events, and things in our formation field. We begin to awaken from illusionary dispositions as we experience the formation mystery and its image within us as the true center of our life. We awaken to the consonant meaning of reality, seeing things from within the formation mystery, as it were. We no longer view the appearances in our formation field as self-contained entities external to the all-embracing mystery, to one another, and to ourselves. Within the mystery of formation, all things interform in intimate togetherness with one another.

Transcendent appraisal and appreciation are thus means to a deeper consonance of the dispositional life. Dispositions begin to foster instead of hindering our participation in the mystery.

One of the most beautiful disclosures of the life of transcendent appreciation is that of the resplendent indwelling of the mystery of formation in the depths of the inner image that grounds our life uniquely. At certain moments the mystery may suspend our movements of appraisal and its sustaining imagination, memory, anticipation, and disposition formation. It may make us feel the mysterious flame of unique life formation, ever glowing within. We are drawn irresistibly into the inner image. The mystery discloses its way with us in the silent depths of the core of our being. What we learned from faithful appraisal now becomes one simple lived experience that transcends all particular appraisals, decisions, images, acts, and dispositions.

A life of transcendent appreciation fosters a life of contemplation. During this life, pauses of imageless and wordless presence may grow in depth and duration. This experience may be so overwhelming that it becomes difficult at times to engage in any appraisal, reflection, or imagination. Our appraisal dispositions are suspended. At such moments we should abandon ourselves to the grace of silent, imageless consonance with the source that lifts us beyond all passing forms of life, all changing situations in the world.

CHAPTER 7

Formative Imagination and Disposition Formation

I n this chapter, we use the adjective *formative* to indicate that the imagination is of interest to our science mainly insofar as it is related to our distinctively human formation of life and world. Formation science would not be interested, for example, in a chance imagining of a geometrical figure if this image had no influence on human formation under its distinctively human or spiritual aspect. By contrast, we may imagine how we can counteract a deformative anti-authority disposition by learning to cope with our irrational anger. In this case we use our imagination formatively. Therefore, we must ask: In what way does formative imagination influence the formation of our dispositions?

In the preceding chapter, we considered the role of transcendent and functional appraisal in disposition formation. In this chapter, we will examine the part played by transcendent and functional imagination. The operation of imagination is transcendent when it supports and depends on our transcendent mind and will. For example, a woman may choose to devote her life to teaching the art of formative living to professional people who feel spiritually abandoned in the midst of opulence and sophistication. This option implies a transcendent appraisal of the meaning of her life as a whole. She has to ponder the spiritual sense of detachment from other, more lucrative occupations. She needs to reflect on the abandonment of spirit that unconsciously depresses many of her contemporaries and cries out for help. Necessary also is an appraisal of the transcendent constituent of such a teaching disposition, for to choose a new way of life means to choose a new set of dispositions.

This appraisal may be sustained by imagining symbolically the beauty of a life dedicated to such a calling. In her imagination she may form the symbol of a prism, analogous to the rich, reflecting power of formative teaching. She imagines that a bright light pervades the prism. This light symbolizes for her the way the formation mystery uses her to reflect its wisdom to others in formative, inspirational teaching. Her transcendent memory may recall images of teachers who have become living symbols of her ideal. In transcendent anticipation she may imaginatively portray herself as a teacher who starts and sustains many others on their life's journey. In this way her imagination enhances and supports her transcendent appraisal and option. If, by chance, she is freely committed to a consonant form tradition, she may find in its sources many other symbols and images to draw upon in her reflection and meditation. These help her to keep in tune with the transcendent depth of her chosen ideal and to replenish her dedication when it is waning.

Such transcendent use of the imagination does not suffice, however, for the formation of concrete dispositions. It has to be complemented by a functional or incarnational exertion of the imagination. The imagination functions incarnationally insofar as it assists functional mind and will in their task of directing the concrete implementation of transcendent ideals in daily life. The teaching ideal should be imagined realistically also. The woman may place herself imaginatively in the concrete surroundings of a teaching situation, asking herself: Will I feel at home there? How would I manage? She may recall imaginative teaching situations in which she participated either as a teacher or a learner. She may try to anticipate what teaching would be like in the future within the society in which she will have to exercise that function. This practical use of the imagination will make her more aware of the kinds of dispositions she should begin to cultivate if she wants to implement her transcendent ideal effectively.

Formative Imagination in the Service of Disposition Formation

In service of disposition formation, formative imagination can create fictitious formation situations or add fictitious aspects to the perception of a real formation situation. People who initiate or cultivate dispositions react and respond to fictitious formation situations as if they were real, even on the level of organismic reactions.

Formative imagination can operate in all five dimensions of our formative presence. Here we will not discuss at length the pneumatic dimension, which is the human transcendent dimension as illumined by the Holy Spirit as speaking in Holy Scripture and Christian tradition and will be the subject of a later volume. Suffice it to mention that formative symbols abound in the Christian tradition. We need only recall the image of the rock in the

Psalms, of the exodus from Egypt through the desert into the promised land, or of the vine and the branches in Jesus' farewell discourse.

In the human transcendent dimension of our formative presence, we may think of such images as the Holy Grail, a national flag, the shamrock of Ireland. In the functional dimension examples can be found in attractive industrial design and in the power and status symbols devised by image makers. In the vital dimension, the West has become poor in symbolic imagination. Mainly physical-sexual imagery has been fostered to see, for instance, an open object as the image of a vagina or a pointed object as that of a penis. Here we become aware of the sociohistorical dimension. The impact of psychoanalytic image formation has influenced popular sexual imagining in our culture. Sociohistorical pulsations form our imagination on every level mentioned. Already a superficial observation makes it evident that such interconscious images and symbols can coform the prevalent dispositions of a specific population.

Formative imagination can be guided by both form reception and form donation. Receptivity can be passive or active. If our form receptivity is only passive, it may spell trouble for disposition formation. Merely passive imagination allows all kinds of formative images to enter into our lives uncritically. We do not actively form and reform our images in the light of appraisal and enlightened choice. Such passivity seems to be fostered in childhood by an early prolonged exposure to television. The child's form-receptive imagination is inundated with images he or she does not elaborate actively. As a result it becomes difficult to activate the child's creative imagination. It may have been better when children were exposed to radio programs only. Enchanted by these verbal stories, children had to fill out visually in imagination what was presented to them only in words and sound. This helped them to cultivate their active-receptive form imagination.

Passive form imagination leads to a passive development of dispositions that are neither unique nor transcendent. It makes for a somewhat dull population, similarly disposed because of exposure from early in life to similar programs absorbed complacently. The pliability of their formative imagination makes them vulnerable to outside influences in later disposition formation. They are easily victimized by any image maker who captures their imagination. A striking example pertains to the vulnerability of large groups of people in Germany to the images created by Nazi propaganda. It disposed them to acts many would never have consented to, were it not for their impressionable formative imagination.

Creative Imagination and Vital Disposition Formation

To illustrate the power of creative formative imagination, let us consider its influence on the vital reformation of dispositions. We choose examples of the formative influence of vital imagination because we can observe clearly its impact on our bodily life. Take the case of a person we shall call Peter who constantly suffered low back pain due to the treatment of rectal cancer. The pain became so intolerable that only three options seemed open to him: effective treatment of the pain, commitment to a mental institution, or suicide. He was lucky enough to have become acquainted with an experienced, well-trained formation counselor. This woman suggested that he should deactivate his present disposition toward pain and develop a new disposition that would diminish his suffering. She proposed to him a project of vital disposition reformation by means of formative imaging. They would first talk through the object pole of the disposition he should reform. She helped him to address himself to the pain, not as an abstract concept or a simple perception, but to form an image of the pain that would express how it really affected him—an image that would not be made up by the mind in isolation but that would emerge from the source of the pain as concretely located in the vital dimension of his life. It should be an image that would tell him something about his suffering.

Under her guidance he was able to form an image of a vicious terrier chewing his spine. It was a nightmarish image, but it enabled him to give form to his pain experience. This visual image in turn made it possible for him to form a verbal image. In this form the pain became available to his appraisal. This appraisal had to be positive or appreciative. The image and the experience it represented had to be seen as a formation opportunity. Only then could he approach it as a point of departure for the initiation of a formative disposition. Then he could begin to work with it. Peter came to this first formative decision: "Yes, I want to reform my disposition toward pain. I am resolved to work with this image, to see it as an opportunity for the improvement of my life."

Once the *formation will* came to bear on this decision, the formation counselor could work with him on the reformation of vital imagination. A process of intraformation was set in motion. Peter was encouraged by her to get in touch imaginatively with the vicious terrier. This should not be an exercise of logic but an imaginary talking to the terrier. In his talking Peter began to find out why the terrier was chewing his spine. His physical pain was amplified because an infrafocal resentment of his profession as an accountant had given rise to bitter feelings of rage and resentment toward

life. He had never been able to admit to himself these deformative dispositions. They were poisoning his life. They found indirect expression in a
deepening of the pain that was already there. The infrafocal, deformative
disposition of rage, revolt, and defiance tried to destroy his life via a deadly
increase in the experience of already existing pain. The vital dimension of
his life became the channel of deformative self-expression. In this way an
unknown disposition was potentially made available through the formative imagination.

When Peter discovered the meaning of the pain, he gradually became
capable of reforming the underlying disposition. In the end transcendent
appraisal and appreciation would lead him to a spiritual disposition of
abandonment in faith, hope, and consonance to the formation mystery.
Functional appraisal would help him to express this abandonment in other
appreciative images that would directly address themselves to the image
of the chewing terrier, representing his self-destructive resentment. In the
end it became possible to make the terrier stop its merciless chewing. With
the taming of the terrier, the disposition of rage and fury against his fate
was slowly deactivated. A disposition of abandonment, surrender, and
trust was initiated. The pain was no longer intolerable. Some of it was still
there, but it had acquired a new meaning through his meaning-giving disposition. The temptation to suicide or to commitment to a mental institution was no longer experienced.

This case study illustrates the power of formative imagination. There
are many examples in primitive cultures of this power. For example, a
medicine man declares that bad spirits have invaded a tribesman. As a
result he will die. Amazingly, the person will not survive this indictment.
No Western treatment can change his fate. The deep formative imagining,
"I have to die," initiates a fatal disposition of anticipation of certain
death. This vital disposition gives form through images to the involuntary
nervous system in such a way that the person dies as predicted.

Something similar may happen in Western civilization. A young man's
father and uncle die in their fifties from coronaries. Deeply troubled and
anxious, this man develops a disposition of anticipation of a coronary
when he reaches that age. Through formative imagination, the disposition
may affect the vital dimension so intensely that the man indeed experiences in that year the coronary he was disposed to expect. The same power
of imagination explains why the laying on of hands by suggestive people
who are either believers *or* atheists may effect healing in those who expect
to be healed.

Incarnation of an Imaginative Reform Project in One's Life

The act of implementation of an image in one's life can be called an incarnation. In the context of our example, such enfleshment applies first of all to the vital dimension; it can then be applied to other dimensions of human formation.

The first condition for effective formative implementation is relaxation. One should let go of all tension, socially, vitally, functionally, and spiritually. Formation science emphasizes in this regard the development of the general form disposition of *gentleness*. At the start of this exercise of implementation of imagination, this disposition will enable us to go through a phase of gentling the force of our vital-functional formation energy. This energy may have been invested, among other things, in deformative imagination dispositions that have to be overcome. For example, I may be disposed to image myself as an overly shy person, a wallflower. I have to overcome this disposition and the images in which it expresses itself. A first step to diminish its hold over my life is to gentle my formation energy. This will indirectly diminish the energy invested in this dispositional image. Now I can distance myself from this disposition.

Once I become gentle, I should foster another general form disposition promoted by science, that of *openness*. Openness in this sense is the same as humility. It is a dwelling in the light of the truth no matter how humiliating or painful this truth may be. I thus withdraw formation energy from its investment in my dispositions. I do so by "gentling down." This makes energy available for openness or humility and for new form reception and form donation. In practice, this withdrawal of energy means for most of us a withdrawal from busy inner and outer functioning. Such agitation is fueled by the form energy invested in our active dispositions.

In the case of Peter and his lower back pain, the formation counselor got him to relax deeply. This relaxation provided him with the necessary distance from his deformative disposition. It freed some of the energy invested in it. He could then be humbly open to the deformative dispositional image. He was able to talk back to it imaginatively under the increasing guidance of his power of appraisal.

Guidelines to Effective Use of Formative Images

How do we influence the formative vital-functional dimension of our life via imagination? How can we make this dimension available to appraisal and appreciation as well as to the power of effective decision? Let us return to the case of Peter. Why did he develop such a disposition of overwhelming rage and frustration?

Peter was an accountant. He never wanted to be an accountant in the first place, but a writer, journalist, or teacher. The formation sessions made him admit to himself for the first time that his was an uncongenial choice of profession. Why did he become an accountant if he did not like this work? It was mainly because his father was a successful accountant who pressured him to take over his company. Peter meekly submitted to this pressure, but deep down he hated the imposition, the betrayal of his freedom. He resented a professional life that was not really chosen or ratified by his own powers of appraisal. As a result, he found his life incompatible with his colleagues who liked their job, with his clients who forced problems upon him he did not want to solve, with his wife and children whose welfare and future compelled him into making a living by means of work he despised.

Because of his infrafocal disposition of resentment, he could not be compassionate with himself or others. Neither could he forgive himself nor his father for having made the wrong decision. He could not empathize with his clients and their worries nor could he feel compassionate toward his wife and children. He was too preoccupied with his own resentment disposition.

This infrafocal resentment would explode at times in sudden outbursts about little inconveniences and irritations that would frighten his family, friends, and clients. There was no proportion between the vehemence of his anger and the smallness of the incident that would trigger it. They could not know the hidden disposition of rage and resentment that was the real cause of these sudden outbursts. No one suspected that a terrier of powerful resentment was chewing the spine of his life. An added strain was his disposition to live up to sociohistorical pulsations. To be a successful accountant and to live comfortably was important in the eyes of his contemporaries and neighbors. This, too, kept him glued to his job.

The disposition of resentment formed a deformative formation field, the meanings of which were colored by his impotent rage. The inner and inter sphere of the formation field was coformed by the father he secretly hated and by the colleagues and clients who forced him to do what he did not like to do. The situation sphere was the accountant's office, reminding him of a position in society he was unable to enjoy. The world sphere of his formation field became darkened by his resentment. He could not see much good in a world that somehow forced him to stay in this niche. The preformation sphere was also affected by his resentful disposition. He felt prefocally that he had been unfaithful to his preformation. He was not made to be an accountant, but something else. So he felt resentful toward himself.

Paradoxically, this resentment turned against the preformation itself, without which he would not have been in this kind of trouble. This contributed to the low back pain and to his suicidal tendencies. It did not cause physical pain, but it contributed to an amplification that made it intolerable. To develop a disposition of resentment toward one's preformation is to be disposed to resent the deepest sources of one's unique life. The impotent rage is directed intraformatively against both the alien, false, or counter life-form and the preformation that gave rise to it.

The first stage of the reformation process was thus to become aware via images of the deformative disposition. The next stage was that of formative appraisal and appreciation. This means that the person has to come to appreciative *imagination* and *appraisal*, for appraisal at this phase is still embedded in the imagination.

The terrier tells Peter in their imaginary interaction: "It is not a career as an accountant that you wanted. You are successful in your job and well-regarded, but you never dared to admit to yourself that you did not want to be there. You have to face your real disposition. It may not be necessary to change your career, but you surely must overcome your resentful imagery and the disposition in which it is rooted."

When this insight had seeped in, the formation counselor encouraged Peter to take time for formative appreciation exercises. He had to begin to appreciate how good he was or could be at what he was doing. He had to ponder how many people are compelled by life to take on a career they do not want. He imagined gifted physicists who became busy housewives and mothers of many children; budding novelists who became secretaries to make a living; potential artists who became house painters; professional people driven from their homes and jobs during wars and revolutions to do manual labor in a new country.

Peter had not freely chosen his professional life, but he could still come to a free acceptance of it. Since this form of occupational life had become his, he could develop a disposition to make the best of it instead of fighting it. He could attain transcendent appraisal by putting his occupation and its problematics in the light of the formation mystery and viewing all that had happened in an attitude of overall abandonment in faith, hope, and love.

After such appraisals, Peter decided to overcome his resentful disposition, to forgive his father, and to forgive himself. Forgiveness is formative. It is a disposition that overcomes resentment most effectively. It helps one to grow in compassionate understanding. Maybe his father did not know any better. He may have been the victim of deformation himself. The people surrounding Peter and influencing him with their deformative sociohistorical pulsations may not be guilty either. They did not ask to be born in this pressured climate for publicly applauded success in life at the cost of one's real aspirations. Parents and neighbors often veil our calling with the best of intentions. If we do not forgive them, it is we, not they, who suffer most in the long run.

Peter came to the decision to accept the present historical situation. He accepted it as a point of departure and as an opportunity. This was the first step in the development of the disposition of "opportunity thinking," or appreciative instead of depreciative thinking. He began to realize that to live in depreciation is to live an unhealthy life.

In the process of deactivation of deformative anticipation, one has to catch in oneself the deformative memories and anticipations linked with the disposition. These tend to evoke, deepen, and maintain its power. During imaginary interaction exercises with the chewing terrier, the answer came to Peter from the terrier: "I will stop chewing your spine." This means the disposition of rage and resentment had weakened sufficiently. It at least did not keep amplifying his vital pain experience. Indeed these appreciative responses were accompanied by an easing of the pain. As a matter of fact, during the following weeks Peter's pain progressively subsided.

The case of Peter makes us aware that when we are in pain, there is some hidden image of pain in us. Of course, we must first try out all the solutions offered by traditional medicine. Only then can we safely apply to chronic pain the formative imagination exercises. What we really do then is to extend our formation powers not only to the voluntary but also to the involuntary facets of the human form of life. If we begin to think and especially to imagine how painful things are, we will feel more pain. We blow our pain out of proportion. It may reach unbearable heights. Our repeated imagining of pain leads to an enduring disposition to expect and feel its sting.

We are in formation at all times through dispositions. These are partly formed by our focal or prefocal images. Sometimes these images are consonant and helpful; they foster formative dispositions. At other times they are dissonant; so they engender dissonant dispositions that have to be reformed. We can put this whole question in a transcendent perspective; the formation mystery helps us to form and reform our dispositional life via consonant image formation.

Vital Physiological Process of Pain Disposition Reformation

Because the reformation of the pain disposition is such a clear example, we can ask ourselves what happens *intraformatively* in this case? The disposition is reformed by means of consonant images. The reformed disposition then gives rise to pain-stilling images. These trigger the release of the body's natural pain killers. Medicine, one of the main auxiliary disciplines to formation science, researches the so-called endorphins. These complex chemicals reform our vital-bodily experiences when they are triggered, among other causes, by appreciative imagery. Their work resembles that of a narcotic.

It may be that Eastern form traditions preserved a kind of operational knowledge in this regard without our present-day scientific explanation. Certain adherents of these traditions were able to walk through fire or over broken glass without pain or injury. They seem to have been able to activate these chemicals by proper imagination and to become immune to pain.

A similar example is the so-called "runner's high" experienced by joggers. This feeling is ascribed to an increased output of endorphins. People may in some sense become "addicted" to jogging. When they cannot run they feel low. This seems to be an indication of withdrawal symptoms. Once the disposition for feeling high through jogging is formed it strives for reiteration, as do all dispositions. A letdown is experienced when this striving is not satisfied. In the case of a chemically sustained disposition, the letdown is felt in the vital dimension in the form of symptoms of withdrawal from the usual satisfaction of this vital disposition.

Consonant Use of Traditional Images

How does one start to give form to life by consonant imaginative dispositions? We may find help in this regard in our form tradition. Various consonant form traditions foster a consonant disposition toward suffering by providing images that lift it to a transcendent level. However, such images have to be used wisely. There is a kind of concentration on images of suffering, like the cross, that can lead to harmful dispositions. One may dispose oneself to appreciate suffering for its own sake. When our disposition is focused in this way, it may intensify suffering. One may begin to revel in pain itself.

A consonant disposition would involve focusing, for example, as an adherent of the Christian form tradition, on the potency of the suffering Christ as enabling one to accept one's own suffering as filled with transcendent meaning. The potency of Christ within the Christian to go beyond suffering as mere pain is activated. Positive appreciative imagination sees the Lord as the victor over grief and agony. As for this disposition, pain and distress are points of departure, not terminal states desirable in and by themselves. The wrong appreciation of pain can become immensely deformative when it is connected with masochistic or sadistic dispositions. The masochistic disposition represents a perverse inclination to experience pleasure in pain, while the sadistic inclines one to find pleasure in inflicting pain on others. These dispositions may be partly innate, partly acquired.

There is a way of talking about symbols of suffering that generates a disposition of hypersensitivity to any potential unpleasantness and exalts it out of proportion. Some types of spirituality exalt any inconvenience that comes one's way as a great "cross" to bear with courage, as a sacrifice to be made generously, and so on. This may lead to a life of imaginatively exalted suffering of things that, for example, the ordinary mother in a large family takes in stride as the everyday business of living.

A consonant disposition in regard to pain and suffering should neither exaggerate it by use of exalted images nor deny its reality. The disposition should help one to relieve pain, if possible. If imaginative intraformative talk can be of assistance, one can engage in it in a relaxed way.

Imagination and the Involuntary Nervous System

As we have seen, the imagination can be used to enable us to give form to our involuntary nervous system. This system is not under the direct control of the powers of formative appraisal and volition. We can learn how to release the endorphins developed in us by the cosmic, evolutionary epiphany of the formation mystery. Such endorphins wrought in us over the millennia by the miracle of formative evolution can reform the intensity of the pain without the side effects of powerful drugs.

We always give form to life by means of dispositions. In the West we may think only of how to give form voluntarily. We may have reduced the art of living to voluntary living only, having forgotten almost entirely that we can dispose ourselves to give form to our autonomic system, too. We can develop dispositions that give us some control over our heart rate, breathing, digestion, and emotional and sexual excitability. Such gentle control can serve our spiritual development.

Our formative autonomic nervous system is connected with both the infra and transfocal conscious dimension of our formative minds. It is also linked with instrumentation of our midbrain and brainstem. The autonomic nervous system is not directly available to focal consciousness. Yet it is in continuous contact with the *infra* and *trans*-dimensions of consciousness. Hence, we can only give form to this involuntary system and its processes in a symbolic and imaginative way. This is the only language by means of which we can form aspects of our life that are not controlled by the focal mind.

What falls under the direct control of the focal mind can be formed by focal command. For instance, I can tell myself to get up, but I cannot directly force myself by mere logical reasoning to become totally relaxed and rested. Here the distinctive formative idiom that is needed is that of images.

Exclusive appreciation of logical and functional rationality leads to the neglect of the development of the formative dispositions of imagination in service of the incarnation of transcendent and functional decisions. The imaginative idiom of such dispositions may be as unfamiliar to us as a foreign language. Yet the restoration of spiritual formation in the West will partly depend on the restoration of this idiom and its underlying dispositions.

Highly developed in our cultural form traditions are the dispositions and idioms of cortical focal life. We neglected the development of subcortical dispositions and idioms, which should not replace but should complement our focal dispositional life. No rational language can speak formatively to our subcortical existence. The autonomic nervous system listens only to images and symbols loaded with affective power. To illustrate this fact, we can perform a simple experiment. We can try telling our mouth with abstract words to form and secrete saliva, making sure not to link any image with the words. The experiment will not succeed. Then we can try, in as lively a way as possible, to imagine a sizzling steak, to smell its delicious aroma, to taste imaginatively the juices of a warm morsel in our mouth. Without any abstract verbalization, saliva will come. Such is the power of imagination.

Had we developed a disposition to evoke certain effective images, they would easily emerge at any moment we needed them. For example, we may have a cholesterol problem. We are not supposed to eat the things we were disposed to love early in life: ice cream, whipped cream, rich desserts, fatty meats. No amount of abstract logical verbalization can lastingly reform the subcortical disposition that makes us crave for them. Now we can try to develop an imaginative disposition in the opposite direction. We image repeatedly in a lively way how our arteries become clogged with this slimy, repulsive, fatty stuff and how the sticky, gluey cream will lie like sludge in our bloodstream. We make the images as vivid, concrete, and repulsive as possible over and over again until the disposition is strongly established. Progressively we will experience the repulsion we need to stick to our diet, to develop a new taste disposition strong enough to resist the lure of imaginative advertisements for these forbidden foods.

Consonant Imagination Dispositions and Higher Dispositions

The faithful initiation, maintenance, and development of consonant disposition of the imagination is in turn dependent on our higher dispositions. We need the foundational triad of faith, hope, and consonance to find the motivation to decide to bear with the work of formative imagination and its patient reiteration. We need the faith that the consonant life is worthwhile enough to do this work, that there is a higher form potency we can trust to sustain us in this effort. For example, if I appreciate in faith that my life is a gift of the formation mystery, I may be willing to get my diet under control via the initiation of the appropriate imagination dispositions.

It is by such imagination dispositions that we can give form to intraformative vital form potentials, such as our endorphins. The appropriate disposition in their regard can reform the pain that was preformed in us intraformatively by our imaginative reactions to all sorts of ailments, from arthritis to angina. Impressive in this area of vital intraformation is the research and therapy of Dr. Carl Simonton with cancer patients. Through the development of healing imagination dispositions, he is able to prolong their life and to decrease their pain.

What can be said of our dispositions for suffering applies as well to our mood dispositions. When we allow depreciative image dispositions to develop, we foster by implication dispositions of dark moodiness. If, on the contrary, dispositions for appreciative images are fostered, they will give rise to moods of appreciation, joy, vigor, and delight in living. All of these image and mood dispositions help us to coform effectively our core, current, apparent, and actual forms of life. They influence deeply what we are and how we appear throughout the day. They affect also our inter-formative impact. Some people with dark, depreciative image and mood dispositions seem to spread doom in their interaction with others. Moods and images are contagious. We are responsible for the images we exude to others, especially to impressionable children with their as yet weakly formed dispositions. Negative image and mood dispositions can numb in ourselves and others the free formative energy flow.

Consider the task of having to write a paper. We should prepare for this task by appreciative imagination. We should imagine ourselves in advance sitting before the typewriter, appreciating what we may do. We highlight imaginatively the advantages. It is much more pleasant to sit here than it would be to dig a ditch, to sit in a dark foxhole during a war, to lie chronically ill in bed. Instead, we have the privilege of working with ideas. While we are typing, we will be growing in reflection, self-expression, and dexterity. We do not allow negative images to creep in, such as "the miserable paper that I doubt I can do." Such depreciative images kill the vital flow we need to accomplish the task. Instead, we should relax and imagine being pleasantly seated. We have only to worry about a line or two. Once we have accomplished that, imagine how interesting it will be to extend these slowly to a paragraph, then perhaps to a page. Writer's block often comes from the neglect of appreciative imaginary preparation *before* we sit down to write our paper.

The in-between moments of a task should be utilized for the prevention or deactivation of paralyzing depreciative images and the promotion of appreciative ones. No amount of willpower can surmount mountains of depreciative image and mood dispositions. They first have to be removed by appreciative acts and dispositions of faith. Once faith has moved mountains, anything seems possible for those who believe appreciatively. An example can be found in medicine. In medical experiments a healing drug may be tried out by administering it to one group, while another group, the control group, receives a pill that has no medicinal qualities, a placebo. To the initial astonishment of the experimenters, many patients who receive the placebo get better: a strong imaginative belief that the pill would help them was enough to cause improvement. This is called the placebo effect.

One striking experiment at the University of California, San Francisco, illustrates this point. Twenty-three dental patients who had their teeth pulled received a placebo that they were told would take their pain away.

The message conveyed to them by the dental authorities was: "If you take this pill, there will be no pain at all." In more than one-third of the patients, the image was so strong that endorphins in the brain were activated and took the pain away. Then a second agent was injected, a drug that blocks the action of endorphins. All the people experienced pain, even the one-third who before had no pain because of the endorphins initially activated by their imagination.

Formative Use of the Imagination

Our imagination can be utilized most effectively for the initiation, maintenance, and development of dispositions by formative gentleness and imaginative visualization. Earlier we indicated the effectiveness of gently letting go. Calming down frees formation energy from the dispositions in which it has been invested and enables us to distance ourselves from dispositions we may have identified with. Another advantage of gentleness is that it liberates us for receptive formation. Images can only have a forming effect if we are receptive, that is, if we are gently ready to receive their imprint in our emergent dispositions and actions.

Because of sociohistorical form traditions and pulsations, we may be the victim of functionalistic dispositions that foster form giving over form receiving. They block the free unfolding of our capacities for receptive formation. This is most unfortunate because the primary way of formation is that of form receptivity. Form giving is secondary; it depends for its human meaningfulness on received wisdom, grace, and insight.

Consonant formation of life and world implies a wholesome polarity between the reception and donation of form in mutual interaction. We can only give, produce, and create meaningful forms out of an inner wealth of gifts graciously received and assimilated. Wisdom is formed in us by the gift of experience as we humbly allow it to enter our formation field without a priori manipulations on our part. We must be open to experience in humility. What has taken form in us uniquely as a result of our receptivity can then flow out in consonant form giving to words, deeds, projects, and behavior.

If sociohistorical form traditions have inclined us to an agitated mode of form giving, we may bypass our need for receptivity. As a result, we become empty people. Our receptivity for images is also missing. Such receptivity is necessary if we want to influence both the voluntary and involuntary nervous systems. Sharing as it does in our overall receptivity, these systems may be disposed by our imagination to act in consonance with our transcendent aspirations, appraisals, and affirmations. In no way can our will directly compel the involuntary nervous system to dispose itself in a desired direction. Yet it can be effectively influenced by the appropriate images. Then it becomes ready to receive other images that progressively dispose it in the appraised and approved direction.

Gentleness presupposes abandonment to the formation mystery and its epiphanies in our life. We must trust the form potencies granted to us by the mystery. Life seen in this light can be compared to a sailboat. If we set the sails in the right direction, the boat will virtually sail itself. The same goes for life. We can engage gently in consonant apprehension, appraisal, and affirmation, and allow the formative imagination to communicate the subsequent form directives to our concrete life in formation on the turbulent sea of the formation field. We need not force anything. Gradually, our life will right itself by the initiation of consonant dispositions.

Gentle abandonment implies the relaxed ability to live in ambiguity. We cannot always know what is consonant. At times we will err. We must trust life and its forming mystery. The mystery may allow us to lose our path temporarily so as to disclose it more splendidly later in life. Everything is beneficial for those who remain gentle and receptive during their formation journey.

Once the process of gentleness has its impact, visual or audio imagination can be used effectively in disposition formation. The visualization can be symbolic or concrete. For instance, to overcome my shyness in public meetings, I may concretely visualize the session I have to attend, the relaxed and open role I have to play during it. To develop a disposition of presence to the mystery, I may symbolically visualize a bright, all-pervading light. My audio imagination may "hear" the mystery as a melody, as the music of the spheres pervading universe and history. If one is committed to transcendent form traditions, one can benefit from dwelling on their visual and audio images, sanctioned and refined by centuries of use.

The Hebrew form tradition, for instance, helps its adherents to visualize the mystery in a variety of images, such as a rock on which to stand, a tent in which to hide, a fortress in which to find strength, a shield that gives protection. Their audio imagination was provided with similar images, like that of a mighty wind or a gentle breeze representing the presence of the forming mystery.

In the realm of vital dispositions, the auxiliary science and practice of medicine has developed many strategies of visualization. Dr. Carl Simonton teaches cancer patients how to imagine their tumor as a dark, dreary mass eating their life away. To initiate a vital fighting disposition, he asks them to visualize something that is tearing away at the tumor, usually an animal. He asks them to engage in such visualization at least three times a day. The fighting disposition has to be initiated and strengthened before the cancer is too far advanced. In a number of patients, this disposition formation led to remission and occasionally to complete recovery.

Form traditions are storehouses of images that can complement in patients the kinds of images suggested by Simonton. Traditional images are charged with sacred powers, filled with transcendent meanings. They connect patients with what they believe to be the source of healing formation as it is disclosed to them by their tradition. Formative readings and rituals may confirm and deepen the patients' original initiation into such symbols.

Exalted Images and Dispositions

Similar visualizations and audio imaginations may be helpful in the reformation of other dispositions. Consider the deformative disposition of religious and social exaltation. The sufferers lose contact with everyday reality the moment an exciting religious or social movement emerges as an accretion of a form tradition or formation community. Such well-meaning people are easily gripped by moods of religious elation and messianic enthusiasm. They are disposed to absolutize, as "the" way for all, any new project, mode of life, social cause, or charitable enterprise. Their exalted disposition blinds their common sense and paralyzes their potency for quiet realism. The exaltation may generate in them a prophetic glow. It numbs their compassionate sensitivity for the everyday moods of more sedate companions.

Seized by such pulsations, they are pulled out of prosaic surroundings. Some may show disdainful pity for those who do not share their particular social or religious concern. Often they strike their common-sense neighbors as good people but pious floaters. They may be irritated by their smiling, sometimes smug insinuation that they know the exclusive path for all true seekers at this moment in history.

The exalted disposition is difficult to overcome. It has subterranean roots in the pride-form and is often powerfully rationalized. Its victims may be able to point to undeniable, ostentatious effects in the peripheral dimensions of social and religious causes. This disposition may fill them with feelings of imaginary divine form potencies. Their pious or social agitation is often sustained by widely acclaimed pulsations in the accretional dimension of a form tradition or in society. It is bolstered by images and symbols engendered by sweeping social-religious movements.

Reformation of exalted dispositions is hindered by one's unvoiced though justified feeling that reentry in common sense life will be a shock. It may disclose, for example, how impoverished they have become in regard to personal spiritual living, to true interiority, to at-homeness in the silent splendor of the hidden life. Estranged from their deepest calling by pulsations that were not personally appraised, they feel as if they have to start from point zero after a collapse of the whole constellation of fictitious exalted dispositions. They dread nothing more than losing their buoyancy and high spirits. The heightened sense of potency and importance that was theirs when they were lifted up by the excitement of some popular religious or social movement subsides. Hence, their exalted disposition inclines them to pounce on the next one that comes along.

Reformation of Exalted Images and Dispositions

A formation counselor may propose various visualizations of such predicaments. She may ask them to imagine themselves as colorful blown-up balloons, filled with the gas of exaltation, drifting idly and vulnerably in the shifting winds of pulsations. They may visualize themselves letting air out by puncturing their balloon, floating down to earth leisurely, feeling pleasantly deflated, finally safely grounded. She helps them to become cautious of anything that may reawaken their exalted dispositions after landing on the earth. They should visualize and imaginatively hear a meeting of zealous people or a speech announcing new religious experiences, social projects, encounters, renewals, and the like. They should visualize how their disposition threatens to abuse such occasions to fill up their deflated balloon again with spurts of elation. They must begin to sense how tempted they will be to join fellow floaters. They should imagine how vulnerable they become when high-sounding sentences begin to flow. They can then visualize their balloon dangerously rising again in the buffeting winds of popular pulsations.

By these and similar images, they may be able to distance themselves from pious or impious crowds and collectivities. Disidentification with their own exalted dispositions may become possible. Released by this detachment, they may become present to their own foundational form of life and revere its silent emergence from the formation mystery as a unique epiphany. Religious or social agitation subsides. Spiritual life comes out of concealment. To preserve this path of detachment, they must spiritually fill the inner void. Otherwise their dormant disposition will tempt them again to stuff their empty minds and hearts with images of the exalted life.

Nourishment of this disposition of transcendent appreciation of what seems unspectacular and trite can be found in one's consonant form tradition and its symbols. One should dwell meditatively on its ancient, time-honored sources. Their affirmation by wise men and women in successive generations offers protection against contemporary exalted pulsations. Some of these ancient images may have been imparted in childhood. They may be dormant now. Awakened later in life, they may play an effective role in the reformation of exalted dispositions.

Functionalistic Dispositions and Suffering

An important cause of deformative dispositions in regard to suffering is an overall functionalistic approach to life. We mentioned earlier that dispositions are not isolated. They are part of a constellation that makes up our empirical life-form. The relation between a general functionalistic disposition and/or a deformative disposition in regard to suffering is one example of the intertwining of dispositions in our empirical life.

People who are functionalistically disposed do not feel in tune with the wider mystery of formation. They tend to exclude the transcendent dimension from their life. Any threat of defeat, loss, death, or betrayal is enhanced by the imagination because of the absence of the transcendent perspective. The more one is isolated from a grander and meaningful whole, the more menacing any diminishment of one's vital-functional potency becomes. We can see this effect on lower levels of transcendence. When children blossom in the abundant love of their mothers, discomfort becomes less painful. Soldiers who are led to believe that their miseries make sense in the light of the cause for which they are fighting are disposed to suffer less than those who do not share that faith. The wider realm of meaning generates uplifting images that diminish the overwhelming impact the isolated image of suffering would otherwise have.

Interformation, Images, and Dispositions

Much suffering finds its source in interformative relationships. Deformative effects and experiences of interformation can influence not only the transcendent and the functional, but also the vital dimension of our dispositions. Recall some of the familiar vital-sensory expressions we use to describe people who interformatively affect us the wrong way. "A pain in the neck," a "constant headache," "too much to stomach," and similar images are lavishly used. We can develop dispositions to experience certain people in this fashion. They may give us real cause to feel that way. Yet if we have to interact with such persons on a regular basis, such dispositions evoke more pain than necessary. They set up in us and others mutually negative dispositions. These may affect us physically more than we realize.

One means for incipient reformation of these *interdeformative* dispositions is the disposition to forgive. This disposition is rooted in the foundational triad of faith, hope, and consonance. We must deepen our faith that people badly disposed toward us are embraced by the same formation mystery that makes us be. We must believe that a unique noble form of life is present in them, at least potentially. We should cultivate the hope that its fuller expression in their dispositional life-form may be fostered by our forgiving love and genuine concern. This occurs when we feel ourselves to be in compassionate consonance with them. We know from our own vulnerability that hostile, offensive, and arrogant people are really hurting. They themselves may be victims of interdeformation somewhere along the way.

Dealing with Depreciative Images and Dispositions

We may experience that through their images depreciative dispositions dominate a relationship that consequently becomes tense and painful. We have to ask ourselves what is the message of that pain? What does it tell us about our interformative dispositions? How can they be reformed? What are the present images formed by memory and anticipation that maintain and reinforce these dispositions? How can we reform such images or substitute more appreciative ones for them?

Interdeformative dispositions, each with their own swarm of images, apply not only to people here and now. Depreciative dispositions may fester in us toward parents, teachers, friends, and others who may have betrayed our trust. There is no use denying the suffering they inflicted knowingly or unknowingly. Only forgiveness can heal the painful memory disposition and the flocks of dissonant images it resentfully holds in our imagination.

A disposition of forgiveness toward others will take away the dark and dreary mass in our infrafocal consciousness. It will no longer poison our life. This disposition of forgiveness must extend to our own life, too. We must live in a climate of being forgiven by the mystery of formation. In the ocean of its forming mercy, our inner misery will be mellowed. The hurt disposition is slowly dissolved in the warmth and light of this love.

Images and Dispositions of Masculinity and Femininity

Among the images handed over to us by sociohistorical form traditions are those of masculinity and femininity. They foster in us corresponding masculine and feminine dispositions, which direct our daily form receptivity and form giving. We need to appraise such images and dispositions critically. Are they restrictive and deforming? Do they serve to release the best in us? Do they foster a consonant life? Consonant interformation implies that we respect one another's dignity as distinctively human. Our humanness transcends our sexual identity. Any cultural image that fosters the illusionary disposition of superiority of one person over another is dissonant.

Interdeformative dissonance generates in turn intradeformative dissonance. It compels us to deny or depreciate within our inner formation the feminine or masculine dimension. Otherwise we cannot maintain our illusionary disposition in regard to the other sex. Formation science distinguishes in the human life form a vital and a functional dimension. It maintains, however, that both are meant to be united in mutual consonance within the higher transcendent dimension of life.

Most sociohistorical symbols of femininity link it exclusively with the vital dimension. Subsequent images promote in women the development of mainly vital-sensory-emotional dispositions. Similarly most popular images of masculinity connect it exclusively with functionality and its subordinate dispositions of functional reasoning, dexterity, technicality, dominance, and willfulness. Few symbols and images point to the confluence of femininity and masculinity in the transcendent dimension and its spiritual dispositions. Our culture is not inspired by the ideal of transcendent, consonant living, as is evident in the battle between the sexes.

Onesided images lead to stereotyped dispositions. They are not sustained by reality. A woman can be rational, logical, and functional. A man can be emotional, sensual, and vitally intuitive. It is hazardous to enshrine the sexes in such exclusive images. Images tend to become true. Deformative images of sexual identity generate deformative dispositions that rob both men and women of the potential fullness of their humanity. How did this deformative stereotyping come about?

Perhaps it originated in an initially favored expression of femininity and masculinity. The biogenetic physiology of the human body teaches us that the female body is linked intimately with the vital process of pro-creation. Once a woman is pregnant, she is more centered in her body than a man ever is. She seems initially more at home in her body. It disposes her to experience the formation field in a more centered fashion. The initial experience of masculinity seems more bound up in our culture with functional physiology.

Some physiologists (for example, F. J. J. Buytendijk) observe the prevalence in male babies of striated muscles over soft muscles. As a result, the muscular disposition of males makes them initially experience the world as resistance to be overcome. The initial prevalence in strength of the soft muscles in female infants disposes them to experience the formation field as nonresistant, flowing, and adaptable. As a result, males tend initially to be more decentered, aggressive, and functional-strategic in their dispositions. Yet in both males and females, vital and functional dispositions should be developed. Vitalism and functionalism should complement each other in both sexes.

The more we grow to transcendence, the more we integrate spontaneously masculine and feminine dispositions in a higher synthesis. Both the transcendent male and female, in their distinctive humanness, can be equally centered or decentered in consonance with the momentary demands of the formation field. Consonant spirituality destroys all stereotypes, also those of an exclusive masculinity and femininity.

Dissonant Images and Dispositions

From the preceding examples and discussions, it may be clear that we can distinguish a consonant and a dissonant imagination. Formation science refers to dissonant imagination also as fantasy. Because fantasy does not have a pejorative connotation for all researchers in the auxiliary sciences, the term dissonant imagination is often used instead. From the viewpoint of formation, images are far more powerful than concepts. Most of our life is guided by focal, pre-, trans-, and infrafocal imagery. Imagery can exert either a consonant or a dissonant influence. It can be our greatest friend or enemy. It can channel the flow of formation energy in consonant directions by means of like images and symbols or it can also dissipate the energy flow in the dissonant ruminations of our fantasy life.

Because the imagination is susceptible to dissonance, we must appraise, when desirable, the consonance of the images that give form to the formation field in which our life unfolds itself. A new life direction may demand crucial change in our formative imagination. Our usual formative imagery has to be apprehended and appraised in the light of a new life direction and the dispositions it demands from us. Imagery should become congenial with the dispositions of the new current life-form. This life-form in turn should be congenial with the dispositions of the foundational and core forms of life.

The process of bringing the imagination into consonance with the dispositions of the foundational and core forms of life demands, at least initially, a formative curbing of one's fantasy and an asceticism or discipline of the imagination. Discipline can help to prevent the erratic ruminations of fantasy life that foster dissonance and disintegration. It also helps us to overcome the hold of formerly helpful images that are no longer in consonance with our new current life-form and with the corresponding disclosures of the foundational life-form in which this current form is rooted.

Consonant formation demands a periodic distancing from our fantasy life and from the concrete dispositions and corresponding situations that threaten to absorb and fixate our formation energy. One means of halting dissonant fantasies and relativizing an overpowering situation is the creation of imaginary situations of diversion. Such diversion may take us momentarily out of our absorption in idiosyncratic fantasies and free us from our absorption in dispositions pertaining to limited manifestations of reality. This liberating function of the consonant imagination by means of periodic diversion can be facilitated by certain so-called servant sources of formation. Travel, movies, television, literature, art, and the like, when utilized discriminately, can facilitate this defixation of the usual concentration of the formative imagination.

Fantasy Life and Fantasy Field

We should be cautious lest the use of media for the relaxation of the imagination becomes in reality a means to foster dissonant imagination. The dispositions of dissonant fantasy life are essentially different from those of the consonant imagination, even in diversion. Dissonant imagination tries to escape lastingly the uneventful regularities of daily life. A fantasy life may take over, fed by unchecked desires, flamboyant ambitions, and floating aspirations. We may day dream about the extraordinary, the exciting, the novel, the grandiose. Such fantasies lead to dissonant dispositions, dissonant because our transcendent dimension has no way to integrate them in the emergent totality of our congenial and compatible formation. They take us away from our foundational life-form and our concrete formation field. The ordinary checks and balances of transcendent and functional appraisals are not utilized. Dissonant imagination fabricates an unreal formation field, replacing the one that is really ours. It is subtly distorted by our fantasy life.

To elaborate and maintain this dissonant fantasy field and its corresponding dispositional life-form, one must be disposed to labor constantly at the falsification of one's real formation field. At the same time, the dissonant imagination must try to maintain and strengthen a whole constellation of protective dispositions and images. These help us to detach and neutralize in advance all the signs that seem to point in the direction of our real formation field.

A striking example of such dissonant disposition and image formation is that of a pseudo-spiritual life. Its victims may have been exposed to the spiritual writings of the masters, to the lives of gurus and saints, and to spiritual exercises, inspiring encounters, and lectures. Somehow their dissonant imagination managed to concoct all of this information into a fantasy field of sublime spirituality. They have disposed themselves to move, speak, and sound as if they were already such masters themselves. They disarm in advance any evidence to the contrary that comes their way. Their performance may be so convincing that even astute people mistake it for the real thing.

Because the fantasy field is borrowed from that of the real masters, it may manifest a coherence, wisdom, and beauty of expression that dissonant persons could never have created themselves. Their own absorption in their imaginary role generates an inner conviction that it is all for real. Like any conviction, this one, too, is contagious. Touched by it, we cannot easily unmask bright, eloquent persons, well-trained in spirituality, deeply believing in their own imagined providential mission. Those less bright and informed would have to construct a spiritual fantasty field by their own powers. They are liable to make mistakes that reveal this field more readily as dissonant.

One should not doubt that many fabricators are genuinely convinced of the reality of their imagined formation field. In the near future, the growing interest in spirituality, combined with the scarcity of sufficiently formed and experienced formation counselors, may help multiply such fabrications. One must always suspect such a possibility in excessively enthusiastic persons who claim an extraordinary depth in spiritual living. One should not trust uncritically the usual manifestations of humility. Well-read people know that they should manifest this necessary sign of authenticity. They can borrow its language from their spiritual readings, albeit unintentionally and prefocally.

Temporary Field of Imaginary Diversion

On the one hand, we note the possibility of an enduring imaginary fantasy field misconceived as one's real field of disposition and action. On the other hand, we note the possibility of a temporary field of imaginative diversion conceived as a passing means of bringing gentleness to one's dispositional concentration. Such diversion can help a person to regain relaxation, critical distance, and freedom. Examples might be enjoying movies, theater, television programs, concerts, or other entertainment that can alleviate our absorption in strenuous life situations or in dissonant fantasy life.

We should clearly acknowledge that imaginative diversion is only an occasional means to relaxation and distancing from our usual task-oriented dispositions and directives. One should take care that such playful excursions of the imagination do not turn into the main source of those central dispositions and directives that are supposed to guide our daily formation. The images sought should not be the kind that lead irresistibly to inner or outer acts and dispositions that are uncongenial with one's foundational life-form; incompatible with one's basic life situation; lacking compassion for the vulnerability of self and others; and inconsistent with the dispositions of the form tradition to which one is committed. For example, an entertaining novel or movie can fulfill the right conditions, whereas promiscuity, brutality, or random destructiveness would not meet the prerequisites.

The formative liberating imagination is marked by its gentle and relaxing effect on our life. No conflicts are created between such diversion dispositions and one's unique life direction. For example, the diversion dispositions of a professional concert pianist should be such that they do not endanger his hands and fingers and the refined sensitivity of his musical mind. He should not develop a diversion disposition for boxing or wrestling. This would endanger the means that sustain the main vocational direction of his life. By the same token, people religiously committed to a celibate life should not cultivate the diversion disposition of watching peep shows as a regular part of their relaxation.

The cultivation of images in one's focal or prefocal attentiveness thus exercises a formative power on one's present and future life. The same is true of the past. For example, the memory image of unjust treatment by a parent may begin to dominate our imagination, as if it represented the whole meaning of life. It becomes a dissonant imagination disposition insofar as it makes us anticipate injustice everywhere. This disposition engenders in turn aggression, overprotection, and suspicion.

To reform them, our consonant imagination, guided by appraisal, has to create images that purify the dissonant images from their isolation and totalization. They should be made relative as well as being integrated into the larger reality of our formation field and our transcendent destiny. In the above example, there is no use denying that injustice happened to us in childhood. This experience alerts us to the possibility of injustice later in life. In the light of our real formation field and the mystery of formation, we are able, however, to relativize the experience of injustice. This means that we reduce it to its realistic proportions. The earlier formative event is no longer generalized as the total explanation of life. We begin to appreciate the positive meanings such an experience can have for our formation. The event is placed imaginatively in the context of our formation history as a whole.

The consonant imagination overcomes the tendency of the dissonant imagination to reduce the whole of life and its disclosures to one overwhelming formation event in isolation. The consonant imagination thus relativizes the totalized events of our formation journey. It integrates them consonantly with the transcendent perspective of the emergent lifeform. Consonant imagination can thus be called the servant of the transcendent dimension of life formation. No event should live on in our imagination as a spiritually unappraised and unintegrated event. Such isolation generates a dispositional life dissociated from our deepest lifeform and its hesitant emergence. Outside this light, we cannot cope with such totalized events. The dissonant dispositions they generate mislead us. We become confused, fragmented, joyless, and desperate. Our journey is thus arrested and we lose our direction.

Dissonant Dispositional Identity

Our true identity is never known to us exhaustively. It is hidden in the foundational image of the mystery deep within us. We are called increasingly to disclose this basic image that we are. We have to bring our primordial life-form to light in the way in which we give form to our second-ary empirical life-form. This secondary life-form can be known imaginatively and focally. It is in principle open to experience. Hence we call it empirical. The dispositional life-form is permeated by our imagination, be it consonant or dissonant. Practically, it is both. Our dispositional identity is a composition of these two aspects, usually one being in ascendancy, the other in remission.

Some people may allow only their consonant or dissonant dispositional identity access to their experience and imagination. Such onesidedness leads to dispositions of excessive optimism or pessimism. People may identify themselves totally with their dissonant dispositions. They may mistake this dissonant identity for their foundational identity. They do not realize that they are dealing only with their secondary dispositional identity.

What are the dynamics that account for this identification with our dissonant identity? They are linked with those of the pride-form, or the quasi-foundational form of life, which by its nature is exalted and exalting. The pride-form tries to prostitute our aspiration for consonant dispositions. It suggests exalted form directives and images that are practically unattainable. People may identify themselves with these exalted dispositions and images. They may mistake them for disclosures of their foundational life-form. To measure up to such exalted dispositions and imaginations is impossible. However, they imagine that they can and should realize in life their exalted dispositions. Their whole feeling of form potency and effectiveness depends on this achievement. They feel crushed by any failure to live up to what they feel they are supposed to be. They demonize themselves for this failure. In disgust they ostracize their weaknesses, mistakes, and limited accomplishments. These look pointless to them in the perspective of their grandiose ideals.

By demonizing, banning, and isolating their vulnerability from the consonant formation flow, they take these human limits out of the integrative dialogue of the spirit. Outside of this dialogue, identification with one's failure to implement exalted imaginations becomes part of one's dissonant identity. The same dynamic leads to an identification of all one's consonant dispositions and images with only the exalted ones that proved to be unrealizable because of one's despised limitations. As a result, one's life-form as a whole is demonized. It is appraised as entirely futile, as perfidious to itself, depraved, deficient, and destructive. This rejection of one's life-form becomes the basis for negative disposition formation. In the extreme it can lead to despair and suicidal tendencies.

Adherents of a religious form tradition who are at home in its spiritual idiom may call this self-rejection humility. Humility, however, is a disposition of relaxed openness to who we are foundationally as a gift of the formation mystery, as a vulnerable composite of consonant and dissonant dispositions, directives, and images in mutual dialogue with one another. Hence, in formation science, we often use the term *openness* to refer to the disposition of humility. This realistic openness is a necessary basis of wholesome, consonant life formation.

Dissonant imagination hems us in. It imprisons us in isolated directives and dispositions. The openness of consonant imagination, on the contrary, shares in the flow and the promise of the formation mystery. It always waits in faith, hope, and love for a new disclosure of this mystery and its preforming epiphany in the great adventure of life. Consonant imagination can always unlock the doors of a formation event that threatens to close us in. It opens us toward the future, toward new becoming. Consonant imagination is thus the mother of opportunity thinking.

Necessity of Intervening Formative Imagery

By now it may be evident that we cannot understand disposition formation without delving into the vast richness of inner images. They are the bridge between appraisal and disposition. All our appraisals and their expressions are replete with imagery. Hence, to reform our dispositions, we should look not only for the focal-conceptual expressions of our appraisal directives but for their formative directive meaning as well. Their dynamic power rests mostly in the intervening images. They are our concrete formation source of appraisals. They give flesh and blood to them, as it were. To be sure, a lot of inner talk goes on before the appraisal ends up in a decision of the will to give form to concrete acts and subsequent dispositions. But this reasoning about formative events is supported by images of which we may be only vaguely aware.

We never appraise without an image, no matter how faint and remote it may be. This unavoidable formative imagery is at least passive. We may undergo the process of image formation unwittingly, without paying attention to it, or we may actively participate in the process, either by receiving or giving form. During such participation we induce some images or reform others in such a way that they may have an effect on our action and disposition formation.

For instance, I may have negative memory images about dieting that constantly remind me of its unpleasant aspects. My doctor may tell me that, due to chronic disease, I should develop a lifetime disposition for a certain selection of foods. I appraise this advice intellectually and decide to follow it. However, I do not reform my prefocal adverse images in regard to this diet. It is only when I make them focal, ponder their inhibitive impact, and replace them with vivid images in favor of this diet that lasting success becomes possible.

Moreover, in the beginning of the formation of this food selection and taste disposition, I must practice the act of dieting in my imagination before I find myself at the table. This may help, but it is still not sufficient. I must complement it with a progressive exposure to tempting foods that excite my customary taste dispositions. In the face of each one of them, I must renew and deepen my new negative appraisal and imagination in their regard. The same applies to my positive appraisal and imagination in reference to the food selection recommended by a physician or nutritionist.

My imagination may be sustained in this endeavor by the vivid example of others who have already developed the desired selection and taste disposition. Their observable incarnation of these dispositions presents my imagination with concrete images. Interaction with them is interformative. Among other things, it can facilitate my own imagination formation.

Dynamic Principles of Formation Science and Disposition Formation

At the end of this chapter, we may ask ourselves where to locate the formative imagination in the intraformative process of disposition formation.

Our description of formation dispositions, their initiation, maintenance, development, reformation, or deactivation is rooted in the dynamic principles of the science of foundational human formation. A relevant principle here is that of the incarnational formative tendency. This principle maintains that any act of formative transcendent or functional appraisal and volition tends to incarnate itself in our life as a whole. This penchant results in form directives, which tend to form in turn suitable images, memories, and anticipations, with their attendant feelings and strivings. Subsequently, these form directives give form to the vital, glandular, and neuromuscular systems of one's body.

Form directives issued by appraisal and volition and invested in concrete imagery prepare these systems, via the imagination, affecting midbrain and brainstem, for corresponding action. Next, they give form to the action itself in the formation field. Finally, by reiteration of these actions, they may give form to lasting form dispositions. According to this principle, every formative image contains in itself a formative dynamic inclination. It is the penchant of this image to incarnate itself concretely in one's process of formation throughout life.

We can strengthen this dynamic tendency in service of the formation of the consonant dispositions we hope to cultivate. A first means is the judicious use of our appraisal potency. We can deliberately focus this power of appreciation on the desired disposition. We try to appraise and deepen our appreciation of motives for this disposition. Similarly we foster appreciation for effective ways to attain its realization. Once this formative appraisal enlightens our will, it may come to a decision in favor of the disposition. Then we stimulate our functional, executive will to incarnate the appraised and chosen form directives in memory images, new images, and anticipatory images that may facilitate and motivate more concretely the chosen acts and dispositions.

These formative motivations and images engender corresponding feelings and strivings. The latter may or may not tap into our vital passions. If they happen to be linked with our passions, their power is increased accordingly. The effective reiteration of the subsequent acts intensifies by formative feedback the original appraisals, choices, directives, images, motivations, feelings, and strivings. It is this reiteration, combined with the deepening of motivation and feeling, that progressively establishes a disposition.

Formation science holds that formative feeling generates incipient formative desire and striving. The stronger the formative feeling, the stronger the striving. Such formative feelings are aroused and enlivened by pertinent images and symbols. They present us with vital roots for lasting dispositions.

There is thus a dynamic intraformative relationship among formative appraisals, decisions, directives, images, feelings, desires, strivings, motivations, actions, and dispositions. These intraformative components facilitate and strengthen one another mutually by their continual interaction. If one of the links in the chain is weak, it may affect the whole chain. This diminishes structurally the solidity of the disposition it tries to generate. In the case of ineffective disposition formation we should try to discover which link is underdeveloped and diminishes our effectiveness. Once we discover this frail component, we should work at its invigoration. Systematic exercises may be helpful. More often than not, it is the formative imagination itself that needs to be awakened and exercised.

This chapter has explored the function of formative imagination. We should add here that people may experience moments or periods of higher, purely receptive transcendent formation in which all thought and imagination is silenced. In such privileged moments of our journey, we are called to dwell in wordless and imageless presence to the formation mystery. Imagination still remains necessary for the concrete implementation in our life of the inspirations received in imageless contemplation. Moreover, one must periodically return to words and images when imageless presence weakens in one's spiritual life. As we shall see in the next chapter, the role of formative imagination is complemented, sustained, and expanded by formative memory and anticipation.

CHAPTER 8

Formative Memory and Anticipation in Relation to Disposition Formation

N ot only imagination but also memory and anticipation influence our disposition formation. All three assist mind and will in effecting, directing, and implementing our appraisals and ideals. Formative memory and anticipation are intertwined with formative imagination.

Interrelationship of Formative Imagination, Memory, and Anticipation
In the preceding chapter, we saw that formative imagination remains operative when we use our powers of memory and anticipation. Both have to be sustained by imagination. To illustrate this interaction, consider what happens when we try to deactivate a deformative disposition, for example, an inclination to dominate in conversation. To facilitate this reformation, we recall situations in which we found ways to be less self-centered during meetings with other people. We try to remember how we succeeded in our attempt at that time. The more we can use our imagination for such remembrance, the more effective our directive memory images become. They begin to influence our interaction with colleagues and acquaintances.

The same can be said for anticipation. We anticipate as concretely as possible the meeting we must attend tomorrow. We visualize the moments in which we will be tempted to take over. We may then be better able to resist the deformative disposition to make ourselves the center of attention. We think of ways in which we can make others feel more at ease, how we can encourage them to take part in the conversation. Our directive anticipatory imagination can give form to the situation as concretely as possible in advance, thus helping us to dispose ourselves formatively.

The same directive power of imagination can distort formative memory and anticipation. For example, we can allow our imagination to flood anticipation and memory with depreciative images: how we failed in the past, how we kept demanding attention from others, how we will surely fail again. Such images foster a depreciation of our potency for reformation. They dim the hope that the higher power of the formation mystery deep within us will sustain our limited powers for change. As a result, both formative memory and anticipation are distorted in their direction. They become deformative, weakening us instead of strengthening us. They confirm our dissonant disposition.

To be sure, we can also recall and anticipate concepts. This, too, has a forming influence. Often we start out with the right consonant ideas; but, from the viewpoint of life formation, images and symbols are far more powerful than concepts. Most of our life in formation, including its exercise of recall and anticipation, is guided by focal, prefocal, infrafocal, and transfocal imagery. All of these are influenced in turn by the interconscious imagery that is alive in our various form traditions. Imagination can channel the flow of formation energy in memory and anticipation. It can do so effectively by means of consonant images and symbols. Imagination can also dissipate our energy flow in dissonant ruminations of memory and anticipation.

Hence we must appraise not only the direction of our memories and anticipations but also the images they generate. Are they congenial, compatible, and compassionate? If not, a reformation of memory and anticipation images will be necessary.

The ever ongoing differentiation and growth from current life-form to new current life-form implies a similar refinement, deactivation, and initiation of memory and anticipation images. They must stimulate and sustain each new formation phase. When, for instance, we enter the phase of responsible adulthood, pleasant images of the carefree life under parental nurturing should play a less directive role in our memory. In our anticipation, images of concrete instances of adult responsibility should be stimulated. We have to apprehend and appraise such images in light of the new phasic refinement of our life direction. Memory and anticipation images should become congenial with each new formation phase. This phasic formation should be congenial in turn with the foundational and the core form of our life.

Relativizing Relaxation

A process of initiation or reformation of memory and anticipation images demands, at least initially, a formative asceticism or discipline of the imagination. Without the flexibility of obedient discipleship, memories and anticipations may become absolutized and fixated. The formation flow will then be halted. Life withers; it becomes uninteresting, stilted, lacking in spontaneity. For this reason we need to practice "relativizing relaxation." This formation technique enables us to disidentify ourselves from our memory and anticipation dispositions. We can apprai ? them in their relativity, or in their periodicity. By means of such dista cing, in gentleness and relaxation, our freedom of memory and anticip. tion is regained. Such detachment is the best means at our disposal to reform memory and anticipation.

Consider the case of a functionalistic career woman. Her memory may have been overwhelmed by images of frantic performance by herself and competing colleagues. Her anticipations are filled with imaginary situations of increasing achievement. Suddenly she falls ill. Months of slow recuperation in the hospital and at home enable her to distance herself from her fixed memory and anticipation dispositions. She realizes: "My dispositional life-form is not the whole me." Her deeper life-form is disclosed to her. Out of this hidden ground grows the power to take a free stand toward the memory and anticipation images that have ruled her days. She now sees the possibility to give and receive form in regard to her life of memory and anticipation in a way she could not do before. Gradually, she may be able to reform the deformative dispositions with which she has falsely identified herself. The retirement imposed by illness facilitates this distancing and disidentification.

It is clearly advisable not to wait for such an event as sudden illness. We should purposefully create moments of distancing in our life. Recollection and relativizing exercises should be engaged in periodically. Formation counseling can be helpful, too. The initiation of new dispositions can be illumined and stimulated, especially by the memory images and anticipations of one's own form traditions. A striking example would be the great memory and anticipation images that have sustained the Jewish people during their survival story in the midst of persecution.

Imaginary Situations as Facilitators of Formation

The potency to detach one's life imaginatively from its usual inner and outer situations is what makes imaginative memory and anticipation formative. We can imagine new situations, which give rise in turn to new memories and anticipations. We can then appraise and decide to give form to one or the other of these imagined situations. Subsequently, we can creatively initiate the memories and anticipations that would foster the realization of this newly chosen situation.

For instance, a person living a life of dissipation may begin to imagine different possibilities of a responsible, dedicated life. She may imagine provisionally various vocational situations, such as that of a graduate student, a business person, a professional athlete. Her mind may carefully appraise what may be most suitable in view of her means and capacities. Finally, she may decide to study medicine. She must deactivate the dispositions of idle dissipation and initiate those of dedication. This process should not be one of repudiation of the past. Rather, it should acknowledge and gradually deactivate suggestive memories of past pleasures and of tempting anticipations of similar pleasures to come. Instead, inspiring memories of past moments of dedication by herself and others and their pleasant consequences should be nourished. Similarly, anticipations of a dedicated life of study and preparation are to be fostered imaginatively.

Detachment from captivity in one's dispositional memory and anticipation images is a necessary condition for formation freedom. Without this conversion, the liberty of formation eludes us. We remain enslaved to our secondary dispositional life. As long as our memory and anticipation images remain rigid and inflexible, it will be impossible to reform our stilted patterns of dispositions and actions. It is through repeated exposure to consonant memory and anticipation images that the boundaries of our dispositional life are opened. A new current life of dispositions becomes possible. Such successive current life-forms enable us to approximate the fully consonant life of peace and joy in congeniality, compatibility, and compassion. Each new current life-form demands a *metanoia*, a change in dispositions. This *metanoia* of formation is facilitated by a change in the images of memory and anticipation. Such images display a dramatic power of formative conversion in our life.

Life in formation is a tension, a polarity, between old and new memory and anticipation images. If our formative memory and anticipation capacity is weak or underdeveloped, we should kindle this power by formative reading or by participation in the imaginative work of others through appreciation of literature, music, theater, or other arts. Such participation can be critically creative. The treasures of our own form traditions can sustain us in this exercise. In this way we can benefit from memory and anticipation images that are already formed. We can share in their meaning for our life. In all of these cases, we must let our formative imagination play upon these images offered by life, art, or form traditions. We must enter into them wholeheartedly, yet in a critical and creative way. They can draw us in and touch us more formatively than our mind alone can.

In a period of painful reformation, past memory and anticipation images tend to converge in protest. They interfere with our incipient new dispositions. At such moments, it is crucial to call to mind newly cultivated memory and anticipation images. This move will be effective to the extent that one has meditatively cultivated these images before or during the onset of such crises of reformation.

Formative Memory

Why do we call memory formative? We have many kinds of memory. One kind, for instance, is rote memory, which helps us to remember things, such as the multiplication tables we memorized in elementary school. Usually this kind of memory has neither a creative nor a striking influence on our personality formation as a whole. Hence, we do not call it *formative* memory in a distinctively human sense.

Each of us has a history of formation and deformation. What happened to us during that history is not totally lost. Certain residues remain to affect the present direction and formation of our life, its dispositions and actions. This affect can be actual or potential.

For example, a dissonant cultural form tradition may have formed in me as a child a deformative superiority feeling in regard to people of other nations or races. This memory may actually make me feel superior when I meet such people. It may be latent and potential. The memory disposition may suddenly be evoked when, for example, an immigrant publishes more than I do in spite of the fact that he did not learn my language from birth. My racist or nationalist background may at once spawn countless reasons why the more successful immigrant is in reality inferior to me as a person in all kinds of other ways. This latent racist or nationalist memory disposition may give rise to gossip about the imagined inferiority of the successful foreigner.

We could rightly call such memories formative. They have given form to our lives in the past, and they continue to give form to them in the present. There is a difference in degree of influence, availability, content, and meaning attached to them. For instance, the racist or xenophobic memory disposition is usually deeper and more conducive to deformative feeling and perception than the memory dispositions of a preference for certain color schemes in one's home. By the same token, the deformative and destructive direction of this deeply rooted xenophobic disposition may be less available to clear recognition by one's focal consciousness.

Creative Tendency of Formative Memory

Another characteristic of formative memory is its creative, flexible tendency. Formation memories change dynamically under the impact of the changing direction of our life and its dispositions. They adapt to what we are striving after. Formation memories organize themselves in memory configurations that serve our present disposition formation. Should I try to develop a more appreciative disposition, memories of the past that were appreciative will come to the fore while depreciative ones will play a lesser role. Memories that focused on the benefits of my childhood and youth will be rekindled; others will not necessarily be repudiated and thus exiled to my infrafocal consciousness, but they will be less active.

Formative memory implies that we are not apathetic in relation to our formation in the past. The dispositions we foster today may give a meaningful new configuration to memories of the past. They show up, as it were, in a new light. The configuration of our memories thus alters when our dispositional life changes, even if only slightly.

Any significant disposition in our life creates an orbit of related meanings and feelings; these dispositional meanings and feelings are mutually associated. Moreover, each significant disposition is connected with all other significant ones. This means that if one meaning in a disposition changes, the disposition as a whole is changed, at least slightly. Similarly all related dispositions change or refine themselves in accordance with meaning changes in their own orbits, as they are affected by a change in the related disposition.

For instance, a child may have developed its faith disposition in accordance with a specific faith tradition. Let us say that this particular faith and form tradition represents a specific Islamic group that holds that nobody outside Islam can be saved. This tenet belongs to the faith disposition orbit of the child. Later in life, when this person is a grown woman, she marries an American and lives in the United States. The memory disposition of her particular faith is still alive in her. However, living with her new friends, colleagues and family who do not share this conviction of her youth, she may experience the erosion of one or another tenet of her faith disposition. Soon enough, the formative power of memory is weakened and eventually deactivated. As a result, related meanings and feelings in regard to non-Muslims are slightly changed. She may manifest a greater tolerance. She still values her Muslim upbringing, though her faith disposition as a whole is noticeably different from that of the girls with whom she grew up, those who still live in her homeland. Having married conventional adherents of a specific branch of Islam, their formation memories have not been challenged. Other related dispositions in this woman also escape total domination by past formation memories. Dressing, appearing in public, meeting men, fasting, appraising Western customs —all change in some measure. She is not a woman without memories of her formative past, but because of a change in dispositions, the configuration of these memories has changed also.

Formative Memory and Formation Continuity

The potency for flexibility is inherent in our memory as formative. Indeed, we-as-formative-memory, as remembering persons, are able actively to guide, form, and reform our memories in the light of our unfolding life direction. This potency for memory reformation is balanced by a potency to stabilize certain consonant memories. The stabilizing power and function of formative memory is as basic for consonant life formation as is the power of timely reform. We-as-formative-memory can give our life a meaningful configuration and continuity, thanks to this holding potency.

Our deepest identity is hidden in our foundational life-form. During our formation history, this most intimate life call may be gradually disclosed to us. We begin to know a little more of who we are called to be by the formation mystery. The memories of such basic disclosures are formative for our empirical core form of life. The core form, or heart, is an integration of fundamental sensibilities and responsibilities that disclose our uniqueness insofar as it has become known to us at any given moment in our formation history.

The specifics of basic sensitivities and responsibilities are not identical in all people. Our core dispositions are in some way unique. Because they are lasting, they enable our life to gain, maintain, and regain wholeness, integration, and continuity. We maintain a certain identity in the midst of the successive current life-forms, formation phases, and situations that comprise our personal and shared formation history.

Without the power of formative memory, we would be unable to maintain these core dispositions. It keeps them in form, as it were. We may refer to this kind of memory as formative *core memory*. It maintains those past personal and shared formative events and our responses to them that have actually formed the enduring dispositions of the core form or heart of our life.

Such formative core memories may be consonant or dissonant. Our lived core memory, moreover, may or may not be available to focal recall or remembrance. Formation counseling may be necessary to make certain dissonant memories avalable to us. It does so most effectively in a sphere of acceptance and confirmation that fosters abandonment to the formation mystery. In the light of such disclosures, it may become possible for people to gain insight into the dissonant dispositions that obscure their life formation.

Memories That Sustain Core or Current Dispositions

Memories that sustain core form dispositions should be distinguished from those that nourish current form dispositions. For example, I may suffer from an enduring deformative sensitivity of the heart which makes me feel worthless and uninteresting. This lack of appreciation of my life may be fed by memories of a childhood in which I did not feel appreciated and loved for what I uniquely was. I felt that others received praise and attention for what they could do, but I did not. The response of my heart was to withdraw. This deformative response was supported by memories of feeling safe in shy withdrawal.

Both of these particular dispositions of the sensible-responsible heart are dissonant. They are uncongenial with the foundational life-form, which should be experienced as a unique gift of the formation mystery deeply to be appreciated. These negative dispositions and their sustaining memories at the core of my life make me enduringly depreciative of the gift I am. They may incline me to continual withdrawal.

An example of memories that make one maintain a periodic current disposition can be found in the case of a student who holds a summer job in a store. She remembers how she was able to sell certain items to clients. This memory feeds into the current disposition she needs during the summer months if she wants to keep her job and to make some money for her tuition. Once she is back in the school of music where her heart really is, she soon forgets about this temporary disposition. It was only part of a current life-form.

Current formative memories are thus those past shared or personal formation events that contribute to the current formation and direction of our life. They, too, may or may not be available to focal formative remembrance.

Central Position of Memory in Disposition Formation

The position of formative memory is central in life's formation. It represents the impact of our whole past formation and deformation. Without it our dispositional life could not be understood nor could it have continuity or unfold as a unifying formation history. Because our memory is not a thing (it is ourself as formatively remembering), we are not merely the passive object of our memories. We can become increasingly the subject of formative memory by raising our memories to the level of free disposition direction and formation.

To reiterate: meditative, formative remembrance can make us the subject instead of merely the object of our memories. We can decisively influence our actions and dispositions by means of formative focal recall. In regard to the apprehension, appraisal, choice, and implementation of a unified meaning for the whole of our life's formation, our modality of formative memory can be instrumental as can no other formation power. It enables our mind and will to take into account the past shared and personal formation events that gave form to our life. Because of this memory, we can develop new integrative meanings for the whole of life that grant a currently significant configuration to both past and present formation events.

For example, if I were to become later in life a formation director or counselor, memories of past disturbances due to deformative family events may gain a more meaningful place in my life's history. I may appraise them as preparatory experiences that enable me to better understand my directees or counselees when they recount similar memories.

Reformation of Formative Memory

As mentioned previously, formative memory tends to change in the light of our present life direction and disposition formation. The factual constituents of the memory of our dispositional life may remain the same. What may change is their configuration and overall meaning, their selective availability. One has only to read the life stories of converts to various religious or ideological form traditions to find a lively example of how they interpreted past situations differently in the light of a newly adopted form tradition. The same applies to people who, during formation counseling or psychotherapy, change their life direction considerably and initiate corresponding dispositions.

The reformation of memory dispositions presupposes the disposition to remember certain formative events in effective ways. This disposition can foster our effective remembrance in three ways: by formative focal recall, by formative remembrance, and by meditative formative remembrance. All three ways directly serve our current disposition formation. Indirectly they may affect our core disposition formation. This reformation can also take place on all levels of consciousness.

Formative Focal Recall and Formative Remembrance

Formative focal recall is the deliberate attempt to bring to focal attention formative and deformative events of the past. Its aim is to apprehend and appraise their influence on our dispositions. We ask: Are these events, in the way we keep remembering them, still congenial with later disclosures of our foundational life-form? Do the meanings we attributed to past events we keep in our memory help us to grow in likeness to our original life call as now disclosed to us? Do they provide us with the appreciation and insight we need for the development of dispositions compatible with our present and anticipated life situations? Do such memories make us more compassionate in regard to our own vulnerability and that of others? Often focal recall is difficult, if not impossible, without the assistance of confirmative and respectful direction in private or in common. In complex cases, psychotherapy may be necessary.

Formative remembrance is less focused than focal recall. It is usually sufficient when we are not plagued by specific formation problems. In times of relative consonance, the memories of past formation events are allowed to flow freely in our life of prefocal awareness. They hover near the border of focal attentiveness. They are available, therefore, to focal consciousness at any moment clear awareness of them is desirable or necessary. Prefocally, they constantly influence our present disposition formation and its maintenance. If necessary, they are instantly available to our formative powers of apprehension, appraisal, affirmation, and functional implementation.

Consider a housewife and mother who has developed a set of dispositions enabling her to relate effectively with her husband and children in a manner that is congenial, compatible, and compassionate. These relations bring joy and peace into her life during a period of relative consonance in her own formation history and that of her family. The set of dispositions that gives form consonantly to her life ought to be left alone. It should not be raised to the level of focal attentiveness. To do so might interfere unnecessarily with the spontaneous flow of her dispositional life, thereby diminishing its natural effectiveness. Should this flow be repeatedly interrupted due to new situations arising in the household or in the woman herself, it may be a sign that the time for focal recall has come, that influential memories need to be examined in a gentle and accepting way along with the disposition they nourish and sustain.

Meditative Formative Remembrance

Different from the usual formative remembrance is meditative formative remembrance. Usually in everyday life, we do not aim at initiating or strengthening certain specific dispositions. Rather, disposing memories flow freely in our prefocal awareness. In meditative remembrance, however, certain memories are selected for special cultivation. We want them to exercise an intensified, prolonged, and continuous influence on our present and future dispositional life.

Say we want to promote a disposition of stillness and recollection. We dwell on memories of moments of silence and solitude we cherished in the past, on memories of what touched us when reading the texts of various form traditions that refer to the peace of the hidden life. We dwell on the impression made on us by refined men and women who could be silent and deeply still at the propitious time. Such meditative remembrance facilitates the birth of a disposition of stillness and recollection in our dispersed lives.

Formative Memory and the Dimensions of the Life-Form

In Volume One of this series, we discussed at length the historical, vital, functional, and transcendent dimension of the life-form. Corresponding to each of these structures is the appropriate type of memory.

Historical formative memory refers to past sociohistorical pulsations that once gave form to our life. As memories, they still influence, at least potentially, our disposition formation. People who, for instance, grow up in a Marxist state under the direction of Marxist parents, teachers, and leaders provide a good example. If most of them are genuinely moved by the historical pulsation of Marxism, the dispositions that give form to their life and world will inevitably be marked by these pulsations.

Historical memory can be made available, at least in principle, to our powers of apprehension, appraisal, and affirmation. This enables us to disclose the sociohistorical component of our shared and unique life direction and disposition formation.

The vital life is characterized by vital pulsions. Our profile of preferred vital pulsions has been formed partially by past vital formation events and experiences. Memories of these may still influence our present pulsion dispositions. We may discover, for instance, an impulsive sexual attraction for a certain type of woman. It may be that she evokes latent memories of real or imaginative experiences of a mainly vital nature with the same kind of woman earlier in our life.

Our vital memory can also be made available to our appraisal powers. Some of our dispositions may be mainly vital; others may have a vital component. Our vital memory, when it is disclosed to us, can help us to appraise this constituent.

The functional dimension of the life-form is made up of our ambition and aptitude dispositions. Formative events in the past contributed to the formation of such functional dispositions, often on the basis of preformed temperament and aptitudes. A temperamental preformation or predisposition for technical performance may have been influenced in its specific direction by the type of technical work one's father was involved in as, say, an electrician. Memories of his dedication, dexterity, success, and satisfaction in his work may influence one's technical ambition and skillful disposition.

Our functional memory makes it possible for us to investigate the functional-technical consitutent of our dispositional life. We may discover that we would be even more effective were we to develop a disposition for another type of technical endeavor.

The transcendent dimension of our life-form is constituted by our preferred aspirations and inspirations that go beyond sociohistorical determination, vital pulsion, and functional ambition. Our first transcendent aspirations and inspirations form the distinctively human summit of our dispositional life. Growing to responsible maturity implies a creative-critical appraisal of our preferred aspirations and inspirations, along with their effectiveness, congeniality, compatibility, and compassion. Our transcendent memory enables us to evaluate the memories that support our appreciation of aspirations and inspirations.

We may, for instance, aspire after social presence to a special formation segment of the population, such as that of factory workers or artists, because we are filled with memories of parents, clergy, or acquaintances, who were temperamentally, physically, and emotionally disposed to serve that segment of the population. As in the case of Vincent van Gogh, who worked among the impoverished miners in Belgium, we may discover nonetheless that our transcendent memory seduced us to initiate an uncongenial disposition. We may become ill at ease and physically disabled, as van Gogh did, and we may finally discover that our aspiration to social presence can only be effectively expressed in another medium for other segments of the population.

Hierarchy of Formative Memories of Life-Form Dimensions

The formative memories pertaining to these four different dimensions of our life-form are interrelated. They form a hierarchy. In consonant life formation, higher-dimension memory prevails in formative influence over lower-dimension memories, yet it takes them fully into account. In this sense, we may speak of a hierarchical value configuration of memory influences.

Let us cite the example of a disposition for social presence to sick people in a hospital. Physicians or nurses who complement medical skill with true social presence may be nurtured by a transcendent memory of warm social presence. They may live in the implicit remembrance of the loving care they themselves experienced from others in the past. Such memories may be deepened by the remembrance of transcendent symbols and images of social presence in the sources of their form traditions.

The functional dimension of their social presence manifests itself in the ambition to learn the best and latest information, to master the best skills they can. One appropriates them not for their own sake or for one's ego satisfaction, but to implement one's transcendent social aspiration. This aspiration should dominate the whole hierarchy of social disposition components. The functional aspect of one's overall social presence is nourished by the memory of how people (including oneself) have been able to help the sick in their suffering, practically and concretely, in a way that radiated transcendent respect, love, and concern.

Vitally one remembers how to keep fit, physically alert, and in a good mood in service of one's higher social aspirations and ambitions. Sociohistorically, one nourishes these aspirations with cultural pulsations that promote social presence among people, not as a pleasant experience of being *in* with some contemporary pulsation but in concrete service of a vital-functional-transcendent social presence to the sick entrusted to one's care. Both vital and sociohistorical components are sustained by corresponding memories. (In a later volume, we will clarify how this human hierarchy of social presence is elevated by and integrated in the pneumatic dimension and its aspirations and inspirations.)

Stilted Formation Dispositions and Stilted Memories

Our form dispositions may be stilted. In that case the memories that help form and maintain these dispositions will be stilted, too. Say we remember a factual event in its formative meaning. The memory of that event cannot be changed as long as we remain faithful to our reality perception. What can be reformed is the meaning the event carries for the formation of our life and world. If this meaning becomes stilted and inflexible, we cannot enhance, reform, or deactivate the disposition that is sustained by the remembered meaning. For instance, people who were once kindly approached, only to be later deceived, may, on basis of this painful memory, form a disposition of distrust toward all manifestations of kindness, no matter how well-intended they are. As long as the generalized meaning of this onesided, fixated memory is not reformed, the disposition of distrust may not be reformed either.

Memories may be more or less available to our appraisal power. They may be repudiated and hence insulated in the infrafocal realm of life formation, or they may be refused and hence exiled in the transfocal realm. For instance, people may have repudiated their sexual pulsion disposition and insulated it in the realm of infrafocal consciousness. This may have happened because of threats from unwise formation persons in early childhood. As long as this repudiated memory is not apprehended and appraised one cannot deal effectively with the fear disposition that feeds on it. Others may have refused a transfocal aspiration or inspiration to create room in their lives for presence to others in transcendent love and respect. This refused aspiration or inspiration, with the memories attending it, remains blocked in the transfocal realm of life. It gives rise to an unacknowledged guilt disposition, which is activated when one's formation field invites such presence. In this case, refused memories are evoked that are no longer available to one's apprehension and appraisal power.

Formative Memory and Feeling

In all of these areas, formation science emphasizes that human formative influences are invested with feelings. This applies also to formative memories. These feelings are the dynamic forces at the core of one's formative memory. No reformation of these memories is possible without getting in touch with our feelings and working them through.

Consider a person who suffers from the deformative disposition of indiscriminate desire to please other people. This disposition may be nourished by memories of family and community situations in which one rightly or wrongly felt that the only way to find confirmation was to please others, no matter what. The deformative feeling tone of these memories, their intensity, quality, depth, and persistence, may not be fully acknowledged. It is, however, the power of such feelings that keeps the memories alive and influential.

The formative feeling tone of a memory is often the result of a variety of emotional reaction and response patterns. In our example, the feeling tone may result from feelings of inferiority, of repudiated anger about one's submissiveness, of false guilt because of misinterpreted tenets or dissonant accretions of one's form tradition, or anxious restriction because one has been victimized by an insuffiently prepared formation director, and so on.

It may take a long time to come to the experiential acknowledgment, acceptance, and expression of such webs of feelings. In complex cases, the formation director or counselor may have to refer people to a psychotherapist. Even then it may be quite a while before the person is sufficiently at home in all of these feelings to be able to reform the memories and dispositions they keep alive.

By contrast, pliable, open, imaginative memories, with their attendant feelings, are dynamic forces of formation. They assist us in the initiation, flexible updating, and implementation of formative dispositions. They enable us to approximate increasingly the consonant life.

Memories will be pliable to the degree that we grow in detachment from our secondary dispositional life-form. We should be detached spiritually, even from our most cherished dispositions, images, memories, and feelings. Our only attachment should be to the formation mystery and its epiphanies in our foundational life-form and formation field. This path of progressive detachment and deepening attachment is the secret of human freedom and consonance. It is the royal road to a life of peace and joyfulness.

Distinctively Human Formation Memories

In formation science only those formative memories are considered distinctively human that give form creatively to the past. They bring our past formation to life again, as it were, not by copying past formation events routinely but by reforming their meaning. Forming memory is, therefore, a reforming memory. This distinctive formation via remembrance should happen in congeniality with one's present disclosures of the foundational life-form; it should be marked by compatibility and compassion in relation to the progressive disclosures of one's formation field.

Spiritual formation cannot be rooted in inflexible memories of past formative events. On the contrary, consonant remembrance implies the creative reappraisal of past events. Their meaning has to be reevaluated and refined in the light of one's present formation history. Imagine being filled with dispositions of anger against one's parents: I may live in the implicit or explicit remembrance that they did not show me the affection and attention I felt I needed. This deformation was a factual reality I cannot deny. My memory may have invested the event with the meaning of bad will on the part of my parents. Later in life I may come to realize that I was an oversensitive child. It was difficult for my harried, hard-working parents to understand my affective needs. Now that I am married with children of my own, I discover that the pressures of a job, the increase of social obligations, and the deterioration of physical strength comprise a formation field that makes it difficult to find enough time to give my own children the affection I would like to show them. The memory of my own lack of sufficient affection as a child is still with me, but its meaning begins to change. I used to think it was due to willful neglect by my parents. Now, in the light of my present experience, I can better understand and forgive them, without repudiating or denying the facts. To be sure, before I attained this understanding, I probably had to pass through a long period of admitting, owning, and expressing the bottled-up feelings of anger toward my parents that were attached to these memories.

Formative Change of Remembered Meanings
with Change in Formation Field

Memory that is formative in a distinctively human way is not just a duplicate of past formative events and their subsequent attached meanings and emotions. It is a reliving of these events in the context of a new formation field. The original event is lifted out of its initial formative meaning and feeling structure. For instance, the cause and effect meaning which I ascribed to an event at one time may be reformed when it is placed in my present formation history and field.

In our example, the initial meaning and emotion structure implied, among other things, that my feeling of affective neglect was caused by willful intention on the part of my parents, as if their intent was the cause of what I was feeling. In the light of a new formation context, I reform the meaning. The cause is now perceived and appraised as a combination of my own oversensitivity and excessive need; of the average, less sensitive capacities that my parents shared with most people; and of the pressure of practical cares in their formation field. The original effect was a disposition to emotional overreaction. I may now overcome this disposition by progressive reality appraisal, compassionate understanding, and forgiveness, provided I am able to accept, express, and work through the accumulation of angry feelings in the wake of my original perception with its consequent memory fixation.

Formative memory thus goes beyond the mere factuality of the initial event. It becomes an intrinsic part of the dispositional life of the person. Its remembered formative meaning and corresponding feeling, unlike its factual meaning, does not stay the same. It changes with the person's formation history. The moment the formative event is past, its conceptual and emotional meaning enters into my history. From now on, it participates in the vicissitudes of this unfolding. Formative memory thus entails ongoing reformation and refinement of meaning and corresponding feeling.

A mere factual recall of a past formative event is not sufficient for reformation of dispositions in service of the consonant life. As long as the initial formative meanings, with their associated feelings, are not lived out and subjected to critical-creative appraisal, no reformation of dispositions can take place. Instead of a distinctively human formative remembrance, we end up with an oppressive repetition of the meanings and feelings of the past. People remain the captive of deformative dispositions because they refuse the work of detachment from these dispositions. Instead of being liberated, they become more rigidly bound than before. Locked into memories of the past, their formation field cannot open up and expand. It remains closed in by stale, confining meanings and feelings that prevent them from disclosing wider horizons.

The consonant life-form integrates past formative events into itself by disclosing and releasing new meanings. It makes these events more consonant with one's changing formation history by granting them a new sense and feeling tone in the light of progressive disclosures. These past occasions of formation find their appropriate place in the changing configuration of one's unfolding life-form.

Focal and Prefocal Formative Memory

The distinction between focal and prefocal formative experience applies also to formative memory. Memories sustain our dispositions, usually prefocally. We do not deliberately think about them or call them to mind. They are usually not the focus of our attention. They simply come to us. Usually they are evoked by prefocal experiences of people, events, things, images, and symbols associated spontaneously with formative events in the past.

For instance, a young man enters military service. The senior officer he meets at once evokes his distrust, anger, and resistance. He does not understand what suddenly conjures up these deformative, depreciative dispositions. Later he discovers that some of this man's features, his voice and manner, remind him prefocally of a schoolteacher who treated him unfairly. These memories were sufficient to activate the dispositions of the past. It is only in bringing them to apprehension and appraisal that he may overcome his prefocal depreciation of the officer that has no ground in reality.

Shared Formative Memories

Adherents of formative traditions share formative memories. What makes them distinct as a group hinges upon this remembering. Their future depends on the remembered past. A form tradition is meaningful only to those who remember creatively its main tenets, symbols, images, historical events, stories, rituals, and resources. We share in the life of a form tradition only when we share in its memories. Forgetting these memories separates us from the formation segment or community and its future, all of which forms around this tradition. Because these memories are already a part of the past history of a form tradition, they will also be a part of its future.

The importance of the memories of a form tradition can be seen in the rites of worship, in celebration, storytelling, music, dance, the arts, festivals, and plays. They are largely acts of remembrance of the formation events that were central in the history of a form tradition. They keep its interconscious treasures alive, reminding the people of the formative beginnings of their tradition.

Formative memory thus maintains the form traditions of a people. Its rites represent a continuing relationship with the formation mystery in its unique epiphany within their tradition. Remembrance is thus intimately linked with our fidelity to a tradition. When our personal memories are insufficient to nourish consonant disposition formation, the memories of our form traditions can play a saving role. Through these memories we may believe that the mystery of formation will not forget us, as it did not forget those who went before us in the shared form tradition. The narratives of the form tradition are meant to remind us of the care shown by the mystery during the course of a tradition's history.

Appreciative abandonment, the cornerstone of a vigorous and trusting life, becomes possible again. Sharing in this remembrance is by no means passive. It implies dwelling in meditative remembrance on the sources of one's tradition. Neither is the act of remembrance totally our achievement. All consonant form traditions maintain that in some way the formation mystery itself makes their tradition be; it reminds adherents of its forming presence within their tradition.

Memories of Form Traditions and Personal Encounter with the Mystery

Form traditions try to develop and expand their memories in such a way that they encompass the whole of human life and world formation. They root them in the formation mystery, which they believe under some name or symbol to be at the heart of their formative memories. These memories are formed around a chain of events that gave form decisively and uniquely to the history of a people. Their remembrance does not restrict itself to the factuality of these events or their past cultural representations. They should direct, illumine, and inspire our own power of meaning formation in tune with our present condition. Our life today emerges from the same formation mystery that gave meaning to our form traditions in the past. Our personal encounter with the mystery of formation happens in our life as we live compatibly in the present-day context. Yet it occurs through the medium of the memory of a form tradition.

This personal encounter with the mystery creates its own transcendent and unique memories. In these memories the formation mystery remains present as one's personal epiphany. Here the mystery abides uniquely as a source of joy, peace, and light to which one can return in faith, hope, and consonance. In its light, we remember the formative events of our life in a new way. We begin to see how the mystery of formation disclosed itself in them as a movement of personal care, how it addressed itself to us in them, drawing us into communication with its continuing presence.

Dynamic and Creative Nature of Forming Memories

This reflection demonstrates again how forming memories are not static images. As formative, such memories are a dynamic, creative appraisal of the meanings of past events. In this case, they are recalled in the light of the memory of the formation mystery present in one's inmost being.

Forming memory is thus an act of appraisal by focal consciousness. This act is faithful to the factual, formative events of the past. It is immensely pliable in regard to their meanings and feelings. Forming memory entails an appraisal made in view of one's changing formation field and history. This field is profoundly altered by participation in the memories of our form tradition; by our subsequent, inner experience of the mystery; and by personal memories that build upon our awareness of this unique image of the mystery in our soul.

We grow to love and revere our foundational life-form by dwelling appreciatively on memories of its disclosures. These memories sustain our growth in empirical, dispositional likeness to the image or form that we already substantially are. They promote a union of likeness or consonance with our foundational life-form in its emergence from the mystery of formation itself. Hence, formative memory leads to a union of likeness with the mystery that is already substantially united with us insofar as it makes us be.

Formative Anticipation

This discussion of the role of formative memory in disposition formation leads to a consideration of the modality of anticipation and its specific place in the formation of dispositions.

Formative anticipation is the power of foreseeing or imagining what lies in the future. All formation powers, dispositions, and actions are somehow dependent upon the foundational formation triad of faith, hope, and consonance (or love). While it is necessarily linked to all three, formative anticipation is especially connected with hope, though not identical with it. Lacking hope for the future, I could not develop the anticipations that give form to my life. However, anticipation does add something different to hope. It mobilizes other capacities in me, namely, those of remembering and imagining what may concretely happen and how I can most effectively deal with that anticipated situation.

For instance, a student may have the disposition of hope that inner and outer resources will help her through her studies this semester. Formative anticipation, nourished by this hope, enables her to foresee some of what will be demanded of her in papers and examinations and how she should prepare herself concretely to make an effective response to these academic challenges.

Forming anticipation tends to organize itself in anticipatory configurations. These are formed largely under the influence of dispositions that are modulated in turn by formative memories. Say a young married couple anticipates buying a home that will be attractively located and tastefully furnished. This anticipation is understandable on the basis of the fact that the couple shares an aesthetic disposition, an aspiration to approach their spiritual unfolding via enjoyment of beauty in their daily surroundings. Another couple may anticipate a rustic house as a point of departure for hiking, water sports, bird watching and other pleasures of nature. Their anticipation is modulated by a shared disposition for the pleasures of living in the wild. One way is not better than the other. They are only different, a difference in disposition that may ultimately be rooted in preformation. In both cases it colors their anticipations and renders them unique.

Anticipation includes those aspects of the past that are relevant to the formation of one's future. Past events represent the contributions of forming memory to forming anticipation. Returning to our example, to anticipate concretely an attractive, aesthetic home may imply the utilization of past experiences in regard to home decoration, while life in a rustic setting will draw upon practical talents in carpentry and home repair.

Importance of Formative Anticipation for Disposition Formation

Formative anticipation is crucial for effective formation. It enables our powers of apprehension, appraisal, and affirmation to evaluate potential or probable life situations as they emerge. What are their challenges, opportunities, and demands? How can we deal with the upcoming situation effectively, compatibly, and compassionately? How do we preserve congeniality with our foundational life-form? How do we maintain some continuity with the unique empirical expression of that hidden image in our past and present core, current, apparent, and actual forms? Do we initiate new dispositions or reform already existing ones?

Future parents may anticipate the arrival of their first baby. What do they foresee as the best environment for the baby? What effect will this birth have on the relationship between the parents? How will they make space for a new life while remaining faithful to their congenial and compatible marital commitments? These and many other anticipations may lead to a modulation of the dispositional life of both parents.

Our power of formative appraisal enables us to develop formation projects. Such projects can only be formed by means of focal attention to our anticipated future. We may pay attention to a project as a whole. For instance, we anticipate the building of a business that will give more consonant form to our life and to the lives of those entrusted to our care. In anticipation, we outline the steps we surmise to be necessary to execute this projected enterprise.

We may choose also to focus only on some of the more relevant aspects of this project, such as the economic factors or the dimensions of social justice and compatibility with our fellow citizens. *Focal anticipation* of such details involves a deliberate attempt to bring to consciousness relevant aspects of our project. We anticipate both formative and deformative events in our personal and shared future. We appraise their meaning for the present direction of our disposition formation. We ask ourselves what dispositions should be developed in service of our projects and in reference to the formative events we foresee as affecting them in the future. These and similar anticipations enable us to appraise what our disposition formation should be at present. They facilitate the choices and decisions of our will in this regard.

We can foster disposition formation not only by formative focal attention but also by *meditative formative attention.* This exercise helps us to cultivate relevant anticipations of a more general nature, both in our focal and prefocal attentiveness. We dwell on them in such a way that they exercise a gentle, continuous influence on our present disposition formation. A pregnant woman, for instance, may cultivate a gentle, caring disposition in anticipation of her baby's birth. She may anticipate the future in which the baby will be hers to care for in a motherly way. In this anticipatory dwelling, a generally loving, caring disposition may be initiated that was not hers as deeply before meditative anticipation.

Formative core anticipations are also important. They pertain to anticipations of such power and depth that they give form to the core or heart of our human life. They may or may not be available to our focal, detailed, or meditative global attentiveness. In our example of the expectant mother, anticipation of the event of giving birth to and rearing her baby may be so profound that it gives rise to a lasting core disposition of maternal solicitude that will color the life of the woman for years to come.

Current formative anticipation would not have such a lasting influence. A girl may anticipate how sweet and amenable she will be during a period of life in which she hopes to attract a man she wants to marry. Once she is married she may drop this disposition since she only developed it as a current disposition for a passing period of effective courtship.

Trancendent formative anticipation pertains, of course, to the transcendent meanings of future formative events. These are formative insofar as they influence our present aspiration dispositions. For instance, a man or woman preparing for a life of ministry in a form tradition may anticipate how this ministry will affect their life of aspiration in the future. This anticipation itself may promote in advance the development of certain religious and charitable aspirations.

Something similar can be said in regard to *functional anticipation.* Functional ambition dispositions may be initiated as a result of one's anticipation of having a function in society in the future. The politician of tomorrow may already develop a disposition of diplomacy today in anticipation of gaining popularity when election time comes.

Vital anticipation can affect the formation of our present vital pulsions. A son or daughter of alcoholic parents may anticipate future inclinations to alcoholism. Hence he or she may already discipline this suspected vital pulsion by dispositions for abstinence and sobriety.

Sociohistorical anticipations enable us to foresee which fads and enthusiasms may sweep through our form traditions and societies in the near future. In view of this anticipated cultural violence due to popular enticements that may absorb our unique call, we may develop dispositions that protect us against deformative onslaughts of popular pulsations on the congeniality of our life's formation.

These different types of anticipation should be progressively integrated in a consonant form of life. They should also be ordered in a hierarchy. Anticipations of a higher form dimension, like the transcendent, should prevail in influence over those of lower form dimensions, such as the functional and vital. This prevalence should not repudiate and insulate the awareness of lower anticipations; it should take them into account in a respectful, critical-creative fashion.

Formative Anticipations and Form Traditions

Anticipations are not formed in isolation but in interformation. They are influenced by our interaction with the people with whom we live, who communicate to us verbally or preverbally their own anticipations. Our anticipations are especially affected by form traditions because they constitute the realm of a vertical interformation, which stretches over centuries. They bring us in touch with whoever and whatever gave form significantly to life and world long before our generation.

Formative anticipation is prominent in every lasting form tradition. A tradition gives us hope for the future. It makes us anticipate how we can give form effectively to our future. This opening to the unknown makes tradition attractive to people. It nourishes their own hopes and anticipations. The deepest reason for this influence is rooted in the link between a form tradition and the formation mystery that one believes to be at its origin. Hence form traditions rely on the ritual, visual, and verbal remembrance of formative events that manifest this special care and concern of the formation mystery.

A dynamic form tradition does not rest in this remembrance. It utilizes it to anticipate the future. An effective form tradition announces the future as opportunity and challenge rather than as threat and defeat. It fosters confident anticipation. This explains why it may instill in its adherents remarkable dispositions of endurance and resiliency, even in the face of persecution and misunderstanding. Great form dispositions kindle hope against all hope. They anticipate the future as ultimately consonant.

Hope and the Timely and Timeless Anticipations Inspired by Form Traditions

The anticipations that consonant form traditions inspire are both timely and timeless. They are timeless because they are rooted in a hope that points to a mysterious fulfillment that lies beyond all generations and their temporary conditions. They are timely because they inspire anticipatory projects that are approximations here and now of things hoped for but not possessed.

These timely anticipations, as well as the beneficial dispositions, acts, and situations they engender, are symbolic pointers to the likeness to the mystery promised by the form tradition. To be sure, each form tradition has its own symbols, images, stories, and legends to express this hope, promise, and anticipation. Each classical religious form tradition has an eschatological thrust. This may be one of the reasons why in times of atrocities and suffering form traditions gain adherents and those already committed seek deeper roots in their tradition.

Because of this anticipatory characteristic, all consonant traditions are forward looking. If necessary they will reform the present in light of their reformulated anticipations. These in turn are rooted in the transcendent hope that the great spiritual traditions keep alive in humanity. Hope and anticipation suffuse every expression of these traditions and sustain the appreciative disposition formation of their committed followers.

Great spiritual traditions that have survived the millennia are not only form traditions of the past but also of the future. They enable us to interpret our formation history in and through the progressive disclosure of future changes in our formation field. The formative meaning of the present formation field and the dispositions it evokes is based on a hopeful anticipatory openness to what the mystery may unveil to us in the approaching future.

Hope is thus intertwined with the anticipations evoked by traditions. The lasting form traditions of humanity foster the faith that an as yet unknown transformation of life and world within the epiphanies of the mystery of formation is awaiting us. According to such traditions, the fullness of this transformation will be disclosed to humanity in an unknown future. We can only anticipate timely approximations of the life of peace and joy on the basis of this hope. These passing anticipatory situations will be marred by ambiguity and deficiency, but the hope engendered by spiritual traditions enables us to live in that ambiguity with gentle courage and patience.

A spiritual form tradition loses its power and becomes deceptive when it fosters the illusion that its adherents will attain the fullness of peace and joy here and now. Either they accept the illusion and walk about in a dream, or they wake up and reject the illusionary tradition itself or the accretions of an otherwise realistic form tradition. Persons form their anticipations and corresponding dispositions accordingly.

If disposition formation is to benefit from the resources of form traditions, adherents should realize that the living wisdom expressed in images, symbols, stories, and formative events operates differently from abstract concepts. Concepts are understood or not understood. By themselves, they have no further formative power. Images and symbols are often not immediately understood in their fullness. Only part of their truth is disclosed to the hearer or reader. They tend, however, to sink deeply in the prefocal and transfocal awareness of the person. By reiterated participation in their meaning, they gradually communicate their treasures to us, slowly transforming our life. The images and symbols of spiritual form traditions usually influence us pre- and transfocally, slowly and subtly, but most profoundly.

Transformation of Dispositions

With this discussion of formative anticipation, we come to the end of our consideration of the main powers of intraformation and their impact on disposition formation. We considered formative apprehension, appraisal, affirmation, imagination, memory, and anticipation in the context of formation and reformation. For the sake of completeness, we would like to conclude these considerations with a few remarks about transformation. This topic will be discussed more extensively in a later volume devoted to the articulations of formation science in explicitly spiritual form traditions of a revelatory nature.

All formation and reformation of our dispositions should be in service of our increasing consonance or likeness with the image of the mystery we deeply and substantially are. This union of consonance is at the same time a union of participation in the formation mystery, which is the source of the unique foundational life-form within us. In this light, all formative dispositions are seen as facilitating conditions for this participation. By themselves they cannot effect participative union. They do not have the power to share in the mystery of formation itself.

The all-encompassing, nourishing formation power transcends the limited powers of formation and reformation. No human disposition is sufficient in and by itself to attain to this union. The formation journey may attain its initial goal of a consonant dispositional life. At that moment the mystery that dwells within us may take over. Formation and reformation now become transformation. A mystery of transforming love illumines and elevates all our dispositions.

We have seen repeatedly how crucial are distancing and detachment for the initial and ongoing formation and reformation of our dispositions. The same basic rule applies to the crowning period of progressive transformation. Detachment for the sake of attachment to the mystery of transformation has to go far deeper. It has to be so profound that we know we cannot effect it by ourselves alone. The mystery of transformation has to bring about this ultimate consonance for us and with us. It must infuse into our core form a faith, hope, and love toward itself that goes infinitely beyond the human faith, hope, and consonance we began to develop during childhood interformation.

The gift of *transforming faith* enables us to detach ourselves from our formative powers of apprehension and appraisal insofar as their operation is based on our own knowledge, logic, insight, and perception. Faith elevates us beyond them to a knowing in love that can transform our life-form into a participative likeness with the mystery itself. The same applies to formative imagination, memory, and anticipation insofar as they sustain apprehension and appraisal.

The gift of *transforming love* or consonance makes it possible for us to become fully detached from our own affections, strivings, and willings so that we may become purely consonant with the will of the formation mystery itself.

The gift of *transforming hope* enables us to rise beyond our anticipations and expectations, and the images and memories sustaining them, and to put all our hope in the mystery alone.

This purification of our intraformative powers transforms our dispositions. At moments of total presence to the mystery, they are suspended in their operation. Yet, at moments of action, they freely and flexibly serve the incarnation of the transforming mystery in our life and formation field.

CHAPTER 9

Fundamental Formation Dispositions of the Heart

F ormation science distinguishes the symbolic heart or core form of life and the physical heart that in some measure resonates with the movements of the symbolic heart. Of all the dispositions that give form to our life and the lives of others, those of the symbolic heart are most enduring and decisive. The symbolic heart is the core form of our empirical life; it is its affective, dynamic center.

In the concluding chapter of Volume One of this series, we provisionally clarified the position of the symbolic heart within the structure of human life formation. Before we expand on the dispositions of the heart, it is necessary to detail more fully the core form, its function, and the essential nature of its dispositions.

Position and Function of the Core Form in Human Life Formation
Human life is called forth within its formation field by the formation mystery. This call is the ground of our personal relation to the mystery. The invitation to share in the epiphany of the mystery and its forming potency in our life fills us with awe for our own participant form potency. Awe is the source of our transcendent dignity within the scheme of life and history. This call resonates in our heart mysteriously. It makes the heart the inspired core of our formation and all its dispositions. These dispositions coform, respectively, the transcendent, functional, vital, and sociohistorical dimensions of our life-form.

Our call to share in the epiphany of the mystery is received by the transcendent and executed by the functional dimension of our life-form. Underlying the functional dimension, and vibrating with it, is our vital dimension. All three dimensions—transcendent, functional, and vital— are pervaded by the more general sociohistorical one. Is it possible that any one of these dimensions can function as the harmonizing midpoint of our unfolding life? Our answer to this question must be no.

165

Neither the transcendent nor the functional, vital, or sociohistorical dimensions can be the proximate integrative center of our formation as a whole. Our symbolic heart, or core form, cannot be identified with any particular dimension of the life-form. It must impartially nourish, sustain, and integrate the consonant movement of all of these dimensions. Functioning as the responsible-sensible or affective middle ground of life, the symbolic heart or core must strive to harmonize our dimensional formation movements in some kind of felt consonance. It should provide a harmonious mosaic of basic and enduring dipositions that affect in a responsible-sensible way our inspirations, aspirations, ambitions, pulsions, and pulsations as they arise in our various life dimensions.

Life Dimensions Cannot Provide an Integrative Center

The pride-form in its exalted autarchy may first of all engender the illusion that our functional life dimension is central. It may suggest that functional ambition and its satisfaction is totally important, that it suffices for life's fulfillment. If we give in to this suggestion, supported as it often is by popular pulsations, our functional concerns may dominate our formation field. We become functionalistic and risk losing our distinctively human centeredness and consonance.

We may be inclined to think that at least the transcendent dimension, as illumined by the spirit, could be the centering middle ground. To be sure, the spirit is highest in dignity and should prevail in the remote direction of our formation. This does not necessarily mean that it can fulfill by itself the function of proximate, practical, lived integration of the diverse dimensions and dispositions of human life.

A medieval monarch may have been the overall wise director of his kingdom. The proximate responsible-sensible daily integration and stimulation of his kingdom was guided, however, by a centralizing heart or ministerial government that reconciled the ideals of the king with the vital, functional, and sociohistorical realities of his kingdom.

Similarly our "royal spirit" gives rise to our transcendent and functional mind and will and illumines them. Their apprehensions, appraisals, and affirmations may generate enduring proximate dispositions of the heart. These live on in the responsible-sensible core and give form consistently to life in the light of the spirit that gave rise to them. Our spirit can also function more directly as a bridge between our preformed foundational life-form, symbolized by the soul, and our emergent empirical life formation, symbolized by the heart.

Our spirit communicates to our heart the hidden preformation of our foundational life-form. It gives reasons to the heart that the mind itself cannot initiate but only appraise after they manifest themselves. While the spirit may at times communicate the movements of one's soul, it is up to the heart to translate them, via proximate dialogue with all the life dimensions, into affective, dynamic, and responsible movements of our incarnated life.

The reader should remember that we are not speaking here about the soul as articulated in the transscientific formative wisdom of certain faith and formation traditions. A later volume in this series will deal with the soul in the light of the Christian tradition and articulate the insights of formation science in the language of its age-old wisdom. Here we use the symbol *soul* to represent the innermost foundation of our unfolding life-form. In this usage the word *soul* is not restricted to its specific meaning in one or another particular form traditions. It refers to what is deepest and most worthy in the distinctively human form of life.

The work of human reformation starts in the heart by means of the human spirit; it is the reclamation by the soul, via the spirit, of its innermost form direction. Gradually the human life-form, through its embodied, distinctively human interaction with a succession of formative life situations, begins to disclose the secret of its hidden foundational life direction or soul. The art and discipline of formation enables us to disclose and implement in our life the epiphany or imaging of the formation mystery in our human soul. In its light we have to engage in the incredibly difficult task of taming and disciplining the chaos in our hearts and minds, in all dimensions of our dissonant human life-form.

Symbolizing as it does our preempirical, unknown, foundational life-form, the soul cannot be a proximate center of integration in and by itself. Only insofar as it becomes disclosed and imprinted in the heart and in its dispositions can its basic directedness exercise an integrating and harmonizing influence in a more proximate fashion.

For all of these reasons neither the soul nor the spirit, directly or indirectly via mind and will, can be the proximate middle ground of daily life formation in all its empirical earthiness.

Can the vital dimension function as the consonant proximate center of all aspects of concrete daily formation? The answer is no. Our vital life dimension represents the bodily forces and directions that give rise to vital pulsions as manifested in impulses, passions, tempers, and temperament. These have to be integrated with the inspirations and aspirations of our spirit, with the functional ambitions and historical pulsations of our life. Without any integration by higher dispositions, our vital pulsions would pull us immoderatly in countless directions. They would disperse and destroy the consonance of our life's formation. Hence the vital dimension itself cannot function as the integrative center of our daily unfolding.

The only other candidate left among the dimensions for this centering function would be the sociohistorical. It would be the most unlikely candidate. If we were to make external social pulsations the exclusive basis of our formation, we would betray our relatively unique interior calling by the mystery. This calling is what we most deeply are. Our sociohistorical center of life would be a center of self-alienation. We would lose ourselves in this surrender to the pulsations of crowd and collectivity.

Often a seductive pious or violent collectivity may claim to be the perfect rendition of community life. It may come to believe its own spurious claim. The consonant community, however, is formed by liberated and generous people. They are masters in the realm of reverence and respect. Envy and competition have sufficiently diminished among them to allow space for the relaxed creativity of unique persons. Their main concern is to facilitate, in faith, hope, and love, the personal integration and modulation of shared ideals without betraying the relatively unique life call of any member of the community.

We conclude from this presentation that none of these dimensions of the life-form can be the proximate center of lived integration. Yet such a center is necessary as a core of integration of our life and its engagement. It must provide the recurrent basic themes of the melody of our existence that are to be taken up and modulated by all the dimensions, acts, and dispositions of our ongoing formation. Because of this necessity, the mysterious movement of preformation and formation of life engenders the core form or heart as the dynamic proximate ground of our emergent dispositional form of life.

Intraformative Polarity of the Heart

Our theory of the formation of the heart in the context of initial formation holds that the basic coformants of the heart are responsibility and sensibility. They mirror in the heart the basic polarity between the transcendent and the vital-functional dimensions of the human life-form. This polarity raises the question of their intraformative integration. The problems surrounding such polarity and integration can cause deformations and dissonances that may mar our formation history.

One main problem can be our onesided understanding and development of the heart. We may be inclined to misunderstand the core form of life as only representing responsibility, as the anxious or rigorous messenger of transcendent-functional reason in isolation from vital life and reality. Or the heart may be mistakenly considered as only the seat of vital sensibility, the arbitrary impulsive or romantic representative of the vital-functional dimension. Such misunderstandings can lead to a deformation of the heart and its dispositions.

Responsibility and Sensibility as Coformants of the Heart

The formation history of the West has been marked by periods of one-sided understanding. At certain times either the responsibility or the sensibility of the heart has been onesidedly exalted as the ideal of life. This may account for periods of a predominantly rationalistic or romantic formation. Formation science, in line with the consonant, classical form traditions, fosters the intraformative polarity of both coformants of the heart. Both are necessary for the consonance of the core form and its dispositions. One cannot be deduced from or reduced to the other. Both contribute their own distinctive feeling tone to the heart. They are affected in turn by the unique affiliation of the heart with its underlying foundational life-form.

In their interplay of intraformation, each plays a different role. They are not of equal rank, so to speak. The sense of responsibility and conviction represents the higher transcendent dimension of life. Hence it should prevail in the mutual permeation of responsibility and sensibility.

Moments of Onesided Prevalence of the Coformant

At certain moments of life, one or the other coformant may prevail onesidedly due to the initiation of a new mode of presence as the specific object of the heart's concern. For example, in the moment of transition from a functional to a contemplative mode of presence to the mystery of formation, the higher response-ability factor may onesidedly prevail. The sense-ability factor may be less active as one passes through the crisis of leaving behind a more sensate mode of presence. Detachment from a no longer effective sensibility mode is facilitated if one's sensate feelings are momentarily silenced and left in the dark, as it were. Once the higher response to contemplation is established, it will both permeate and elevate once again the sensibility of the heart. It now becomes a higher, more refined sensibility.

Consonant, mature responsibility and sensibility operate in intimate collaboration; they engender an inwardly felt stability of basic mood and feeling. A quiet peace and wisdom of heart begin to mark the best moments of life. One experiences an inner at-homeness, a gracious, relaxed feeling of at-homeness with the mystery, a calm certitude of mood and life direction.

The responsibility and sensibility of the heart are related to one another as are the different dimensions of the life-form they represent. This basic polarity manifests itself already in the apparent form of life. No other life-form on earth stands erect as humans do. Transcendent vision and vital earthboundness are expressed in human appearance. This fundamental tension between spirit and body, transcendence and immanence, is represented in the polarity of the responsibility and sensibility of the heart.

The personal center of our life in formation can only be understood as the consonance of both factors in the midst of their polarity. The initial opposition between them is progressively overcome. A striking example of this consonance can be found in the experience of distinctively human love. It manifests the integration of loving transcendent responsibility and vital affectivity in regard to those who are loved and cared for in a mature fashion.

Ascendance and Descendance of Dimensions into the Human Heart

Formation science views the transcendent responsibility feeling of the heart as a fruit of the spirit. The spirit may directly generate responsibility feelings in the heart. It does so as a messenger of the soul or foundational life-form with which the heart is also directly affiliated. The spirit may also influence the heart via mind and will, which the spirit itself makes possible and illumines. The latter is the transcendent dimension of the life-form. Only in relation to this dimension can we speak about a descendance into the heart. The seeds of formation created and affirmed by transcendent thinking and willing sink into the proximate middle sphere of life that is our affective heart. This is a benign invasion, followed by a settling down of these seeds into the fertile affective core form of our life. This descendance of the transcendent into the fertile open heart deposits the results of its movements of apprehension, appraisal, and affirmation. The heart in turn can influence these transcendent movements.

Response Ability of the Heart: Descendance Movement

The response ability of the heart is basically a felt conviction that one is able to respond to the formation mystery as it discloses itself within the limits of one's formation field. Formative response ability marks each person's formation history insofar as it is consonant. We respond to the epiphanies of the mystery by wanting and striving to give form to our life and world in accordance with its disclosures.

To what does the word *ability* in the term *response ability* refer? The answer is that it refers to the implicit experience of our formation potency. This potency is rooted in our participation in the higher form potency of the mystery itself. Such participation makes it possible for us to respond consonantly within our limits. Both our potency and its limits are given to us by the formation mystery. The quiet conviction of our limited yet effective form potency is thus rooted in our being called upon by the mystery. It is not grounded ultimately in our functional or apparent achievement or failure. To build our security on the latter is to live an anxious, vulnerable life, no matter how powerful and effective we imagine ourselves to be.

Sense Ability of the Heart: Ascendance Movement

Sense ability of the heart represents the ascension, purification, and elevation of the fruits of our vital dimension into the consonant core of our life. If purification and detachment do not occur, the heart will be dissonant to that degree. The ascension of the vital complements the descendance of the transcendent. Vital sensibility, thus elevated, coforms with transcendent feelings the enduring core of our central formative mood and feeling life. In short, the heart becomes the affective, transcendent-vital center of our formation.

This ascension or elevation of vital sensibility does not destroy or dimenish its essential animating power. What changes by this elevation, purification, and detachment is the exclusive dependence of our vital feelings on the somatic roots we have in common with animal life. Instead our vital feelings become dependent on the felt-responsibility that progressively pervades them within this feeling core of life. It becomes a spontaneous, responsible sensibility.

Without this vital sensibility, the center of our formation would become estranged from our bodily life. It would become alienated from incarnated, earthbound life itself. The heart becomes anxiously compulsive when it is dominated by responsibility feelings that are not balanced by vital affectivity.

Neither can the heart be the consonant core of life when vital moods and feelings onesidely prevail. The heart is then lacking in affective order

and wisdom, that is to say, in the determination, courage, and perseverance that gently and firmly discipline the vital moods and sensations of
our heart in the midst of life's vicissitudes.

We can conclude that apprehension, appraisal, and affirmation engender certain foundational dispositions. They do not remain outside the
heart. They sink into the heart as its enduring dispositions. These are the
source of the affectively preferred specific apprehensions, appreciations,
depreciations, and determinations of the human heart. They reside in our
interiority as basic affective and effective powers of formation. They constitute together the dynamic core form of our life of disposition and action. Wisely integrated within these core dispositions of responsibility are
the vital mood and feeling dispositions that have been raised to the level of
the responsible heart. They provide the heart's vital sensibility, its incarnational dynamic power.

The somatically rooted vital sensibility grants us the psychophysical
feeling of individual form potency. The transcendentally rooted responsibility feeling gives us the conviction of participation in a higher form
potency. Both foundational experiences complement one another in the
consonant, well-balanced heart.

Hidden Formative Nucleus of the Human Heart

This intraformative polarity is the foundational condition of a distinctively human life formation. It is not the only foundation nor is it the
deepest foundational condition. The heart knows a still deeper foundation that helps prevent this polarity from becoming a dualism.

Responsibility and sensibility are not separated in their mutual intraformation. They are marked in the process of mutual intraformation by
the mysterious nucleus of our heart, consisting in its direct, natural affiliation with the unique foundational life-form and the spirit that is the
summit of this foundational form as well as its bridge to the empirical life
as a whole. This hidden form radiates its forming power into our heart via
the spirit. The nucleus holds the anonymous secret of our relative uniqueness. It is the link of the heart with the specific image or personal epiphany
of the formation mystery we always already are substantially, if not yet
fully in empirical likeness.

This founding form and its subtle radiation into the human heart are ineffable. They are hidden not only from others but also from ourselves.
This affiliation could be called the "umbilical cord" between our heart
and the depths of our being. Along with our relative uniqueness, it explains

many experiences. It illumines for us a deeper aspect of the distinctively human love experience about which we spoke in relation to responsibility and sensibility. The depths of our founding form of life mark uniquely and mysteriously the feelings of our heart. Distinctively human encounters in love are rooted in this secret affliation of the human heart. Hence we are unable to explain the depth and power of an experience of profound love and spiritual attraction that comes as a gift and surprise. It may happen at once or after a period of encounters in depth in which the heart discloses itself. Somehow we are taken over by a mysterious affinity we sense in one another without being able to give it a name. It is hidden in our founding form of life. Some of its mystery may be disclosed to us in the course of our togetherness in spirit. Yet it will never be fully known in our focal consciousness. We enjoy its fruit in the spontaneous deepest feeling tone of our heart. Yet it remains partly anonymous, as does the hidden image that always remains hidden in some measure in this life.

The same affiliation with the inner image or personal epiphany of the mystery opens the heart to its felt faith experience of the transcendent mystery of formation. Because of this affiliation, we may say that the consonant heart is in principle the empirical-dispositional core expression of our foundational life-form.

Summary of the Structure and Relationships of the Core Form of Life

The core form is distinct from transcendent and functional knowing and willing as such. Yet it is not isolated from them. Their fruits sink into the responsibility dispositions of the heart. Likewise the core form is not identical with sociohistorical pulsations, vital pulsions, and functional ambitions. These dimensions keep their relative independence, yet the heart is not isolated from them. Their fruits can be elevated to dispositions of the heart in intraformative interaction with the responsibility dispositions. Nor is the affective core form of life identical with our foundational life-form. The heart could be called the empirical proximate core form of our dispositional life as distinguished from the foundational life-form, which could be called in this context the remote core form of life. Still the consonant heart is affiliated intimately with this remote core form. This epiphany or image affiliation itself is the nucleus of the heart. It is, so to speak, the heart of our heart. Hence we use the expression, "What do you feel in your heart of hearts?" This affiliation contains the secret of our relatively unique life direction.

The core form is thus a proximate center of integration of our life formation. As such, it is the dynamic ground of our empirical life-form. As a relatively stable, enduring center, it is clearly distinct from that in life which is not its center. Our actual life-form, as it concretely manifests itself in its daily appearance, is more than this center. It comprises beyond this lasting center our less-central, less-enduring current and apparent forms of life. These in turn have their changing transcendent, functional, vital, and sociohistorical dimensions and articulations. These, too, are less enduring than similar dimensions and articulations of the human heart itself. They are coformed by changeable dispositions and acts. All of these manifestations of formation beyond our center should be related to the core form as the spokes of a wheel to its axis or as the musicians of an orchestra to its conductor.

Heart or Core Form and the Soul or Foundational Life-Form

Formation science makes a similar distinction between the soul or foundational life-form and its empirical expression in the emergent integrative core, current, apparent, and finally integrating actual form of life. The foundational life-form, symbolized by the soul, can be increasingly expressed in the empirical life-form without being absorbed by it. The same can be said of the relation between the core form and its dispositions, on the one hand, and, on the other hand, the successive, integrative current, apparent, and final actual integrating forms of life and their dispositions.

Predispositions and Dispositions of the Core Form: Presupposition of Essence

We will discuss later the main formative dispositions of the heart. To do this meaningfully, we have to start from two presuppositions that may seem self-evident. Unfortunately, some existentialistic and positivistic currents of formation seem to neglect or deny these presuppositions, and it is necessary to affirm and explain them again as basic in formation science.

Each formation scientist starts from the presupposition that anything that *is* has an *essence* that can be described at least in principle in the language of concepts we have in common. Predispositions and dispositions *are*. Hence they have an essence that can in principle be described in common concepts that people can understand.

If this were not true, it would be impossible to make any sense out of the people, events, and things that emerge in our formation field and out of what emerges in ourselves as participants in that field. Everything inside and outside of us would be absolutely individual, exclusively unique. They would not have any specific characteristics in common. We could not compare them at all because there would be no point of comparison. Nor could we speak about their differences since we can only see differences on basis of some similarities.

We can apply the same line of thought to our predispositions and dispositions. If each person had only unique dispositions, we could not compare them with other dispositions in other people. It would be impossible to speak about such dispositions. We could not say anything meaningful about them. We could only say that a person's dispositions are an unknowable and totally unavailable secret. We ourselves could never have a disposition comparable to the disposition of another. One could say nothing about dispositions as such, nor even use or invent the term *disposition,* because using the term already presupposes that people have something in common, in other words, that they are not exclusively unique. Among other things, they have in common what we call dispositions.

Without *essences* of dispositions and their conceptual expressions, we could not speak about any specific dispositions. Words such as the dispositions of awe, faith, hope, consonance, congeniality, compatibility, compassion, gentleness, and firmness would make no sense. No one would know what we were speaking about. Neither could we meaningfully discuss disposition formation. If, for instance, the disposition of awe in one person had absolutely no similarity with that of another person, then the formation of awe in one would not have the slightest thing in common with the formation of awe in another. It would then be impossible to speak about disposition formation or reformation or to develop a science of formation. Any collection of form dispositions in a person would then be a chaos of totally unique phenomena that would remain closed to our human powers of apprehension and appraisal.

To avoid such absurd conclusions, we must accept that dispositions, like all other things that *are,* have certain modes of being in common. These can in a certain measure be comprehended in concepts such as awe, gentleness, firmness, detachment, simplicity, respect, communality, and privacy. Such a common mode of being could be called the essence of a disposition.

Formation scientists who would say the opposite would end up contradicting themselves implicitly. Imagine that they would pose the thesis that each human life-form has its own exclusively unique, totally incomparable dispositions. According to them, these could only be understood intuitively but never comprehended in common concepts. What they say here is a judgment. Such a judgment, like every other one, is formed by concepts. Moreover, it is a universal judgment. They assert something that should be valid for each human life-form and for all dispositions. This judgment demonstrates already that human forms of life and their dispositions are not absolutely incomparable, that they can possess not only unique but also universal-typical characteristics. By their negation of essential concepts, they contradict themselves implicitly in the universality of concepts implied in their own statement.

One reason to emphasize this possibility of universal-typical descriptions of formative dispositions is to distance ourselves from the tendency to see only an *exclusive* uniqueness in human forms of life. It is true that a certain uniqueness is typical of the human life-form and that this trace of uniqueness manifests itself also in our distinctively human dispositions. Without our acknowledgment of this relatively unique aspect of each human form of life and its dispositions, our insight into a person's dispositions would be onesided, limited, abstract, and schematic. What we object to is the assertion that human life-forms and their dispositions are absolutely or exclusively unique, that they have nothing whatsoever in common.

The formation scientist or practitioner who through study, experience, and observation has gained some insight into the essence of the human life-form and its potential or actual dispositions, can grasp what in the individual person is unique or somewhat different and personal in comparison with the universal-typical dispositions of all people. Formation scientists or counselors who did not have the slightest insight into the essences of the human life-form would be unable to distinguish a unique aspect of a person's dispositions.

We do not deny the relative uniqueness of persons and dispositions. We only object to the claim of the exclusiveness and absolute incomparability of such dispositions. To grasp the unique characteristic of a disposition presupposes that one apprehends the common typical or essential aspects of the disposition in question. Formation scientists who would deny the possibility of knowing, necessarily in an imperfect, limited fashion, the essence of the human life-form, its formation, and its formative dispositions, would end up with some form of skepticism or agnosticism.

We must conclude that the universal and necessary distinguishing marks of the predispositions and dispositions described by the formation scientist are necessary characteristics. Descriptions of formative dispositions that would represent only superficial, cursory, and accidental impressions are without basic value for the science of formation.

CHAPTER 10

The Disposition of Awe

The disposition of awe has a primordial place in the hierarchy of dispositions of the heart. This disposition is transcendent, that is, it goes beyond dispositions that are primarily directed to those aspects of the formation field available only to our sense perception. Dispositions that are merely vital-functional cannot in and by themselves be the source of awe for the mystery.

The disposition of awe is primordial, meaning that it should be first in our hierarchy of dispositions; it should be pervasive, gradually influencing all other dispositions of the human life-form. Awe and its object pole, the formation mystery, will be considered at some length because both play a central role in formation science.

Awe, Mystery, and Positivism

To raise the question of awe and mystery is to pose the problem of the position of the science of formation in relation to the philosophy of positivism. The epistemology of positivism dismisses questions of awe and mystery as pseudoproblems. For scientists who adhere to this philosophy only questions that can be answered by reference to sense perceptible aspects of the formation field have validity. Accordingly, they would consider the central questions of the formation scientist regarding awe and mystery as issues without meaning.

To respond to them, we must state in advance that the science of formation is an integrative-hypothetical provisional science. This means that it tries to bring together provisionally, in a systematic, critical-methodical fashion, all we can know at this moment of history about distinctively human formation. Formation scientists must be open to available past, present, and future knowledge about formation. This accounts for the provisional character of formation science. Such relevant insights can be prescientific; they can come from the natural and human sciences and from the transscientific wisdom of formation traditions and their formationally relevant philosophical and theological clarifications.

This integrative discipline is called a science for three reasons. First it uses a critical-objective methodology for the elucidation of the pre-scientific formation experiences it critically objectifies and analyzes in service of the development of its integrative constructs. Second, it applies a critical-objective, integrational-dialogical methodology consistently to the disclosure and integration of formationally relevant insights and findings of other disciplines. Third, it fosters a methodical attempt to keep the accurate formulation of prescientific formation experiences and of trans-scientific traditional formation wisdom in consonance with the rigorously validated findings of the natural and human sciences that become available to humanity.

This dialogical openness generates the respectful readiness of the integrational formation scientist to disclose and integrate any formationally relevant insight and finding, no matter where or by whom it is offered, as long as its validity can be demonstrated. The science gratefully acknowledges and integrates also the formationally relevant facts discovered by scientists and philosophers of a positivist persuasion in regard to the sense perceptible aspects of the human formation field.

What an integrative science of formation must never do is take from any philosophy of science a statement that would restrict its ability to integrate relevant formation findings from areas or disciplines of human thought and experience arbitrarily excluded by such a philosophy.

It is true that the questions of awe and mystery cannot be adequately answered within the restriction of the positivist position toward sense perception. What is invalid, however, is the contention that such questions are thus meaningless. Formation experiences and the wisdom of tradition are as old as humanity itself. Countless people throughout the millennia of human history, including our present era, have been asking these questions in various ways. They did not find them meaningless at all. They arose as a result of the experience of aspects of their formation field that were not merely sense perceptible.

It is an empirical fact that such transcendent questions arise again and again as meaningful in the human experience of the formation field. People who honestly believe that such questions cannot have any meaning seem to have lost contact with some significant aspect of this field. Their meaning simply escapes them in spite of their often remarkable mental power and learning. Something may have happened in their initial or ongoing formation that cuts them off from the experience of field dimensions that, for thousands of years and still today, have been of utmost meaningfulness for the overwhelming majority of people.

This is not to deny, of course, that some positivistic philosophers and scientists are geniuses in regard to the knowledge of the sense perceptible aspects of the formation field still available to their experience. Their exclusive concentration on these material aspects may make them even more insightful in this limited realm of formation. Their findings and insights should be carefully scrutinized for potential contributions to the integrative science of foundational human formation.

Awe Disposition and Myth Formation

The primordial formation question is not about the essence of any particular sense perceptible aspect of the formation field. Transcending such particular questions, it inquires into the founding and forming mystery at work in all such appearances. This distinctively human question is inherent in the preformation of our transfocal consciousness. When people pay attention to this question, they may begin to evolve more elaborate questions that become part of the questioning transcendent dimension of their life-form. Their elaboration is influenced by the sociohistorical dimension of their formation in time and space as expressed in their prevalent form traditions. Hence, the transcendent elaboration of awe and mystery does not appear in the same form at all moments in the history of human formation. Various historical situations give rise to various modes of experiencing the mystery and its epiphanies. Its apprehension and appraisal, and the expression of its subsequent awe disposition, varies from utmost simplicity to complex differentiation.

The formation scientist can trace the awe disposition from its expression in periods of primary experience of the cosmic epiphany of the mystery, through its transitional nuances, to its expression in periods of the experience of distinctively human and transhuman epiphanies of the mystery. Such different experiences give rise to nuances in the elaboration of the disposition of apprehension and awe-filled appreciation of the formation mystery.

In periods of presence to the cosmic epiphany of the mystery, awe moves people to symbolize by means of myths the mysterious founding and forming of their life and world. They form their shared disposition of awe by means of a story that relates appearances in their familiar field to other intracosmic events or things that are depicted in the story as the founding and forming sources of initial and ongoing formation. Often these stories may be filled with mythical priomordial events and with gods and goddesses.

The formation myth is the main means such people use to form in themselves and upcoming generations a disposition of awe that responds to the questions alive in their own transfocal consciousness, even if they are not yet able to articulate the primordial question of the meaning of the mystery as such. As they advance in disposition formation within the context of their experience of the cosmic epiphany of the mystery, they may gradually begin to refine their apprehension and appraisal disposition by a corresponding refinement of the formation myths. Shorter myths may lead to the apprehension and awe-filled appreciation of the highest formation source, symbolized as the origin of all formation in the cosmos. At such moments in the formation of the awe disposition of humanity, the simple story may be complemented by mythical speculation.

Certain advanced populations may become aware that their formation of myths is a tentative answer to a question that is inherent in the structure of their own transcendent consciousness. As a result, they may begin to ask themselves if their myths are a consonant expression of the questioning they now become focally aware of in themselves. On the basis of this disclosure, they may begin to compare different formation myths according to their suitability as an answer to the inner question of questions. Later on in the history of human formation, myths and mythical speculation may be radically changed under the influence of the distinctively human and transhuman epiphanies of the formation mystery.

New insights into the mystery and into the nuances of the awe disposition to which these insights give rise are not immediately familiar to all members of a population. They are first disclosed by people who are unusually creative and original in regard to the experience of the formation mystery. Among these persons are saints, prophets, and deeply reflective thinkers. They seem to be especially gifted with what formation science calls an "epiphanic apprehension." Their expression of these insights may enter into the formation history of humanity at large. It can effect the emergence of a new religious formation tradition or refine an existing one, which, in different degrees, may influence the formation of the awe disposition.

The formation scientist, who specializes in the study of such form traditions, is struck by the fact that they do not arise without objections, resistances, deformative accretions, misinterpretations, reformations, or further refinement. Often the first witnesses to new disclosures of the disposition of awe pay with their lives for their message.

Awe Dispositions and Arrogance

Having considered the historical formation of the disposition of awe as it arises out of its predisposition in the transfocal consciousness of humanity, let us now reflect on its present manifestations in those who have cultivated this disposition.

When we cultivate awe as a transcendent disposition of the heart, we may be wholeheartedly involved in everyday endeavors while at the same time transcending them. To be disposed to awe enables us to be beyond all things and yet wisely engaged in them. Awe disposes us to a life of enlightened presence to the mystery of people, events, and things in their deepest being. Hence awe generates dispositions of reverence, respect, abandonment, congeniality, consonance, compatibility, compassion, gentleness, firmness, communality, and privacy. We will reflect on these dispositions of the heart in the second part of this volume.

The opposite dispositions can be traced to arrogant self-exaltation under the influence of the pride-form. Arrogance disposes us to lose respect for the formation mystery and its epiphanies in the people, events, and things to which it gives form. It inclines us to infringe upon the integrity or mystery of our formation field. To the degree that we lose awe, our formation is marred by arrogance, violence, and willfulness. These deformative dispositions may manifest themselves in manipulation of self and others and/or in discrimination against other formation segments of the population or those who adhere to form traditions different from ours.

While awe disposes us to progress, graciousness, and consonance, arrogance disposes us to cruelty, ugliness, and dissonance. Awe and arrogance are contesting dispositions, constantly vying for ascendancy in our formation field. Our life-form grows in consonance only to the degree that we are able to reform our dispositions of arrogance, violence, and willfulness into such dispositions as gentleness, congeniality, compatibility, compassion, and reverence.

The disposition of awe opens us to the mystery that can fulfill our most intimate aspirations; it endows our life with the assurance, graciousness, peace, and wholeness given to those who have discovered the Infinite in the finite, who have accepted the personal epiphany of the formation mystery in their own soul as an invitation to union with their deepest ground.

Awe and Faith

To be sure, doubt, anxiety, failure, and suffering may mark our formation journey despite our primordial disposition of awe for the epiphany of the mystery. Awe has to be lived in faith, no matter how darkened it is by doubt. The radiance of the formation mystery may pierce this veil. It may emerge out of its concealment in our formation field and overwhelm our consciousness at moments of undeserved enlightenment.

Usually, however, awe makes us present to the mystery and its epiphanies in the darkness of a faith that does not feel this presence intensely. The disposition of awe in this sense represents a commitment of the deepest core of our life-in-formation, an awe-filled commitment of the heart.

Awe and Other Dispositions

The disposition of awe is a mysterious force in the core of our being; it is a principle of consonance and unity. Awe gives a new and profound meaning to the other formative dispositions, not by making the partial meanings of these dispositions superfluous, but by rooting them in our deepest center. Awe helps us to be truly alive in all these dispositions without becoming their captive. It is the secret source of our consonance, our peace of heart, mind, and body; it is the spring of faith, hope, and love, of firmness and courage in the midst of adversity.

In this light, the consonant life-form can be appraised as the harmonious integration of dispositions that have developed at any given moment of our formation history. Such integration should follow every meaningful differentiation of our life. Subsequent, repeated integration can only be consonant if it is based on a primordial form disposition that is fundamental and comprehensive enough to include the other differentiating dispositions of our life. Such a disposition has the effect of centering our formation insofar as it recollects or gathers together, in a modulating way, the variety of excessive or deformative acts and dispositions that tend to disperse our formation energies indiscriminately. The formation scientist believes that the disposition of awe is just such a basic disposition.

Peace has always been considered not only as tranquillity but also as consonance. We cannot be peaceful, serene, gentle, and relaxed if we empty ourselves in the numerous exaltations that mar our everyday involvements. We feel fragmented, dissected, and torn in diverse exalting and exalted directions, no longer whole and centered. Still we feel an inner aspiration to be present to an ever widening horizon that transcends all separate meanings of our engagements in the formation field and gathers them together in consonance. Thus centered, we will be at home with the epiphany of the mystery in our life and in our formation field in the midst of distractions. There is no disposition that can do this better for us than the disposition of awe.

Essence and Expressions of Awe

Let us go deeper into the meaning of awe and find out how it saves us from dissonance. Awe disposes us to be present to the formation mystery and its epiphanies in the universe and in history as well as in our daily life. This presence tends to center all our experiences within the one experience of awe. In this way awe can make us whole, experientially speaking, and therewith consonant with the epiphanies of the mystery in our soul and in our formation field.

Adherents of various form traditions will express this awe-filled presence in different ways. Jews may speak about their presence to Yahweh and his law; Muslims about their presence to Allah and his will; Buddhists about their presence to the wonder of all-pervading being; Christians about their presence to the Trinity and its highest epiphany in Christ. The disposition of awe refines itself in accordance with one's faith and form tradition and the segment of the population to which one belongs by birth or choice. In all of these refined dispositions of awe, a fundamental awe-filled presence to the mystery of formation is experienced by anyone who is so disposed.

Bypassing for the moment these nuances of the various faiths and form traditions in regard to the awe disposition, let us focus again on the essence of awe as presence in ultimate reverence and wonder to the mystery that gives form to life and world.

Full and Diffused Experience of Awe

At certain moments, the disposition of awe may give rise to an experience so profound, fascinating, and overwhelming that it seems to inundate our full field of consciousness. Other engagements, cares, and concerns seem to evaporate. The experience of the mystery may momentarily absorb our receptively forming energies.

During everyday engagements this experience is more diffuse. Awe cannot be experienced as the absorbing center of our forming energies during our task orientation. It becomes more like the underlying concealed source out of which new energy flows deepening our main attention to the task in which we are engaged and through which we experience implicitly the companionship of the mystery. The disposition of awe is still there in our core form of life, but it has released its exclusive hold over our focal consciousness while at the same time inserting itself inconspicuously and diffusively into our engagements.

Disposing our daily formation in this hidden fashion fosters consonance in our experience; it exudes, as it were, a mood and atmosphere of gentle respect and reverence. We may be dimly aware of this transforming gentle force of consonance and feel confirmed by its veiled presence.

Corresponding either to our full or to our diffused disposition of awe is the way in which we apprehend and appreciate our formation field. When the disposition of awe takes the center stage of focal consciousness, we feel fully present to the mystery dimension of people, events, and things. Their mundane aspects seem to disappear; only their actual or potential consonance with the mystery, which forms them most deeply, touches our apprehension and appreciation. For example, instead of experiencing a sculpture as a decoration on our desk or as a gift from our family, we appreciate it mainly as a pointer to the mystery of formation, as one of its countless epiphanies. Some moments later, we may have to handle this sculpture in practical ways, dusting it or finding another place for it in our bookcase. In these moments the focus of our attention is no longer on the epiphanic mystery concealed in this work of art, but on a multiplicity of mundane concerns that announce themselves in the practical dimensions of our everyday formation field.

The disposition of awe does not disappear when its activation is less full and focal. The residue of its past moments of more explicit actualization somehow lingers like the scent of incense long after it has been burned in a place of worship. While it is true that we may have to move a piece of sculpture in a functional fashion, it is also true that the way in which we apprehend and appreciate the sculpture functionally is somewhat different from our approach before we were disposed to be touched by its mystery. Our handling seems to be coformed by a newly gained respect that resonates implicitly in our functional disposition and its activation.

Here we see a demonstration of the relationship that exists between our primordial disposition of awe and other transcendent, functional, vital and sociohistorical dispositions. In the measure that they become consonant with our primordial disposition of awe, these others diffuse the directive and formative power of awe throughout our life-form as a whole and its movement in our formation field. Formation science refers to this occurrence as the diffusive power of higher dispositions due to their implication in lower ones in the hierarchy of consonant dispositions. It is important to notice here that such a relationship of forming implication does not take away the specific forming power and orientation of the subordinated dispositions.

The primordial disposition of awe should be filled and deepened periodically by a full and focal presence to the formation mystery. This fullness of actualization cannot be forced in the same way we compel the actualization of certain functional dispositions. It is a gift of the mystery itself.

We can prepare ourselves for this gift by creating favorable conditions for form receptivity in periodic moments of meditative stillness so that the mystery does not find our awe disposition lying dormant when it wants to manifest itself to us.

Transfocal Knowledge of the Predisposition of Awe

Without the enlightenment imparted by certain faiths and form traditions, people may not know at all what the mystery of formation represents. Even those who enjoy such traditional enlightenment can never fully grasp it. Otherwise it would no longer be a mystery. And yet, while not knowing it focally, we may know it in not knowing. We refer here to a transfocal kind of knowledge. The human life-form is endowed in its transfocal consciousness with a predisposition of awe for the forming mystery. Were this not the case, the formation scientist could find no explanation for the empirical fact that the overwhelming majority of people over thousands of years of formation history have continued to ask about the mystery in a variety of ways and have experienced a sense of awe that never fades in humanity. Even the anxious denial of the mystery, or the refusal to admit the possibility of its epiphanies in our formation field, manifests the hidden predisposition for awe in the human life-form. Only humans can refuse and resist what appears in their transconsciousness and tries to break through the boundaries of its pre- and focal consciousness.

The more formation scientists study the history of humanity, checking carefully the information available from the auxiliary sciences, humanities, arts, and form traditions, the more the human life-form appears to them as endowed with an implicit transconscious predisposition of awe for the formation mystery. The unfolding of dispositions of wonder, admiration, respect, reverence, abandonment, obedience, detachment—or their deformations in mindless fascination, fanaticism, gushing adoration of heroes, slavish submission to impressive people—can only be explained on the basis of this admitted or refused predisposition.

Nothing in our formation field deserves our reverence and wonder as long as it is appraised in isolation from its deepest ground, the mystery that grants every person, event, and thing potential respectability. To grow in ultimate consonance implies the awakening in us of this dormant disposition for awe in face of the mystery. Distinctively human life should thus include a continuous attempt to foster and implement the hidden predisposition for awe that we already are.

Disposition and Predisposition of Awe

Formation scientists distinguish between a *predisposition* of awe, which is already in the depth of our transconsciousness in a dormant, concealed, or refused way, and a liberated, explicit, freely developed *disposition* of awe for which we have freely opted. The transfocal predisposition will guide the unfolding of the disposition of awe that should be formed and enriched in the course of our formation journey in dialogue with successive life situations. If there were no such predisposition in us to begin with, we could not ask for the meaning of this inclination to awe nor seek its formation as a free disposition in our consonant life.

All that we do and are in our formation journey can be understood ultimately in the light of a search for a suitable object pole for this hidden dynamic predisposition to surrender in awe before the mystery. Every formation attempt is a concealment or an unconcealment of this fundamental predisposition of our transfocal consciousness; it is a direction or misdirection of this innermost tendency of our transcendent life.

This basic predispositional striving does not express itself identically in every particular human life-form. The basic search for an object of this predispositional striving for adoration and surrender is realized in terms of our own unique formation field. The human life-form also establishes its own relatively unique ways of resisting, refusing, or falsifying the predisposition for awe that is the basis of its distinctively human formation.

Circular Process of Consonant Life Formation

We may say that consonant formation is in a sense a circular process. We are already in a predispositional way present to that which we seek to give form to in our life. There is already deep within us what we hope transconsciously to find, namely, the mystery whose personalized epiphany, image, form, or likeness is already concealed in our soul and generates our predisposition of awe.

Consonant life formation consists, therefore, in releasing that preempirical, concealed form of the mystery into our empirical life. We move from a vague, implicit predisposition to an explicit, articulated disposition of awed presence. If we belong to a specific religious faith and form tradition, the transscientific formation wisdom of our tradition is meant to articulate more explicitly what the unfolding of this disposition means in our life as adherents of that tradition.

The circular process of distinctively human formation implies that we grow from one current life-form to another, that we move in an ever widening spiral of increasing articulation of the disposition of awe-filled presence to new epiphanies of the mystery in ourselves and in our formation field.

We will never be able to understand distinctively human formation that is consonant by observing it from the outside only, by reifying it as if it were merely an object of scientific research, or by trying to imitate the external behavior of people who seem to have reached a consonant life. All such attempts to grasp the circular movement of consonant formation are doomed to failure.

The formation of human life is not first of all an externally imposed system or world view. Awe is a predisposition within us to be disclosed and released over a lifetime with the illuminating assistance of the formation wisdom of consonant form traditions. Only by abandoning ourselves to the predisposition of awe that we already are can we grow to consonance.

Primordial Predisposition and the Study of Formation

The study of consonant life formation implies first of all the elucidation of the primordial availability in awe to the mystery of formation that we already are. This research begins by making explicit what is already prereflexively contained in our fundamental predisposition to awe-filled abandonment; it is a laying bare of the concealed ground of the consonant life that is our implicit substantial union with the epiphany of the mystery within us and a making manifest of this epiphany.

The fact that we are endowed with a predisposition for awe-filled abandonment to the mystery of formation is the basic experiential fact underlying all attempts at consonant formation. It is the irreducible foundation of a distinctively human science of formation. Any consonant disposition or act of the distinctively human life and any question of a formation theory of personality can be traced to this basic experience of how we are already predisposed to be in relation to the formation mystery.

If it is true that human life in the most basic sense is a search for the mystery and its epiphanies, then everything in our formation, including our religious or antireligious dispositions and acts, can be explained in this light. Otherwise the predisposition to awe-filled abandonment would not be the most basic one in human formation. This is not to deny that the human life-form may and often does replace awe by another basic principle of formation, the pride-form, and its irreverent, arrogant expressions, or its tendency to idolatry. The formation scientist sees such a displacement as a secondary deformation, a faulty response to the primordial formation question. The study of formation history makes it obvious that at certain periods whole populations may succumb to the secondary principle in which they are initiated in early childhood, when there is no practical possibility of resisting deformation.

Formation science sees the search for the awesome mystery as the inescapable, innermost meaning of consonant life formation. Dispositions and actions that are at variance with this meaning could be unmasked as deviations and deformations of our basic predisposition for awe. People who escape or falsify their predisposition for awe usually do so in ways that are partly personal and partly inspired by the cultural form traditions in which they participate.

Every form tradition, formation segment, and individual person develops specific forms of escape from the predisposition to abandonment to the mystery. Formation science makes these deviant forms the object of its study, without reifying them in objects amenable to mere natural scientific research.

Primordial Predisposition and Formation Counseling

One of the main tasks of formation counseling or direction, either in common or in private, is to disclose and clarify such escapist dispositions and their protective safety directives that may become deforming dispositions. The formation practitioner must be aware of the avoidance dispositions typical of certain form traditions, formation segments, or personality types. Formation counselors should make clear to their counselees or directees that this disclosure of their preferred avenues for escape from the awe disposition does not mean that these tempting escape hatches cannot reappear. They will always remain with them as a potential force of deformation.

Influenced by the approach of the natural sciences (an approach that is appropriate to their own objects of research), one may be inclined to reify the preferred avoidance dispositions as if they were things. One may feel the same about the disposition of awe for the mystery. As soon as it is activated and established, for example, in formation sessions in common, one might want comfortably to forget about it as if it were a thing we possess as we own the furniture in our room. The formation director has to remind the directee that the disposition of awe-filled presence to the sacred is a formative life disposition; it is not a thing, but a dynamic mode of presence to be cultivated, renewed, and, if necessary, refined in daily fidelity.

Our general considerations of the nature of dispositions in the preceding chapters have taught us that they may wither and die when they are no longer activated. This applies also to the disposition of awe. Fortunately, the *predisposition* of awe can never die, and the formation counselor can trust that the basic possibility for reawakening the dormant disposition remains in essence always present.

Formation counselors should encourage counselees to attend to this predisposition as a steady invitation to actualize one's reverential presence to the mystery. They should make their directees aware that this predisposition of awe will become a formative force in their lives once they assume it as a free personal disposition. They should, therefore, initiate their counselees in the process of apprehension, appraisal, and free, loving affirmation in regard to the awe disposition.

The formation counselor realizes that such a basic decision is not necessarily conceptualized or reasoned out. It may involve a prefocal conversion of one's basic dispositional form of life. This conversion entails a change from one's preoccupation with surface appearances in the formation field to a silent fascination with the formation mystery and its epiphanies in and through these appearances.

When counselees adhere to some religious form tradition, it may be crucial to point out to them that a rigid style of mainly formal conformity to the externals of their tradition is not without merit, but that it may dull their dynamic awe-filled presence to the mystery itself as presented by their faith and form tradition. They may be more or less caught in the concealment of their predisposition for intimate religious presence when they live the precepts of their tradition only formally.

The formation director cannot stress enough that the decision to abandon oneself in awe to the mystery of formation, and to the faith, hope, and consonance that it engenders, is the first and foremost decision of their life. They should put their entire past, present, and future formation into a loving will to abandonment to this mystery. Such resolve grants them the necessary distance from the immediate influences of the secular form traditions of their culture, family, friends, and colleagues.

The deepest quest for the sacred, which we are, cannot be measured by the dispositions fostered by secular form traditions, no matter how popular the pulsations are that support them. The formation counselor should also foster a reasonable compatibility between the expression of one's awe disposition and one's contemporary culture and surroundings. The essence of this disposition should never be compromised in such adjustments, but the concrete embodiment of its expression should wisely take into account the formation segments of the population to which one belongs. At the same time one's awe disposition should transcend such segments. It should appreciate the finest manifestations in word and symbol, service and worship, art and culture, that have been developed by many segments and generations. They, too, may deepen the disposition of awe.

Many aspects of the awe dispositions have been disclosed in their formative power by the science of formation. They manifest the ecumenical formation experience of humanity. However, we should not be so absorbed in the manifestations of other periods and segments that we lose contact with our own. The consonant life incarnates awe and its manifestations, first of all, compatibly and compassionately in its own surroundings.

CHAPTER 11

Formative and Deformative Expressions of the Awe Disposition

W hen we cultivate our predisposition for awe, we may be blessed with moments filled with light and joy, moments of full focal presence in awe. Focal experiences of the transcendent range from rapture to peaceful appreciation of the forming mystery in our lives. At such moments daily cares linger in the shadows of our consciousness without enlisting our concern. We feel like holiday travelers absorbed in the beauty of woods and mountains, unperturbed by the problems that beset us in office or family. Our troubles are still there, but they do not interfere with our inner peace.

To be fully present to the mystery is to experience participation in its forming potency. We feel at home in the unique epiphany of the mystery we are in the inmost sanctuary of our being. We believe that the mystery in us is the root of the awe predisposition that has been ours since birth— a predisposition we can refuse or freely accept. The disposition of awe is more a mode of readiness than achievement, of surrender than mastery, of silence than speaking.

Awe in the Night of Faith

We cannot force at will the lucid appearance of the mystery. This realization prepares us for its silent presence paradoxically in the night of its absence. We must accept its seeming withholding in faith, hope, and consonance. For long periods of time its abiding may remain veiled to the awe disposition deep within us. We must believe in darkness in a nearness that reserves its lucid manifestation for the right seasons of our journey. Awe waits patiently in the proximity of the mystery's self-withholding until out of this nearness its lucid epiphany may be ours again.

When we live in the night of the mystery's self-withholding, we can only apprehend in faith that the people, events, and things in our formation field are vessels of the mystery, heralds of the holy, epiphanies of the sacred. Sometimes our functional and vital dispositions themselves conceal the epiphanic depth of actual reality. A prevalence of functionalism may needlessly extend the time of desolation during which the mystery withholds its manifestation.

Formation Counseling and Homecoming to Epiphany

Formation counselors are called to help fellow travelers who have lost their way to disclose again their own epiphany and its ground. They try to grow daily in the art of appraising the myriad ways in which people hide from the mystery. They realize that their role is to foster the unfolding of the awe disposition in people. The more they become servants of the forming mystery, the more they are able to unmask in themselves and their directees counterfeit forms of life that substitute falsely for the true and only object of awe.

Joy, serenity, and equanimity, the gifts of the sacred, should permeate the ways in which formation directors are present to their directees. Their presence should give people a taste of the peace promised in the life of the spirit. This peace will sustain people in their waiting presence to the light that seems to hide itself. Because intimacy with the mystery is a homecoming, we do not have to travel far to meet it. It will manifest itself to us in the everyday events of life's formation.

Awe and the Formation Field

Formation counselors should help people find themselves within their own formation field by learning to be simply present to everyday events. They should make their home in the daily rhythm of form donation and form reception. In utmost simplicity, they should deepen their faith that the mystery they are seeking is already coming to meet them.

The mystery of formation is the most intimate aspect of our life and its field of daily presence. People, events, and things in that field are apprehended in a new way. The field is no longer appraised as mere resistance. Neither is it primarily seen as a complex maze geared to the pursuit of advancement and competition. The formation field becomes the locus of manifestations of the mystery as it allots everything its proper place. Each appearance stands in the brightness of the mystery like a still guiding light on our formation journey. A joyous vision begins to dawn: every event has its proper place in the history of formation.

Many dissonant appraisals lose their hold over our lives once they are exposed to the light of the spirit. People of faith seem less inclined to re-place the forming influence of the transcendent by their own functional intelligence and willfulness. Pragmatic directives, dispositions, and pro-cedures are not idolized as if they were the ultimate source and object of awe. Such idolatry would be a parody of consonant formation. To meet the transcendent in awe, we should not be attached to functionalistic con-cerns as ultimate. The mystery does not manifest itself as such in func-tional concepts but in the actual as actual, in the concrete as concrete. Homecoming in awe means returning to the nearness of the transcendent in our own everydayness.

Inverted Awe

As long as we remain imprisoned in functional satisfactions and vital pleasures, we will remain alienated from our predisposition of awe. This crippling state is unfortunately the common lot. Sociohistorical pulsations combined with our own blindness incline us to center our formation field around the pride-form and the counterfeit life it generates. We cannot be present to the mysterious ground of all formation that grants each thing and event its own goodness, truth, and beauty. Awe inclines us to see all that is in its concreteness as a unique epiphany of the mystery. By con-trast, the pride-form generates a kind of inverted awe. We are in awe not of the mystery but of our autonomous self in isolation from the sacred.

Inverted awe inclines us to appraise all appearances mainly in schemes of achievement and self-enhancement. As long as our appraisal is domi-nated by inverted awe, we are blind to things as gifts of the mystery that forms them continuously. The moment we are present to them in this light, we set them free from the web that binds them in a system of pur-poses that serve a perverse transposition of the ultimate object pole of awe to some passing person, event, or thing.

The disposition of awe nourishes a respectful caring presence. It is like a loving gaze under which life can unfold itself congenially. Awe renews our apprehension and appraisal. It deepens our quiet concentration and inner joy. The pride-form obscures our awe disposition by its inordinate ambition, jealousy, envy, lust, and competition. We tend to live in anxious comparison based on limited categories that catch only isolated aspects of the appearances in our field, bypassing their inner richness and nobility.

Inverted awe generates a mere anthropocentric categorical stance. It compels us to appraise repeatedly only those facets of life that enhance our self-actualization. It leaves no room for the free unfolding and manifestation of the mystery that is the basic form of each consonant appearance in life and world. Anxiety about our form potency, and the dissonant tendencies it may at times generate, loosens the connection between the mystery and our power of appraisal.

Awe enables us to let our formation field be in its own right and uniqueness. It makes us more acute and realistic in our appraisal, also of the practical facets of life. We see potentialities in people and situations that we missed before due to the self-centered pride-form. Awe liberates us from the tense awareness of self to which the pride-form gives rise. Lessening the power of inverted awe makes us less self-conscious. We experience anew consonance with the mystery and its epiphanies. We feel, act, and function more graciously with refreshing spontaneity.

Inverted awe causes the opposite to happen to us. It makes us anxious, insecure, overeager to please others and gain their confirmation at any price. The pride-form in its anguished self-centeredness makes us lose our graciousness of speech and movement, our carefree presence to our task and to others. Inverted awe splits us off from the mystery that unites us intimately with the other forms it generates simultaneously in our formation field. We experience alienation from ourselves and from other persons, events, and things. Our formation does not flow easily and spontaneously from gracious interaction. We worry more about how well we will perform in the execution of an assignment. We ask ourselves fearfully if others will confirm the inverted awe we feel for our own isolated form potencies.

Awe and Formative Wisdom

Wisdom is formative insofar as it directs our form reception and form donation via the power of appraisal. Wisdom is rooted in the primordial disposition of awe, for it disposes us to appraise our formation field in the light of our awe for mystery. The activation of the awe disposition depends on our primordial appreciative or depreciative abandonment option. (This option was discussed at length in Volume One of this series.)

The wisdom arising from awe sets our appraisal powers free from their encapsulation in dissonant pulsations, vital pulsions, ambitions, aspirations, and inspirations. It endows our appraisal with such dispositions as openness, detachment, equanimity, and inner freedom, the conditions of true wisdom. We gain thereby in our capacity to be congenial, compatible, and compassionate in our formation field. Consonant wisdom demands a gentle disciplining of our formative strivings. This wise and gentle discipline, its victory in our life, is an outstanding preparation for any formative direction we may give to others who want to walk a similar path.

Wisdom in awe liberates us from credulous trust in any human formation field or potency as ultimate. It goes beyond the functional appreciation of the average person, who may live in the naive illusion that all things can be controlled and formed adequately if one uses one's logical-functional mind well enough, supported if necessary by the insights of the natural and human sciences and by advanced technology

Awakening of Wisdom-in-Awe

People who are captivated by naive trust in the powers of functional formation alone may be shaken out of their complacency by transcenddence crises. These crises are marked by the destruction of one's current, primarily functional appraisals, on which one has built one's life formation. The shattering of current appreciations, memories, anticipations, and imaginations brings one face to face with a void of formlessness and form impotence. One does not know any longer how to give form to life functionally in a way that makes sense. The experience of threatening formlessness and form impotence evokes formation anxiety.

Formation Anxiety and Formation Fear

Formation anxiety differs from formation fear. In the latter case we are afraid that we cannot give or receive form in regard to this or that specific formation event. Formation anxiety emerges when we are faced with the threat of absolute formlessness and form impotence. In formation anxiety we are confronted with the spectre of total formlessness. We experience an emptiness of all form potency, not only in ourselves but also as available through any other power that could and would assist us. This dread should be distinguished from the experience of the mystics, who sense the awesome formlessness of the mystery that transcends all forms yet is itself their formative ground.

Formation anxiety may awaken the dormant predisposition of awe for the mystery and its power. It transcends our everyday vital-functional formation powers, yet is immanent in them mysteriously. It may kindle our faith in the formless, all-embracing formation power that is now experienced as the reality that directs and forms our formation field in spite of its teeming variations.

Formation anxiety generates a wisdom that entrusts itself to the veiled form direction of evolution and history. No longer does the cleverness and astuteness of our functional, logical, scientific mind prevail. Transcendent wisdom is rooted in awe whose object cannot be controlled by logic and science. This wisdom is neither antirational nor dissonant with the factual findings of the sciences. It transcends naive trust in our power to function well in the formation field. It lifts us beyond the anxiety generated by formlessness and form impotence when our formation field seems totally shattered.

Formation wisdom-in-awe is thus the relaxed acknowledgment of our actual or potential formation anxiety, combined with the knowledge of how to transcend this anxiety in the light of the mystery. It gives us the confidence we need to seek a new current form of life by turning obstacles into formation opportunities. Wisdom-in-awe rests in ultimate abandonment in faith, hope, and consonance to the formation mystery.

Forming Epiphanies of the Mystery and Consequent Dispositions

The formation mystery manifests itself in its three main forming epiphanies, namely, transcendent truth, goodness, and beauty, each of which evokes a corresponding disposition of awe. The mystery as transcendent truth awakens the predisposition of the mind for awe-filled transcendent speculation, meditation, and contemplation. As transcendent goodness it inspires the predisposition of the will for transcendent aspiration in awe and transcendent incarnational functioning in prudence. As transcendent beauty it awakens in our heart the awe-filled aesthetic predisposition.

Where do the forming epiphanies of truth, goodness, and beauty manifest themselves? Respectively, in the cosmic, human, and transhuman realms of reality as we know them in our shared and personal formation fields.

Awe for Cosmic, Human, and Transhuman Formation

The interformative cosmic processses that pervade our daily formation fields are by no means experienced as always consonant. At times, for instance, we become acutely aware of dissonance in certain microcosmic form changes in the organismic cells of our brain, nervous system, and other organs. These changes can generate discomfort, irritation, pain, and illness. Yet we also have faith in a consonant tendency in the overall, ongoing processes of cosmic interformation. The forming mysterious power in and behind these processes may fill us with awe. At certain privileged moments we detect the manifestation of truth, goodness, and beauty in nature, in the formation of clouds, mountains, stars, seas, or flowers.

We apprehend these appearances with our senses or by means of such instruments as microscopes and telescopes, through listening devices or the astounding disclosures of theoretical physicists. We may apprehend this cosmic harmony directly or indirectly in representations by artists and scientists.

Truth, goodness, and beauty as epiphanies of the forming mystery are manifested to our wisdom-in-awe when we behold the distinctively human epiphany of the mystery. In this realm we are also confronted by many deviations from what is true, good, and beautiful. The vision of wisdom, however, detects a deeper tendency that goes beyond such aberrations. At gifted moments we may be awed by the truth, goodness, and beauty a human life can manifest as an epiphany of the holy. The same wisdom-in-awe directs us to seek ways to enhance the potential manifestation of the truth, goodness, and beauty in our own consonant life formation.

Over the centuries countless people in a wide variety of form traditions have reported on special manifestations of the truth, goodness, and beauty of the formation mystery. They believed that such manifestations went beyond their own natural power of form reception and donation. Such manifestations were revealed and believed to be transhuman. The more people grew in wisdom-in-awe, the more they were open to such transhuman epiphanies.

Sedimentation of Wisdom-in-Awe within Form Traditions

The formation wisdom of generations can become sedimented in form traditions, which are rooted in turn in religious or ideological faith traditions based on direct revelation or on a primordial intuition. Form traditions embody in word and other symbols the formation wisdom-in-awe of generations. If adherents freely assent to them in faith, they are open to the potential or actual epiphanies of the formation mystery in their life and world. Formation science assumes that one basic dimension intrinsic to all human life-forms is the sociohistorical dimension. Not only individuals but also generations of people develop together a form tradition rooted in a shared formation field that is marked intrinsically by the sociohistorical dimension. This dimension also influences the formation of the wisdom-in-awe disposition fostered by a specific tradition.

On the basis of this dimension, we can explain the variety of forms of wisdom dispositions that have developed in the course of humanity's formation history. The formation wisdom of the Eskimos, African tribes, American Indians, Eastern sages, medieval Christians, and ancient Greeks and Romans shows remarkable differences, as do their subsequent form traditions. This variation is not surprising to formation scientists. They see wisdom-in-awe first of all as a foundational predisposition of the human life-form. Secondarily, they posit that this distinctively human predisposition, like all others, must be given form in concrete human life as lived in a formation field. Both the empirical human life-form and its formation field are intrinsically differentiated in the concretely lived sociohistorical, vital, functional, and transcendent dimensions. All influence the concretely lived dispositions that are the incarnation in time and space of the preempirical predispositions.

In other words, any concrete dispositional formation is intrinsically interwoven with sociohistorical styles of life formation to which people are exposed within their form traditions. Even those who critique the dominant form traditions necessarily do so in the context of such traditions and their consequences. Their opposition could not be understood without an understanding of the sociohistorical context. Formation science thus holds that dispositions, when shared, become the basis of formation history in various sociohistorical form traditions.

Necessity of Empirical Implementations of Wisdom-in-Awe

Wisdom-in-awe transcends all particular insights and functional directives. This fact does not contradict the assumption of formation scientists that any *predisposition* can only become a *formative disposition* when its concretization is rooted in the sociohistorical dimension of the life-form and its field. Only then is such a predisposition able to give form to specific form traditions that incarnate concretely this transcendent wisdom in lived time and space.

Such sedimented formation wisdom enables adherents to participate in a certain social and/or historical formation segment of the world population during a certain period of time. This wisdom further enables them to hear the silent call of the formation mystery, to appraise its presence in awe, and to form their life and world accordingly. In this way wisdom-in-awe gives form to consonant religious or ideological traditions. Secondarily, it coforms in some measure the economical, political, cultural, and social-psychological formation field shared by adherents of such form traditions and their sedimented wisdom.

In this sense, wisdom-in-awe becomes incarnated in the life formation of a population. Resonating in the formative interconsciousness of a people, it generates a certain popular wisdom that is a more or less faithful reflection of the form tradition itself. At times dissonant accretions may turn popularized formation wisdom into a tradition that is a caricature of the wisdom-in-awe that was its origin. A special problem in this regard involves false, self-centered ideologies that are disguised as true expressions of consonant, classical form traditions.

Wisdom-in-Awe and Ideological Form Traditions

Formation science holds, as we have seen, that religious form traditions are rooted in religious faith traditions. Similarly, consonant ideological form traditions are based on corresponding, distinctively human, faith traditions. As in the case of a faith tradition and its theological propositions, so, too, in the case of ideological faith traditions: there can be no directly logical deduction from the philosophical propositions of the ideology to the concrete form tradition it generates. Here, too, the formal object of the formation scientist is not the underlying ideological faith tradition but the corresponding form tradition that develops in dialogue with concrete formation events.

Because religious and ideological form traditions may share certain foundational formation problems, facts, and insights, an interformative dialogue between them is possible. This may lead to a convergence of certain formation insights.

Transcendent and Vital-Functional Ideological Form Traditions

Formation science distinguishes between transcendent and vital-functional ideological form traditions. The vital-functional traditions are rooted neither in a religious nor in a distinctively human ideological faith tradition. They are not really directed by revelation or by a distinctively human point of departure. Their real starting point resides in sociohistorical pulsations, vital pulsions, and functional ambitions that may or may not be appraised, corrected, and complemented in the light of transcendent, religious, or other distinctively human principles they claim to represent. The latter might be used merely as a cover-up to initiate or maintain a life-form and formation field that serve mainly self-centered, shared, or individual pulsations, pulsions, and ambitions.

Examples of Relatively Consonant Ideological Form Traditions

Examples of incipient ideological form traditions would be the Freudian, Jungian, Adlerian, Skinnerian, Maslowian, and Rogerian ideologies. Each starts out from its own intuition about the nature of the human life-form and its formation field. Around this intuition a faith tradition is developed by the founders and their followers, mostly in an implicit fashion. The corresponding form tradition is developed systematically in dialogue with scientific data and insights.

The underlying intuition of each of these important ideologies touches some basic aspect of the human life-form and its formative influence on all other forms. A scientific elaboration of such aspects offers valuable material for the formation scientist in service of the development of an open-ended foundational theory of human life in formation.

Misdirection of Awe by Vital-Functional Ideologies

Not all ideologies are distinctively human. Some are merely products of vital pulsions, functional ambitions, and corresponding pulsations; deceptively they play on the human predisposition for awe. Their slogans and symbols attempt to disguise their objectives, means, and strivings in such a way that they falsely evoke awe in people. Enthralled by such quasi-transcendence, people may be misled. They may mistakenly believe that such ideologies are in tune with distinctively human aspirations. An historical example would be Nazism. This movement tried to initiate its own form traditions. Exalted propaganda, exciting mass meetings, and youth formation were used for such ends.

Vital-fuctional ideologies may emerge also within well-established transcendent form traditions. Each form tradition has adherents who do not live by its ideals. Such persons may be inclined to use the ideals and principles of their tradition to disguise for themselves and others their designs of self-indulgence, greed, power, and oppression. Oppressors may abuse the aspiration for awe in underprivileged adherents of the same tradition. Awe-filled subservience to themselves, their status and power, is the aim of their ideology. An example would be Christian imperialists who exploited other peoples in the name of an ideology of divine predestination.

Criterion of Consonance of Form Traditions

There are form traditions that have shown themselves to be truly formative for generations of people. Periodically we witness the emergence of new faith and form traditions. Novel cults and systems of wisdom are propagated. Reformers and founders of new religions appear on the scene every age. Are they to be taken seriously? Are their visions and efforts formative or deformative? What critical questions need to be asked? We have to discover whether such form traditions enhance the possibility for the greatest number of people to live a more consonant life. Do they foster the wisdom-in-awe that makes it possible for people to live and die in inner and outer harmony and equanimity? It may not be possible to appraise this effect immediately. Only in the course of the history of formation may the consonance or dissonance of the formation wisdom offered by new prophets be manifest.

Questions testing the degree of consonance might be the following: Can the formation wisdom be translated in concrete forms of everyday life? Are such forms of life in tune with the formation mystery and its epiphanies? Do they deepen and expand wisdom-in-awe in those who live that way? Is their life more congenial, compatible, and compassionate? Do these forms foster inner peace, freedom, joy, and equanimity?

When a form tradition bears these fruits its wisdom may be acknowledged by successive generations. It will endure because it is relevant to distinctively human aspirations. If it manifests continuously such aspirational power it may give rise to a popular wisdom-in-awe.

Insufficiency of Science and Philosophy for Proximate Life Formation

No natural or human science, no philosophical or theological system, is sufficient to endow people with consonance. The knowledge that science, philosophy, and theology impart is of great importance, but it needs to be complemented by a more proximate wisdom, nearer to life as lived in its immediacy. This kind of wisdom is sedimented in consonant form traditions developed by generations over and beyond their faith traditions.

Formation science acknowledges this necessity, for it is at the basis of two of its main methodological aspects. First of all, the science of formation tries to integrate within its theoretical frame of reference the common wisdom of consonant form traditions. It can only do so insofar as it can establish their convergence. The methods of foundational tracing and integrative dialogue are the main means employed in this search for a possible convergence of basic formation insights in various form traditions.

The convergent wisdom thus gathered will always be limited. It can never present us with the depth and richness of those consistent insights and symbols of formation wisdom-in-awe that we find within the fullness of a form tradition to which we personally adhere. Hence the formation scientist or practitioner often advises people to complement the compact and inadequate wisdom of formation shared by the adherents of many traditions with that of their own basic form tradition. Universal formation wisdom ought to be embedded within the consistent systems of teachings, stories, symbols, rituals, and exercises offered by their own form tradition, developed over centuries and deeply rooted in a faith tradition to which they are committed. Formation scientists who belong to a specific tradition should support their coadherents in this effort.

Essential Limits of the Ecumenical Formation Wisdom of Humanity

To be sure, the ecumenical formation wisdom of humanity is important. It can sustain a rich variety of consonant form traditions. We should be respectful of any form tradition that strives in principle to be consonant. We recognize in these traditions true attempts to live out the human predisposition of awe toward the transcendent as well as the wisdom of formation gained in light of this aspiration over many generations. Yet as we shall see in the next chapter, ecumenism can never fully represent the unique richness of each of these form traditions. A deeper insight into the source of the variety of form traditions will clarify the possibilities and limitations of a foundational ecumenical formation science.

CHAPTER 12

Awe, Formation Traditions, and Culture

E cumenism in and by itself can never replace the highly refined formation wisdom-in-awe that characterizes each consonant form tradition in its own developed art treasures, stories, rituals, and symbols. The reason for this unique wisdom and expression can be found in the course of each form tradition's history. Each tradition grew by means of historical dialogue with the relatively unique formation fields in which they originated and slowly unfolded. Both founders and adherents had to establish concrete formation dispositions of their own. Such dispositions had to be effective answers to what was disclosed to them in their encounters with their formation fields. The arena of formation for American Indians, Arabs, African tribes, Australian aborigines, Chinese, Japanese, Europeans, and South Sea Islanders differed in countless ways. This difference accounted for the many nuances in their formation wisdom-in-awe in response to the epiphanies of the mystery.

Source of the Variety of Form Traditions

The endless variety of form traditions is rooted in the essentiality of the sociohistorical dimension of human life. The human life-form, as we have seen, is sociohistorical through and through, as are its formation fields and form traditions. The human life-form is a finite form potency bound to a finite formation field. Part of that finitude manifests itself in the sociohistorical limitation of each formation field in which people are born and raised. The human formation journey continues in dialogue with new, finite, sociohistorical situations, circumscribed by limited time and space. Hence one can never predict with certainty what nuances our form traditions may assume. Nor can one foresee what new form traditions may emerge in the future.

This necessary proliferation of form traditions does not imply an absolute relativism of human formation. On the contrary, formation science is based on the premise that it is possible for form traditions to approxi-

mate increasingly in awe the right path to consonance. This ongoing refinement of form traditions may bring their adherents closer and closer to
the truth, goodness, and beauty in which the formation mystery discloses
itself via various historical epiphanies.

Formation science tries to facilitate an empathic apprehension, a critical-
creative appreciation, and a volitional affirmation of the universal ecumenical formation wisdom emergent in various consonant form traditions. It
aids the efforts of form traditions to purify themselves from dissonant accretions that are not distinctively human.

Formation Scientists in Relation to Their Own Form Traditions

An experienced formation scientist or practitioner may become an astute observer of the form tradition to which he or she personally adheres.
On the basis of a lifelong concentration on the historical development of
form traditions, formation experts may rightly or wrongly surmise that
their own tradition is on the verge of a breakthrough or reformation.
They may feel that a new refinement is immanent or necessary. They may
ask themselves if the time has come for the disclosure that certain form
directives, which up to now were considered essential, are only accretional.
Here they should be guided by wisdom-in-awe for the ancient form tradition
and its treasures, for its primary authoritative custodians, and for the
secondary theological or ideological guardians of its corresponding faith
tradition. They should be concerned about the vulnerability of its adherents. A humble distrust of their own limited opinion and insight will
prevent them from airing their personal doubts before such time as authorities, theologians, and adherents have historically become ready for
such communications. Are such scientists ahead of their time or are they
victims of contemporary pulsations or hidden impulses? Wisdom generates an attitude of waiting in patience until the time is ripe and the evidence becomes irrefutable.

In the meantime, such a growing personal conviction cannot remain
without influence on the scientist's private life. Denying this inner persuasion as though it did not exist could lead to a painful experience of dissonance. Admitting to the conviction without integrating it in one's personal
wisdom-in-awe would be even more destructive. To live it out indiscreetly
or to communicate it prematurely would disregard the principles of reasonable compatibility and compassion, which formation science extols.

The only solution may be to live privately in congeniality with these new
disclosures if the population with whom one lives abides by the opposite

conviction. A more public manifestation of one's new persuasion, especially if it partially or wholly conflicts with the authoritative guardians of the tradition, may be impossible. For instance, certain Muslim intellectuals may have to adapt to form traditions in their home country that seem at odds with Western scientific convictions. When they live in Western countries, however, they may not have to hide their scientific convictions.

Similar examples can be found in Christian form traditions. At a certain period in the history of Catholic and Protestant form traditions, people with certain psychotic or hysterical symptoms were thought to be possessed by the devil and were condemned to the stake. There was at that time no empirical scientific basis upon which to evaluate the symptoms that were appraised to be demonic by the form tradition and its passing accretions. Some people may have entertained genuine doubt about this aspect of the form tradition. While they could not be scientifically certain that they were right while the contemporary understanding of the tradition was wrong, their persuasion may have been compelling enough to allow them in conscience to withhold information from tribunals in order to save people from the stake.

Awe, Fear, and Reverence

The disposition of awe is coformed by holy dread and reverence. Dread is evoked by the overwhelming majesty of the mystery that continuously coforms universe, humanity, and history. Human life-forms feel vulnerable in the immense cosmic expanse of ever falling and rising forms. If we look with the eyes of the physicist, we realize how dissonant we may appear in the tiny niche of the universe called Planet Earth. We often feel and act disharmoniously in contrast with the consonance that seems to mark the subatomic formation field, which is the basic cosmic epiphany of the mystery. No wonder we ask ourselves anxiously whether this all-encompassing mystery is beneficent. This question generates a pervasive and reverent holy dread.

Sense of Dissonance and Deficiency

Awe makes us apprehend the dissonance between human formation and the well-attuned formation of the universe. Our failed attempts at consonance seem to signal to us a certain deficiency in our form potency. Our formative consciousness, touched by awe, reflects upon itself. It appraises how we may direct our formation of life and world more consonantly. In this appraisal the human life-form senses increasingly that its formation tends to be dissonant and its form potency insufficient.

Formative reflection is interformative. This appraisal evolves and deepens in dialogue with past and present human life-forms. Through this continuous dialogue, formative reflection feeds on the apprehension and appraisal of a shared sense of dissonance and deficiency that pervades humanity. The results of humanity's dialogical reflections are sedimented in faith and form traditions. Initially they are couched in the language of myth. Many of them communicate in archaic stories how dissonance and deficiency emerged in the human formation of life. Other myths symbolize paths of reformation and transformation, of healing and salvation, in the face of this original predicament.

The sense of dissonance and deficiency, which formation science traces throughout human history, is in principle as fundamental and universal as the sense of awe that precedes and accompanies it. The human life-form is free to deny and refuse this awareness. We are inclined to such denial under the pressure of the pride-form of life, which tends to exalt human autonomy and self-sufficiency. Yet such willful withdrawal from a spontaneous sense of insufficiency is like whistling in the dark. One must keep convincing oneself that everything is under control or that humanity shall master life and world perfectly in the not too distant future.

Much formation energy may be used in the maintenance of such pretenses. When this basic sense of dissonance and deficiency is admitted, it engenders a search for ways that enable the human life-form to transcend its disquieting condition and the hidden anxiety it constantly breeds.

Awe and the Sense of Insufficiency in Human Interconsciousness
Formative reflection on our life's awkward formation in the face of awe may vary in intensity among individuals. The accumulated wisdom of centuries of reflection on formation is sedimented in the interconsciousness of humanity by means of shared faith and form traditions. Both basic dissonance and the paths to consonance are expressed in the myths, rituals, stories, symbols, and doctrines of such traditions. This interconsciousness is embodied in human societies, which are influenced by these traditions. Personal reflection on one's sense of dissonance and deficiency both strengthens and is strengthened by this living interconsciousness. Those who deny this basic sense of insufficiency defy an awareness that is both universal and personal. Their denial is an implicit response to an inescapable human apprehension they can only dismiss secondarily. Faith

and form traditions are partly based on the elaboration and sometimes on the codification of such movements of formative consciousness.

Basic Dynamic of Formation

We are faced here with a basic dynamic of formation. To apprehend and appraise this dynamic is essential. Without such apprehension we cannot understand the distinctively human formation of individuals as well as of their form traditions. Consonant form traditions keep the awareness of deforming dissonance and deficiency, as well as the search for consonance and its pathways, in the forefront of consciousness. The pulsations of everyday life in our functional-vital societies try constantly to drown out this awareness. At times only small groups may keep awe alive. Some creative expressions of their fresh awareness of awe may be embedded in the objectified forms of myths, stories, rituals, and symbols. This creativity expresses the continuing unfolding and refinement of faith and form tradition. Such enlightened small groups function as centers of distinctively human formation. They radiate their message into society at large. They are reminders of what is buried time and again in forgetfulness of the mystery and the awe it inspires.

The sense of dissonance and deficiency is accompanied by a sense of distance from the mystery. At times this sense may deepen to a felt absence. Yet within this absence the mystery reminds us repeatedly of its presence through its manifold epiphanies. These provide, as it were, a cosmic and historical outline pointing to the Distant One. They evoke awe in spite of hiddenness. To bridge this sense of absence, religious form traditions develop paths of proximity to the mystery.

Awe and the Beginnings of Religious and Ideological Faith and Form Traditions

The basic human sense of awe thus implies holy dread, reverence, dissonance, deficiency, and distance. Such dispositions are embodied in specific types of formative apprehensions and appraisals. These generate corresponding form directives and dispositions. Together they give birth to various religious and ideological faith and form traditions. Each of them developed diverse ways of regaining consonance, of complementing or restoring deficient form potency, and of overcoming distance between the human life-form and the mystery at its core.

Every form tradition has a beginning. Transcosmic faith and form traditions claim as this beginning a revelation; cosmic ones an experiential enlightenment about being; ideological faith and form traditions, such as the Freudian, Jungian, Adlerian, Marxian, Maslowian, Skinnerian, to name only a few, start from a primordial intuition as their hidden point of departure. The term faith in regard to ideological faith traditions is used here in an analogical sense. The faith aspect of the ideological intuition does not reside in the fact that the object of that intuition is not verifiable in reality. Usually it is. Faith refers to the ideological conviction that this undeniable aspect of human life formation is exalted as the most basic one in the light of which all other formation aspects should be understood exclusively.

Form traditions are living treasures of formation wisdom. Formation scientists cannot disassociate their research from such sources. Traditions enshrine and carry the most fundamental formation insights of humanity. They image them in their concrete expressions as no abstract philosophy or experimental science could ever do. Without them, it would be impossible to grasp the formation even of so-called secular cultures and societies.

Awe, Dissonance, Form Reception, and Form Donation

The awareness of dissonance and deficiency in response to awe generates an inspiration for consonant life formation. The human life-form unfolds itself by ongoing formation in dialogue with its formation field. The two main modes of formation are form reception and form donation. Consonance of life can be approximated by both modes in mutual collaboration. Certain persons seem predisposed to be formed prevalently by the mode of form reception. People who are congenially contemplative are an example. Others seem predestined to approach consonance mainly by the mode of form donation. This style, due to its predominance in the West, is expressed almost everywhere. The majority of administrators, executives, scientists, business people, teachers, and laborers live a life of active form donation.

Form traditions may develop mainly around one or the other of these two modes. An example can be found in the basic difference between the Judeo-Christian and the distinctively Eastern traditions. We say *distinctively* Eastern to distinguish these traditions from the monotheistic Islamic tradition, which is profoundly influenced by the earlier Judeo-Christian tradition. This may explain why the Islamic awe disposition, as expressed in form donation, gave rise to a disposition of personal and communal responsibility for the direction of history that is typical of the forming directives of the Judeo-Christian tradition. Form donation accounts for the impressive spiritual, cultural, ethical, scholarly, administrative, and military achievements that in certain historical periods excelled the Judeo-Christian formation of life and world in the West.

Distinctively Eastern traditions, such as those of Hindus, Taoists, and Buddhists, developed mainly around the receptive mode of formation, whereas the Judeo-Christian tradition developed mainly around the donation mode of formation. The lasting empirical impact of both modes is first of all on the symbolic heart or core form of life. Sensibility and responsibility, we recall, are the basic dispositions of the heart. In this regard, sensibility is related to the receptive, responsibility to the donation mode of formation.

Form traditions that have grown around the receptivity mode are marked by the sensibility dimension of the symbolic heart. Those that have grown out of the donation mode are profoundly influenced by the responsibility facet of this core form of our empirical life.

Ambient Radiation Fields of Form Traditions

Such sensibility or responsibility directives of form traditions may become immanent in the interconsciousness of large populations. Yet the same populations may seem to be alienated from these form traditions. The influence of form traditions may stretch beyond the explicit interconsciousness of the adherents of the tradition itself. Once traditions are at the root of a culture, they tend to keep radiating their basic directedness into the formative facets of the shared formation field of the population, whether or not people still approve of the original form tradition. They may rebel against it, deny its hidden influence, or remain reluctantly aware of its formative radiation.

Formation science calls such relatively indifferent or alienated orbits of form traditions their *ambient radiation fields*. Such fields are wider than those that belong explicitly to the form tradition itself as its inner circle of influence. Usually such neutral or estranged orbits are not acknowledged as such in the self-apprehension and self-appraisal of the faithful adherents of the original form traditions. On the contrary, these divergent orbits may be denounced and opposed by them because of the deep resentment such orbits may manifest toward the form traditions they try to shake off. Yet these ambient fields remain in some way an undeniable, albeit deformed, extension of the forming power of their original traditions.

Original form traditions remain the hidden nucleus of these ambient radiation fields. They help to shape the formative interconsciousness that emerges from them, albeit often in divergent manifestations. Unlike their ambient radiation fields, the form traditions themselves remain explicit in their self-preservation by means of internal self-apprehension, appraisal, and affirmation.

Formation Science, Transcosmic Faith, and Form Traditions

Each transcosmic faith tradition underlying a specific form tradition is a unique elaboration of faith in a revelation regarding the object pole of awe. Ultimately the revelations they claim cannot be scientifically compared with one another or graded as if they were identical. Neither the formation scientist nor the theologian could analyze away the uniqueness of a revelation claimed by the adherents of a transcosmic faith tradition to be the mainspring of their awe in face of the mystery.

By contrast, form traditions lend themselves more readily to analytical and integrative research. Formation scientists can study individuals and populations insofar as they are formed practically and concretely by such assumed revelations and insofar as they receive and give form proximately to their lives under their ultimate accepted or rejected influence. The unique transcosmic revelations regarding the object of awe are not as such the research object of the science of formation; they are the object of theological studies. Formation science concerns itself primarily with doctrines, myths, stories, symbols and rites insofar as they influence proximately the formation of people and their cultures. Formation science not only compares their apparent manifestations, it also examines the depths of formative apprehension, appraisal, affirmation, and symbolic imagination where such basic form directives take shape in the spirit, mind, and heart of people.

Assumed revelations concerning the object pole of awe and corresponding appraisals of human dissonance and deficiency, complemented by paths to consonance, reside in the sociohistorical intra- and interformative consciousness of populations and individuals. This process of assimilation does not leave unchanged the inner and outer expression of such revelations. It implies necessarily some reformation of the formative expression of the revelation concerned. For example, the same revelation will be differently felt, expressed, and applied in Italian, Irish, Asian, African, and North American populations. Hence even identical revelations generate considerable nuances within common form traditions shared by many individuals and communities.

Families of Form Traditions

Our various religious and ideological form traditions are different from our faith traditions. Each form tradition is a self-consistent whole of dispositions and corresponding form directives, feelings, moods, and expressions. Within widespread cultural circles, certain religious and ideological form traditions may be interrelated. They share certain identical dispositions. We could call them families of form traditions. An example would be the various Christian form traditions and their ambient secular, ideological Western form traditions. They are far more like each other than, for instance, the families of Hindu and Buddhist form traditions. Such a family of traditions points to certain common primordial dispositions that each member of the family elaborates on its own in accepting such dispositions totally or in part. Some of their ambient secular ideological traditions may reject all or part of such dispositions. Yet the very emergence and typical elaboration of their specific opposition manifests the influence of the prevalent traditions they resist. The elaborate structures of rejection and opposition demonstrate their tremendous preoccupation with the same dispositions and their forming power. This formation process on the basis of common dispositions can be demonstrated in a comparison of all Western religious and ideological form traditions with those of the Far East.

Awe and Eastern and Western Form Traditions

To apprehend and appraise the difference between distinctively Eastern kinds of traditions and those of the West, we must return to the fundamental distinction between form reception and form donation, and the dispositions of sensibility and responsibility that emerge accordingly in the symbolic heart or core form of life. As we have seen, all such form traditions can function within their ambient sociohistorical field as powers of formation. They radiate into that field certain formation dispositions that may unwittingly move even their opponents. Such dispositions and their manifold directives and expressions seem to endure even when the form traditions that engendered them have lost their hold on a population.

What is most remarkable is that some of the form directives implied in the original form traditions may begin to blossom in new historical formation movements that rebel against the form tradition that contained these directives potentially in its own dispositions in the first place. This demonstrates the extraordinary form potency contained in great form traditions. For instance Rousseau, Voltaire, Comte, the French encyclopedists of the Enlightenment, Schiller, Goethe, Schelling, Kant, Hegel, Fichte, Marx, Freud, Adler, Jung, Erikson, Horney, Skinner, Maslow, and Rogers, to mention only a few, have given form, compatibly or adversely, often excessively and onesidedly to some basic Christian dispositions and thought patterns. Their ideological faith and form traditions would be unthinkable in the distinctively Eastern formation history of society and culture.

Similarly, natural and human sciences, industrialization, massive organization, evolution and revolution, technology and cybernetics, could take form only in a sociohistorical formation field profoundly influenced by the original Judeo-Christian disposition for creative form giving, for responsibility for a meaningful development of history, for respectful presence to the individual. The same holds for the dispositions of anxiety, guilt, and performance-preoccupation that tend to accompany those of form giving and responsibility for the course of history.

In contrast, the ambient radiation field of distinctively Eastern form traditions is influenced by the disposition of almost passive-receptive openness to what is given in the cosmos and the corresponding appreciation of a tranquil sensibility of the heart. Such dispositions do not breed social and scientific revolutions, anxious concern about the course of history, or enhancement of uniqueness in individuals. They generate timeless ways of receptive presence, of highly sensitized and alert awareness of what always is and will be, of an appreciation of the eternal recurrence of the same in cyclic time, of the cosmic absorption of individuality, of transcending the "illusion" of material and cultural progress.

Awe, Traditions, and Consonant Culture

Awe is the wellspring of consonant culture. It generates form traditions that facilitate the presence of people to reality in reverence. Reverence is the spontaneous beginning of worship. Consonant culture fosters via its traditions the reverence that may move people when listening to music, looking in wonder at art and beauty, climbing mountains, walking along the ocean's shore, or dwelling in the silence of the forest. Consonant culture makes people feel humble in the face of such beauty and majesty, yet somehow they do not feel alienated, forlorn, or threatened. They feel carried by nature and its mirroring in composition, painting, poetry, and sculpture. Awakened people experience life in awe as a fleeting moment in the immense and continuous whole that extends itself indefinitely. Humbly acknowledging their position, they experience reverence.

Reverence is the flower of consonant form traditions. Its source is the awe-filled fascination we feel in the presence of the epiphanies of the mystery. Everything worthy of dedication receives its appeal from an epiphanic affiliation with the mystery intimated by consonant faith and form traditions. Outside this mystery, each manifestation of reality loses its inner light. It fails to awaken the awe dormant in our silent soul. Awe is neither instinct nor custom. Chancing upon the unknown or the epiphanic, we may initially feel dread, but form traditions facilitate the refinement of this dread into awe by loving abandonment to a higher presence that embraces us as a mystery of beauty and generosity.

Awe is dread become reverence under the transfiguration of a loving abandonment to a mystery that draws us by its beneficence while keeping us at a humble distance by its majesty. The more traditions form us in awe and its manifestations, the more it permeates our apprehension, appraisal, and affirmation. Awe at the root of our life's formation may grant each of our acts its deepest epiphanic meaning.

Awe and Worship

Traditions form us in the awe that generates worship when they open us to the ground of this mysterious universe. They inspire a consonant culture to reflect the epiphanies of the mystery in art and beauty. They disclose us as emerging from the mystery. Traditions point to the hidden source of cosmic, human, and transhuman unfolding. They remind us of the limitations of our successive cultures in space and time. Our awe disposition may be refined by faith in a personal mystery in and beyond us that is the transcosmic and transhuman source of our own being and thought. We feel holy fear in this presence, whose forming energies give rise to countless variations in universe and history; simultaneously we feel attracted by the effusive love that makes us be.

Awe permeates us. Before the mystery of formation we feel as nothing. At moments the mystery becomes overwhelming, fascinating, filling us with holy apprehension. The worship fostered by religious faith and form traditions is the appreciation and affirmation of our dependency on this all-embracing mystery. Awe is, therefore, the root of consonant culture and humanization. The response that flows from reverence is congenial, compatible, and compassionate; it is the fecund source of a living culture.

Isolated Fear and Free-Floating Anxiety

The holy fear or dread inherent in awe, though mitigated by the aspect of reverence, may be isolated from this original source. When people fall away from awe for the mystery, they are left with a free-floating anxiety whose source has become unknown to them. Deep down in the infrafocal depths of their consciousness dwells a repulsed dread for some unknown threatening power.

A dissonant culture may have made them refuse, perhaps already as children, the spontaneous acknowledgment of the awe dwelling in the transfocal dimension of their consciousness. They never allowed it to become focal. Hence it could not sink into their prefocal consciousness or become a disposition of their heart. The silent dread that fills a dissonant culture generates anxious reactions that are unfree and fixated. These reactions hamper mutual respect and love, stifle joyous trust in our form potency, and poison leisure and playfulness. They paralyze culture and make us anxiously dependent on technical civilization alone.

Because cultures remain in some measure the ambient formation fields of their original traditions, some human respect may remain. This remnant of awe may save the last outposts of culture from the encroachment of mere technical civilization. However, this remnant may be lost if it closes itself off totally from its own possibility to deepen awe and to renew its presence to the mystery and its epiphanies. Technical civilization is a great blessing if it is subjected to a consonant culture rooted in awe.

Refused Awe and Idolatry

When a dissonant culture refuses to keep itself open to the possibility of awe, it will exalt one or the other isolated appearances of cosmos or civilization as the central meaning of human existence. The falsification of repudiated awe penetrates from below into our prefocal and focal consciousness in distorted forms. Such exaltation develops into idolatry.

For example, people in a dissonant culture may invest their distorted awe disposition exclusively in relation to sports heroes or movie stars, in their career, in a political party, in possessions, in the power structures of a church, in their country, or in some ideal or vested interest of their family or the formation segment to which they belong. Idolizing such values in isolation instead of enjoying them as limited epiphanies of the mystery leads to the neglect of fidelity to other demands of one's formation field and its surrounding horizon.

Our cultural respect is rooted in awe for the mystery that transcends culture and civilization. This mystery inspires consonant unfolding and grants every value its proper place. It opens us to the objective demands of formation in each of our cultural acts and creations. Loss of awe means loss of cultural responsibility, of openness in reverence to transcendent values. The disappearance of respect and responsibility, resulting from the death of awe, leads also to an increase in free-floating dread. Dread instead of inspiration becomes the source of a merely technical civilization, protecting with its military defenses and devices anxious citizens against equally anxious citizens of competing technical civilizations.

Deepest Ground of Consonant Culture

The deepest ground of consonant culture can be found in awe as nurtured in the great faith and form traditions. Awe implies that each consonant act of culture carries more than the mere functional meaning of effecting an observable change. Awe implies a minimal awareness of the epiphanic meaning that transcends immediately observable effects of cultural acts. Presence in awe becomes a listening in reverence to the deepest meaning of our formation field. It manifests itself in loving obedience and abandonment to the mystery speaking in all events, in interformative compatibility and compassion, and in respectful presence to things.

Awe makes us tend beyond the veil of appearances to penetrate the mystery of formation as it emerges in its manifold epiphanies. We see all people, events, and things flowing forth in the splendor of their uniqueness out of the ground of the sacred.

Consonant culture nurtures our potency to be receptive to the epiphanic dimension of all that is. Yet it keeps us humbly aware that our powers of apprehension, appraisal, and affirmation can be overwhelmed and blinded by immediate appearances. Consonant culture forms us in vigilance against demeaning demands on our affections, time, and formative energies. Consonant acts and dispositions are ultimately rooted in awe. Their symbols and appeals coform consonant cultures via their underlying faith and form traditions. Such basic consonance of a culture embodies itself differently in different dimensions of the human life-form.

Consonant Culture and the Dimensions of the Life-Form

Most basic in a culture is consonant obedience to the formation mystery and its epiphanies. This obedience generates in the transcendent dimension of life the consonance of respectful congeniality with the disclosures of the unique epiphany of the mystery in each person's foundational life-form. It nurtures in the functional dimension the flexible congruence of form reception and form donation with aptitudinal affinity and consonant ambitions. In the vital dimension, consonance respects and fosters a formation of life and world that is congenial with the vital endowments and limits of people as gifts of the cosmic epiphany of the mystery. In the sociohistorical dimension, consonance promotes compatibility with the situations in which the mystery allows people to be inserted successively. Consonance with the historical manifestation of the mystery makes people share in its all-embracing compassion for the fallenness and vulnerability with which people are faced daily in the formation of their own life and that of others.

Awe, Consonance, and Celebration of a Festive Meal

The many faces of consonance could be exemplified in the celebration of a festive meal pervaded by the graciousness of a distinctively human culture and its underlying traditions. A prefocal reverence, rooted in the sediments of unspoken awe, may linger almost unnoticeably in the dining room among the guests. They express mutual respect in gracious dress, word, and manner. Occasionally, an appropriate blessing at the beginning of the meal may make our pre- or transfocal awe for the mystery and its gifts focal and tangible.

Respect for congeniality is manifested in the invitation and seating of the guests in tune with their congenial affinity in regard to company and conversation. Regard for functional congruence is expressed in the practical arrangement of napkins, plates, utensils, and the well-timed serving of drinks and dishes. The functional-aesthetic coformant of the celebration is facilitated by the attractiveness of the table setting; refined table manners; the graciousness of the host, hostess, guests, and servers; and the quiet flow of pleasing conversation. The vital congeniality of consonance finds fulfillment in a choice of well-prepared drinks and dishes of sufficient variety to satisfy the vital needs and tastes of the concelebrants of this occasion.

In these embodiments of prefocal awe, a certain hierarchy prevails. For example, vital acts and dispositions of nourishment are modulated in their execution by the higher dispositions of gratefulness to the mystery of formation and of mutual respect. The table conversation, too, is influenced by the compatibility and compassion inspired by this particular sociohistorical celebrating, which is coformed communally by its participants during this enhanced moment of their formation history.

This ritual of implicit awe is not isolated from the ongoing formation history of humanity and the world. In some minimal way it sustains the history of consonant human formation as a whole. In contrast, dehumanizing ways of celebrating meals would somehow diminish the flow of distinctively human formation in a culture. It could signal the possible erosion of prefocal formation codes in which a consonant culture expresses its implicit rootedness in awe.

This description of a festive meal exemplifies how a culture is consonant and distinctively human insofar as it facilitates, via its consonant form traditions, the opening up of people to the possibility of expressing awe in the various dimensions of their life formation in their proper hierarchy.

The process of cultural humanization could be continuous were it not steadily disrupted by dissonant forces. These may halt, reverse, or distort the upward movement of form traditions that foster the consonant cultivation of our life and world. One main source of dissonance is an exclusive dominance of the functional dimension of the human life-form. Another is the exalting and isolating pride-form inherent in human life. As a quasi-foundational life-form, the pride-form hinders the gradual disclosure of our authentic foundational life direction, symbolized by the soul in many form traditions and intimately interwoven with our predisposition for awe. In the next chapter, we will reflect on these basic modes of distortion or refusal of the predisposition for awe and on means to overcome their deformative consequences in our culture.

CHAPTER 13

Cultural Obstacles to Awe and Means of Recuperation

I n the beginning of its formation history, the human race was probably less afflicted by discord between its functional form reception or form donation and its formative celebration of the disposition of awe. Rituals of planting, harvesting, hunting, dancing, tribal defense, birth, and burial spontaneously expressed tribal awe for the mystery, especially in its cosmic manifestation. The tribe apprehended, appraised, and affirmed such endeavors as interwoven with the awe-filled mystery of the birth and rebirth of nature, cosmos, tribe, and family. The carvings on their tools, the symbolic embellishment of their bodies, the designs on the walls of their caves, their totem poles—all were functional, aesthetic, and transcendent manifestations of awe and its traditional impact on tribal formation. Aeons before our overemphasized formation of the functional dimension, they had found the secret of a living integration of awe and functional formation. Their form traditions approximated a certain unification of life and world.

Awe, Functionalism, and Culture

The contemporary history of formation shows a remarkable advancement of the functional dimension as manifested in the informational sciences and technologies. The accelerating explosion of informative knowledge enables us to give form concretely within our cultures and civilizations to distinctively human formation ideals. It can help us to provide opportunities for the greatest number of people for a distinctively human unfolding of life that is congenial, compatible, and compassionate.

However, the same proliferation of functional skill and information may blind the human race in this phase of its history of formation. Humanity may lose touch with its own predisposition for awe. Awe should liberate, sustain, and guide our pilgrimage of human disclosure and appraisal in the universe. At this juncture of our history, functional formation of life and world may preoccupy our race onesidedly. This may lead to a depreciation of the distinctively human dispositions that flow formatively from the disposition of awe. The latter are the soul of a consonant culture. The distinctively human dispositions generated by awe are threatened by mere functionality. They can also be overshadowed by an exclusive emphasis on formative dispositions that are lower in the hierarchy of life's formation but still essential.

For example, scientists, theologians, or technicians may be overinvolved in functional-rational endeavors. They may neglect the demands of their vital dimension for timely nourishment, relaxation, and recreation. Functional dispositions may prevail at the expense of vital ones. People may be so enamored of their careers, sports, power-seeking, or socializing that they do not sufficiently take into account the concerns of their family. This marks a diminishment of consonance in one's multivalent expression of awe. The cause is again a onesided concentration on the development of functional dispositions.

Consonant family formation should be one of the concerns that guide and motivate our awe-inspired functional dispositions and actions in regard to spouse and children. The same applies to other dispositions implicitly rooted in awe, such as the social, the aesthetic, and the transcendent. The higher (and therefore the more distinctively human) the disposition from which consonant cultural acts emerge, the more it may be threatened by the functionalistic pulsation that sweeps through contemporary life.

Distortion of the Awe Disposition by the Pride-Form of Life

Our pride-form is another basic threat to the life of consonance, marked as it is by a balanced hierarchy of dispositions rooted in congenial, compatible, compassionate, and competent embodiments of the disposition of awe. On the scale of dispositions, each one nearer to the wellspring of awe should influence subordinate dispositions by implicit implication. Yet it should not take away the unique contribution each lower disposition has to make to consonant life formation. Dispositions subordinated to awe should neither be reduced to awe nor take its place. Exercising the body, socializing, celebrating human love—all have their own meaning and value, yet they can be integrated in awe for the mystery that grants us these marvelous form potencies.

Awe discloses the transcendent meaning of each distinctively human act or disposition. This applies not only to personal formation but to the formation of form traditions, subsequent cultural formation fields, and formation segments and communities within the population. The transcendent meaning disclosed by awe is implied in a consonant culture. Such implication alone can guarantee a culture's consonant unfolding.

For example, vested material interests of formation segments or of individuals should be lower on the scale of dispositions to be embodied in a cultural formation field than spiritual, social, and aesthetic dispositions. Endeavors that are exclusively motivated by vested material interests delay and distort the consonant unfolding of humanity. Such dispositions are rooted in the exalting and isolating pride-form of life. This inherent predisposition to self-centeredness tends to close people and societies off from dispositions of awe and their implications in subordinate dispositions.

People may be dominated by dissonant, isolated dispositions for status, popularity, and material possessions, thereby sacrificing the consonant unfolding of their culture. The pride-form, which all people share, may even become the basic disposition of a culture, thereby displacing the disposition of awe. A functional-vital type of humanism or scientism may dominate such a dissonant cultural formation field.

Only openness to the disclosures of awe, together with commitment to its implicit implementation in other dispositions, will enable people to transcend the pride-form in themselves and their societies. Awe saves their cultures from dissonance and self-destructive tendencies.

Form Traditions and Awe Radiation

Each human life-form is called to develop its own unique profile of life. In such a profile, one or more basic dispositions will prevail, while other fundamental dispositions, though less emphasized, will not be lacking entirely. The total lack of one or another fundamental, distinctively human disposition would mean that one's formation is dissonant. By means of such distinctively human dispositions, every person remains open, at least implicitly, to the basic disclosures of awe. However, it is difficult for people, especially when they live in a dissonant cultural formation field, to remain available to such disclosures. Hence the role of consonant faith and form traditions is essential. They highlight and radiate the disclosures of awe in a concentrated and symbolic way.

When a culture loses its consonance, its members can fall back only on their faith and form traditions for restoration to wholeness. Distinctively human dispositions, rooted in awe, may be lived implicitly by most members of a culture. In this case, such dispositions are less threatened by forgetfulness, extinction, or neglect, even if a number of people are not explicitly involved in the faith and form traditions that underly their cultural formation field.

A culture conducive to consonant life formation is one which fosters a variety of institutions and interests implicitly related to the disposition of awe. For example, the literary life with its many teachers, publications, poets, novelists, and literary critics helps to maintain and promote the sensitive poetic disposition of the human life-form. As many cultural groups as possible should be encouraged to focus on the formation of specific dispositions, be they transcendent, functional, or vital; all dispositions imply the typical awe disposition for the mystery and its manifold epiphanies. Each cultural group should keep the population in consonance with an epiphany of the formation mystery that might otherwise not be apprehended, appraised, and affirmed.

Formation Institutions and Cultural Formation

The process of consonant cultural formation implies that society sets certain people free to focus on the formation of human dispositions. Some may concentrate on vital dispositions of health, exercise, nutrition, healing, athletics; others on functional dispositions of competence, scientific research, logical reasoning, sound ambitions, aptitude development; others again on transcendent dispositions of wisdom, philosophizing, poetry, religious presence. All are called to pursue excellence in the dispositions that they are to foster in a special way, while implicitly rooting them in the awe disposition and not entirely neglecting the formation of other dispositions that are equally human.

An exceptionally gifted person may attain an unusually deep formation in a particular disposition. But cultural institutions that are called to highlight the formation of particular consonant dispositions within the cultural formation field are for the most part made up of people of average giftedness. For example, average teachers of ballet emphasize the musical-poetic form potency and disposition of the human body as a transcendent-vital expression of many explicit and implicit modes of awe. They will not attain the same outstanding formation of this disposition of the human life-form as the great masters of ballet who appear periodically in our formation history. However, average ballet teachers and dancers will enhance this disposition formation immensely if society enables them to focus together, in mutual interformation, on the unfolding of this specific disposition in the light of the form traditions inspired by the great masters of ballet over the centuries.

Need to Foster a Balanced Presence of Specialized Formation Institutes

Contemporary society has especially fostered functional dispositions, often in isolation from the awe disposition and from other dispositions that are less functional. To balance the important dispositions for effective functionality, society should complement them by fostering centers that call attention to other human dispositions. Otherwise they might be forgotten in the universal exaltation of dispositions of competent functioning.

For example, society should encourage specialists who accentuate the vital dispositions. Such people as medical doctors, nurses, nutritionists, masseurs, and exercise experts remind the population of the importance of vital dispositions that may easily be neglected under the pressing disposition to be functionally effective in one's formation field. Similarly, people are set free for the cultivation of functional-psychological or aesthetic dispositions in the cultural formation field. They may be social workers, psychotherapists, counselors, educators, poets, architects, ballet dancers, sculptors, painters, composers, musicians, designers, or teachers of art appreciation.

A more foundational calling to cultivate formative dispositions entails bringing into relief the basic human dispositions that are pointed to by the great religious and ideological form traditions. Their adherents witness to the dimension of awe that should be implied in all other dispositions. People set partially or totally free to witness to such transcendent dispositions radiate them into the cultural formation field and into the dispositions it advocates. Their concentration on these particular dispositions may awaken in others the dormant predisposition for awe that should be reflected in all their dispositions if life is to be fully consonant.

Wavelike Movement of Cultural Disposition Radiation

The radiation of any disposition could be imagined as a wavelike movement in the cultural formation field. The forming wave starts from the concentrated formation center that cultivates specific dispositions. Initially it affects people who are most ready to disclose in themselves similar dormant predispositions. They form spontaneously a cluster of similar disposition radiation around the formation center concerned. They generate the next formative wave insofar as their disposition formation may awaken in others around them a similar disclosure of neglected predispositions. These people in turn may influence those in their own circle in the same direction. In this way, a wavelike disposition movement is fostered in the sociohistorical formation field as a whole.

This movement could be illustrated by the cultivation of the aesthetic disposition. The core of people committed to the formation of aesthetic dispositions is coformed by such people as dancers, sculptors and painters, poets and composers, teachers of literature and art, conservators of museums and patrons of art exhibitions. The formative cluster around them is coformed by people who are not called to dedicate their life mainly to the cultivation of the aesthetic disposition. However, as form-receptive participants in this core, listeners and onlookers become awakened to their own aesthetic predispositions. They promote the aesthetic disposition in the cultural formation field as a whole by the manifestation of their own awakened aesthetic disposition. The overall result in the cultural formation field may be a more acute awareness of the importance of the aesthetic disposition, no matter how simply expressed in the choice of furniture and dress, the beautification of one's garden, or the graciousness of bodily movement and speech.

Radiation of the Foundational Awe Dispositions

Committed adherents of fundamental form traditions witness to the modes of formative awe as they have been developed by these traditions. Each form tradition develops a specific style of awe-filled life formation. The transcendent meaning of people, events, and things can easily be overlooked in a cultural formation field in which the demands for functional effectiveness may be overwhelming at times. Yet if awe is lost, life loses what makes it basically worth living. In spite of the onslaught of functional and vital-emotional problems, humanity must keep open its transcendent disposition.

Consonant foundational form traditions guard people against becoming enslaved to their functional and vital-emotional dispositions. They help them to create moments of transcendence of functional and vital care. The adherents of such form traditions gather together periodically to deepen their dedication to the disposition formation developed by their tradition. They bear witness for each other to a transcendent openness in awe that sustains the distinctive formation of the human form of life as human.

Beneficial Influence of Consonant Form Traditions

The greatest benefit for any culture or civilization is the all-pervasive presence of consonant form traditions. They purify the cultural unfolding of humanity by silently exposing mere self-centered interests through fostering a fundamental presence to the transcendent meaning of the culture.

The disposition of awe, inspired by the great form traditions, is first of all a disposition that is form receptive. Presence to the mystery is a gift not a conquest. The more people are open to the gift of awe, the more their cultural dispositions will seem to share the luminous quality of light. Their presence to the sacred meaning of consonant culture will become increasingly spontaneous and gracious. Those who do not yet share in this receptivity may be inclined by many functional preoccupations, by their prefocal needs for popularity, power, and possession, to live more peripheral lives. The dedicated adherents of a consonant form tradition may initially strike them as different, yet they may be touched by the gracious ease and naturalness with which they seem to be present to play or performance. It may be difficult for them to understand why such people seem less preoccupied with status and success, especially when these have become the primary purpose of their own involvement. Gradually compelled to admit that the committed adherents of a consonant form tradition grow in stability, serenity, and integration, some may begin to suspect that there *is* another unseen dimension to the cultural task that, though it still eludes them, must be the explanation of the passionate yet serene engagement in manual labor, science, play, art, or social justice and mercy of those relaxed adherents of the great form traditions.

Gradually the mystery of formation may unveil to them their own predisposition for awe and its potential implication in every consonant cultural endeavor. Once this happens to them, they may begin to see their cultural task in light of the all-encompassing mystery of formation. The hidden presence of the formation mystery in consonant cultures is disclosed to them. They may discover that the various modes of participation in a consonant culture do not generate isolated dispositions to be integrated laboriously into a unified form of life. Rather their presence in awe to the mystery becomes the hidden ground from which emerge consonant dispositions of cultural participation. They manifest and radiate awe for the mystery at the core of their life's formation.

Awe and Consonant Participation in a Culture

As consonant participants in a culture, we should be deeply compatible, compassionate, and competent, yet at the same time transcendent. Compatibility, compassion, and competence presuppose a rich sensitivity to the immediate aspects of our cultural situations, companions, and tasks. Transcendence has to permeate our sensitivity insofar as our cultural participation is also an act originating in the disposition of awe that keeps us present to the mystery.

Awe should transform the most transient and seemingly insignificant events into *formation events* with a transcendent meaning. They are at once what they are, and yet something more than they seem to be. Awe lights up everyday reality. To live in awe is to pass beyond appearances and attain the unseen mystery in daily events. This experience occurs when the simplest of acts are elucidated by the light of the spirit. Thus illumined we become an invitation to others to discover the spiritual in the cultural. Our disposition of awe as manifested in our mode of presence may disclose to them the source from which all people are called to draw meaning in life. Participants in the great form traditions of humanity should not offer themselves as obvious exemplars of the consonant life. Their life should be a silent invitation for people to find within themselves their own hidden life call, which they themselves should want to disclose and unfold in awe as their own unique epiphany of the mystery.

Historical Forgetfulness of the Mystery

In some periods of formation history, people may be closed to the message of the mystery. The adherents of the great form traditions may find themselves unable to awaken the dormant predisposition for awe. It is precisely during such times that the few remaining outposts of the great form traditions are more needed than ever.

This situation may be compared to the human predisposition for the aesthetic dimension of life. Because of functional overinvolvement, people may become insensitive to their own predisposition for aesthetic presence. Artists are not superfluous in such periods. On the contrary, if there were no artists left as lonely guardians of the aesthetic disposition of humanity, it would be far more difficult for people to find their way back to their own aesthetic predisposition when they reawaken to this deeply human possibility of life and world formation.

The absence of artists and artworks for a long period of time would also mean the loss of concrete styles and modes of beauty. It is true that in such times of forgetfulness of the aesthetic dimension of life, lonely masters of awe-filled beauty may not enjoy the eager reception of a delighted audience, but neither are they robbed of the possibility of joy. For the time being, lonely masters may find an even deeper joy in art itself, in the celebration of form and color, tone and timbre, melodious word and fortuitous phrasing, in their own solitary presence to all that is disclosed to people who dedicate their lives to beauty.

Similarly, dedicated adherents of the great form traditions are sorely needed in a cultural field of formation that tries to forget the mystery and the awe it engenders. They are called to guard the distinctively human disposition of awe. When people are once again ready to allow this predisposition to blossom in their lives, they will find to their delight that the paths of spiritual formation disclosed over the centuries are still available. They are still alive in forgotten corners of their culture, kept silently open by the adherents of the age-old form traditions who reflected on them, who lived them almost unnoticed in the conspiracy of silence erected around them by a functionalistic culture.

Awe and Initial Formation

Initial formation is affected by awe. If awe is absent, parents may overly impose on children their own dispositions. Some of these may silence the child's innate wisdom of mind and body. This implicit wisdom flows from the child's seminal awe for the mystery of formation. Their parents' repudiation of what they most deeply are becomes a force of duplicity in their life. They begin to disposses themselves of some of their own feelings, apprehensions, and appreciations. Inwardly they become divided by a proliferation of safety directives against disapproval by adults. No longer are they in consonance with their own formation field as it manifests itself to their spontaneous apprehension and appraisal.

Distortion of one's own life-form implies distortion of one's field of formation. Diminishment of awe for one's form potency means an erosion of awe for the unique opportunities in one's world. Children must distort the message of their own field in order to maintain with some conviction alien dispositions that mainly please their parents. Their own apprehension, appreciation, affirmation, and action is continuously blocked by those who do not respect the mystery in their small lives. They do not encourage the assimilation of their children's own experience, their awkward experimentation with their own possibilities, their tentative search for their own inner call.

As we know from our reflections on the disposition of firmness, children should often be restrained in service of consonant formation. They must learn discipline. But restraint becomes deformative when it is merely a result of parental fears and anxieties, of pride, of dissonant accretions from their form traditions, of personal idiosyncracies. These deformations veil parental faith and hope in the mystery at work in each child; they paralyze parental awe, which is the source of consonant child formation; they dull parental sensitivity for the unique vulnerability of each child.

When awe is absent, fear prevails—fear of failure in the countless things we may substitute for the mystery, such as our prestige in the neighborhood, our spotless home, our perfectly behaved sons and daughters, their successful future, our moral or social superiority. If children threaten by word or deed any of these concerns, we become upset. Sometimes we may explode. We fear desperately that they may not form their lives in the image of our reverence for the idols that have replaced the mystery as our object pole of awe.

Children have to carry the burden of parental anxiety. They are forced to absorb formation fears that are foreign to them. These cannot be related to any of their spontaneous pulsions, ambitions, and aspirations. This makes it difficult for them to expand naturally and to refine their own formation field.

Parental Confirmation of the Awe Disposition in Children

Like all human forms of life, children have to be confirmed in their sense of awe for their own form potency. They need to believe that they themselves have received from the formation mystery the power to give form to their life in cooperation with loving adults.

If this spontaneous awe of children for the power of life in them is not repudiated by parental overprotection, they feel stimulated by this potency. It inspires them to try to unfold their own primitive version of human existence. Their initial efforts to express what they are may be erratic and awkward. Yet to strengthen their faith in their form potency, they must experience that their personal efforts are worthwhile in their parents' eyes.

Children's predisposition of awe prepares them to honor their own gifts as undeserved potencies. This implicit awe can only be awakened by the awe of the parents genuinely manifested in their mode of presence. To give form to their life in the light of such gifts, children need the forming assistance of the mystery as manifested in its awe-filled representatives:

their parents and significant others. We cannot go far if we are not allowed to nurture a humble awareness of the gifts the mystery generates in us. Hence one of the great tasks of parents is to make children feel that they are loved by the mystery of formation, represented to them by their parents.

Children are endowed with gifts that make them worthy of respect and reverence. They must unfold the form potencies they have received. Formation is not a lonely linear development; it is an adventurous journey with the always surprising mystery. For children this mystery is imaged in their own parents who manifest it in their awe disposition.

The only way children can obtain an awe-filled sense of their own giftedness, its power and its limits, is by accepting the faith, hope, and consonance of their parents in regard to their own form potency. Unfortunately, the opposite is also true. Children may be unnecessarily curtailed in the experience of their potential. They may be forced unwisely to abide by their parents' commands, even if they happen to impede innocuous actions that could disclose to them something of their own giftedness for living. These actions could make them experience their potency to give form to their own life in their formation field. This field may be for them their parents' house and garden, their neighborhood, and the homes of family and playmates they visit.

Children are inclined to go along with this parental blocking of their innocent initiatives. They feel afraid that they may otherwise be abandoned by their parents. They cannot risk losing their love and respect, since they are dependent for survival on the adults around them. Caught in the necessity to conform in order to feel secure in their confirmation by adults, they may form in themselves uncongenial dispositions to please adults. They shape themselves not in the epiphany or form of the mystery hidden at the center of their life but rather in the image of their parents and the other adults around them.

Children may repudiate many of their own innocent actions, sound initiatives, unique potencies, and joys if they fear that their manifestation would displease their parents. Rather than fashioning themselves in an image or form that is pleasing to the mystery, they develop an image that is pleasing to people. They become anxious people-pleasers, not joyous pleasers of the epiphany of the mystery in the center of their being.

Duplicity of Initial Formation
The basic duplicity of initial formation starts when children form dispositions mainly to please their parents. Some of these may be at odds

with what they are called to become. Children may be made to feel anxious, guilty, or ashamed when they do the very things they are predisposed to do. They are made to feel at peace, good, and acceptable when they follow indiscriminately the dispositions borrowed anxiously from adults.

We are not referring here to numerous necessary dispositions in which children should be formed by their parents and by the faith and form traditions parents rightly represent, ideally in a relaxed yet awe-filled fashion. We are pointing only to imposed dispositions that are not foundational or necessary. Such alien dispositions oppress without reason children's own initiative, those genuine feelings and experiences that are compatible with the foundations of their tradition, if not with its parental version.

In this way children may not learn to listen in awe to the mystery as speaking in their own formation potential. They may learn instead to close themselves off from given predispositions. Rather than making them their own in respectful obedience, they become mere mannequins of parental formation. Their parents do not serve them in awe as servants of the formation mystery and its vulnerable disclosure in their children. They impose their own image and what they imagine to be the pure fundamental image of the formation tradition in which they themselves have been raised.

To establish and maintain some sense of form potency and worthwhileness, children may adopt a life of duplicity. They are fearful of these "giant adults" who are continuously correcting anything personal that comes out of them. The parents are not necessarily to be blamed. The majority of them are of good will. Often they themselves are the victims of the duplicity engendered in them by their own formation, for they were not shown the awe that results in relaxed faith, hope, and love.

Unavoidable Duplicity

For most of us it seems impossible not to develop initially a certain duplicity of formation. It is part of our fallen condition, which militates against awe in those who initiate us in life. This duplicity causes prefocal tension and a loss of awe that diminishes our joy as well as our experiential oneness with the epiphany of the formation mystery deep within us.

All of us are inclined not to be centered in the unique image or form hidden within us. Initially we do not allow it to be the revered source of our basic dispositions and actions. After our initial formation we tend to make popular pulsations, the media, our peers, political figures, and sports and entertainment heroes the successors of our parents. They, not the limpid treasure in the depth of our being, become the source of our ongoing formation of life and world.

We are thus off-center. In some way, awareness of our true potential is blocked. Disrespectfully we bury our talents; we refuse to be the responsible stewards of what has been given to us uniquely. Somehow we delegate this stewardship to others—to models presented by society; to successful figures in our environment; to pressures in family, neighborhood, and work place; to idle dreams of autonomous self-actualization in the image of fame and success. Onto these we transpose the aspiration of awe.

This duplicity or counterfeit form of life is something under which we all suffer in some measure. When we become aware of this problem, we may feel embarrassed and confused. Fear and shame could overwhelm us if we think we are different from other people—but we are not. Almost everyone suffers some duplicity that stems from childhood experiences. In the vulnerable period of initial formation, adults may have imposed on all of us at least some of their own dispositions, though they were uncongenial to us. They did so simply because they were not formed in awe themselves.

Because we are incarnated spirits, our transcendent dimension awakens fully only later in life. The vital, bodily dimension prevails in the period of initial formation. Foreign dispositions, imposed on us irreverently, are written into our bodies. Parental refusal to let our own giftedness shine through, filters into our cortical and subcortical, hormonal, and neuromuscular systems. These dispositions may still sculpt our movements, posture, and facial expressions, at times making us tense and angular in our vital appearance.

The vital body has been disposed this way by usually well-meaning parents, but it is a vital body at war with the epiphany within. This deformed body is the substratum of a rigid standardization of some foreign social image or form. Yet our true form, encased in the tight configuration of a dominating or submissive apparent life-form, keeps calling us to be something more than a sociohistorical product. The mystery is calling us. Awe-filled listening to its voice may set us free.

Compassionate Response to Duplicity

We should be compassionate with ourselves and others in this regard. At this period of the formation history of humanity, some duplicity of formation seems almost unavoidable. We can reform, but not totally prevent, the absorption of foreign dispositions. We all are crippled in some degree. The epiphany of the mystery in us is veiled to our awe. We are attached to our duplicity because it enables us to obtain confirmation by others of our form potency, provided we pay the price of blind conformity. Others pat us on the head because we are able to accomodate them so perfectly. Smilingly they approve of us because we manifest the superficial potency of adjustment to all popular criteria and customs.

Because we all feel the need for confirmation of our form potency, we become oblivious to our own duplicity, to our betrayal of the voice within. Our focal consciousness is no longer aware of the form we give to our life so as to enhance our sense of form potency in the eyes of others. We can say that this duplicity of life results in a kind of mindlessness or a formation ignorance cultivated since infancy. In some measure we relinquish the awe-filled apprehension, appraisal, and affirmation of what our formation really should be like.

This counterfeit form and the formation ignorance that accompanies it are maintained because we feel that we have to go on living in a way that is effective by popular criteria. We hunger for confirmation by others to assure ourselves that we are not impotent. Paradoxically, the very repudiation and refusal of our true potencies make us prefocally fearful of our hidden impotence. This fear deepens our dependency on popular confirmation by others and therewith strengthens our duplicity.

Compassion with our shared predicament of duplicity is deepened by the insight that children are too young to realize that they are formed in a certain way. They do not know what is happening to them. They do not yet have the symbols or the language available that would enable them to apprehend, appraise, and affirm the dispositions being formed in them by others. Without symbols, they cannot handle the deformative signals slipped into the cortical, subcortical, neuromuscular, and hormonal prepersonal forms of their life. These signals tell them how they should give form to their life, without knowing why and how their form giving is related to their unique life call.

Such is the tragedy of the human life-form. Yet the mystery of formation can overcome the duplicity of our formation. It can lift us beyond crowd and collectivity. It can help us to find our true face, given to us before we were born and before we were deformed by an early imposition of dispositions foreign to our secret destiny. Often this mystery may lead us to seek formation counseling or some form of therapy to help us regain our rightful potency.

Parental Repudiation or Refusal of Awe Questions

Another impediment to the awakening of children's disposition for awe is the repudiation or refusal of their first spontaneous awe-filled questions. To ignore these may set the stage for a lifetime of rejection of their inner aspirations.

Awe makes us receptive to the mystery that embraces life and death, to the emergence of all that is in and around us. Faith in the mystery of formation holds the beneficent answer to the great hidden questions that fill us with fear, foreboding, and silent prefocal dread as long as we cannot rest in appreciative abandonment to this ultimate response. How and why did I come to be on this planet? Who am I as this unique form of life? How and why must I give form to my brief journey and to the fields I am called to traverse with my fleeting presence? Where do we come from, where do we go? What is the point of it all?

If we keep open to such questions that rise from the transcendent dimension of the human form of life, we must admit that the ultimate answer is a total mystery. Science enables us to analyze a few links of the great cosmic formation chain that makes us emerge in the universe. But neither these few observable links nor the cosmic chain in which they are embedded satisfy our quest for ultimate forming sources.

Such deeply human questions, which are at the root of awe, emerge already in a most elementary fashion in children. They are touched also by the distinctively human dread of helplessness and vulnerability, of a vaguely surmised mortality. They concretize it in fear of witches and animals, of darkness and shadows, haunted houses, spectres and ghosts. Fairy tales and stories may help children to make such fears concrete and hence less overwhelming.

When children ask where they come from, they ask this question not as students in biology but as unfolding forms of life, haunted already in embryonic fashion by the basic awe questions of the human race. We must be able to answer them with deep and warm conviction that the great formation process out of which they came is basically a beneficent mystery that nobody can totally dissolve. If we happen to be adherents of one of the great faith and form traditions, we should use their magnificent symbols to describe this loving mystery. While we may tell them something about the few intervening biological processes science knows something about, we should not be surprised if they are bored by such technical details. Onesided knowledge of such instrumental biophysical factors may veil the mystery itself. To reduce our answer to biophysical processes alone is to indirectly belittle, repudiate, or refuse the deeper question of the child. It may not be asked again. Children may feel that their hesitant transcendent curiosity may look silly in the light of this technical reduction of life and death by omniscient adults. We teach children indirectly by our cynical disposition that there is no forming mystery in the cosmos, life, or history. We close the door that opened ever so slightly. We prevent the awakening of awe or the human sense of mystery. We barricade their first door to the sacred. Some may never find it again.

When the sense of mystery is ignored, children may be engaged for a lifetime in the struggle to keep refusing the awe question, which becomes more and more threatening. They may feel compelled to find the answer to the why and how of their life in anxious empirical justifications of their existence. They may be obsessed by the need to prove how important, great, lovable, successful, or clever they really are all by themselves.

Another awe question, intimately related to the first, arises in children on the occasion of a death in the family or among their acquaintances. We should help children in their sadness to share in our own conviction that, in spite of this unexplainable happening, the forming mystery of life and death is beneficial. Here again a mere technical explanation of what biologically happens at death is not an answer to the deepest concern of the child. Here, too, our faith and form tradition can give us the symbols, rituals, and stories that facilitate immensely our pointing to the mystery.

If this awe question is not answered, awe may die. A lifetime may be spent in the proliferation of safety directives and protective dispositions against the threat of awareness of a mortality that cannot make sense. When finally the question becomes inescapable, the person may be totally unprepared for this reality. The end may be terrifying in its desolation, for without awe life loses not only its luster but its closing consolation.

CHAPTER 14

Awe Disposition in
Transcosmic Formation Traditions

O ur considerations thus far have led to the conclusion that awe
disposes us to be present to the mystery in and beyond all things.
Somehow all people seem *predisposed* to meet the mystery, but not all of
them actualize this potency in the *disposition* of awe. Among those who
do, there are striking differences in the way in which the awe disposition
unfolds. Some people feel disposed to love and be loved by a personal
God. Others are disposed to find the mystery only in their own heart and
in the awesome appearances and powers of nature. Both kinds of people
may be sustained by corresponding faith and form traditions. We could
call these, respectively, the transcosmic and cosmic traditions. An example of the former would be Jewish, Islamic, and Christian; of the latter,
Buddhist and Taoist.

Differences between Cosmic and Transcosmic Form Traditions
What may confound us at first sight is that both types of form traditions often use similar language. They foster the awe disposition and profit
directly or indirectly from each other's formative writings. Our confusion may give rise to a few key questions. Are these traditions basically
different? If so, are they still related to each other in some respects? Are
the awe dispositions they foster comparable in any way? Do the pro-
ponents of cosmic form traditions and those of transcosmic traditions
mean the same thing when they speak about the mystery, the holy, the
sacred, the numinous? If not, what is the difference? Should followers of
transcosmic form traditions reject totally the cosmic way of speaking
about the mystery? Or do some of their expressions point to certain
manifestations of the mystery celebrated also in transcosmic rituals and
writings? Do cosmic form traditions perhaps totalize such particular appearances? Can transcosmic traditions relativize such totalized facets of

the mystery and integrate them in a transcosmic vision? How does this nuance in disposition affect the actual symbolization, expression, and life and world formation of people? What dangers loom for adherents of the two form traditions when confusion arises between those two modes of presence to the mystery?

We must address these questions to ensure that our emphasis on the awe disposition and the formation mystery will not compound the already existing confusion in this regard among a number of people genuinely interested in the spiritual life. Adherents of transcosmic form traditions must not belittle those who are initiated in a cosmic form tradition. They are concerned, however, with people who are freely committed to one or the other type of tradition and who can no longer distinguish the differences and similarities between the two types.

For example, people belonging to transcosmic form traditions may distort the transcosmic personal mystery by identifying personal and cosmic images with the impenetrable transhuman and transcosmic mystery itself. This could be seen as a form of unintended idolatry. Some insight into the difference between the mystery as cosmic and transcosmic may help such adherents to purify and illumine their subjectivistic symbols and images and the arbitrary transpositions of their own strivings and feelings onto the mystery. Such purification, when aided and finally completed by the mystery itself, may open to them the way of union with the personal transcosmic mystery in whom they believe.

Cosmic form traditions foster an awe disposition that limits itself to an intimate human experience of the mystery dimension of the cosmos and of one's own life as interwoven with this mystery. Some cosmic traditions may use the same language as transcosmic ones. The Jungian ideological faith and form tradition may speak, for instance, about God, Christ, the transcendent, the father figure, but these words do not mean the same as they do in transcosmic faith and form traditions. Jungians will not necessarily use these symbols as representing an objectively existing transcosmic personal reality beyond human experience and cosmic imagery, such as an independent creator and ruler of the universe.

Transcosmic traditions would see the mystery dimension of the cosmos and of this religious human experience as only one manifestation of the mystery opened up by the awe disposition. Formation science would call this manifestation the cosmic and human *epiphany* of the mystery. Transcosmic traditions go beyond this to refine and expand, as it were, the awe disposition. For them, the object pole is not only the mystery dimension of human life and world. They believe in a transcosmic personal mystery. This belief has a transforming impact on the lives of their adherents. It expands their awe disposition, enabling them to acknowledge and celebrate a personal God proclaimed by transcosmic faith and form traditions in writings and rituals. Their life formation differs considerably from those who follow cosmic traditions. This difference is due in great part to their aspiration for personal interformation with a personal God in love and obedience to his word.

Yet, this orientation to a personal incomprehensible mystery does not lead to a repudiation of the mystery dimension of life and world that is available to human experience. This mode of presence to mystery seems to be basic to any human awe disposition. Transcosmic believers do not deny this mode. They complement it with modes of awe-filled adoration and loving interformation with the mystery as transcosmic and transhuman. For them the merely human disposition of experienced presence to the mystery opens only to a cosmic manifestation, appearance, or epiphany of a transcosmic mystery in ourselves and in nature. They believe that the awe disposition attains its fullness only when it is coformed by all three modes of presence to the mystery: the cosmic-human, the transcosmic, and the transhuman modes of adoration and of personal loving interformation.

Three Aspects of the Transcosmic Awe Disposition

We can now summarize three aspects of a fully formed awe disposition as aspired to by adherents of transcosmic form traditions. They are the disposition to be present to the forming mystery as it manifests itself to our human experience in its cosmic epiphanies; to be present to it as a personal power who absolutely transcends our cosmos, our potential or actual human formation fields and their cosmic horizons, and all our human knowledge, experience and, expression; to be present to this personal mystery as to a mystery of loving, caring, and demanding interformation with humanity. In the fully refined awe disposition these three aspects are organically interwoven with one another.

We find these three facets expressed in the formative language and other symbols of committed adherents of transcosmic form traditions of all ages and cultures. Explicit and unambiguous expressions of personal adoration and personal loving interformation with a totally Other beyond this cosmos and beyond human experience are obviously present in transcosmic faith and form traditions.

Relative Relevance of Cosmic Form Traditions for Transcosmic Believers

This does not mean that transcosmic believers cannot learn anything from cosmic form traditions. The human awe experience for the cosmic epiphany of the mystery remains an integral part of their own awe disposition. Insofar as cosmic form traditions can help them to deepen that aspect, they remain relevant to those who have expanded their awe disposition beyond its cosmic dimension. If they want to remain faithful, however, to their own tradition they must always subordinate this cosmic-human facet of their awe disposition to its transcosmic adoration and interformation facets.

Transcosmic believers should periodically rekindle the cosmic-human aspect of their awe disposition. This will help to keep it alive. This aspect of the disposition provides the indispensable human and intracosmic base to be taken up and transformed by the transcosmic aspects of the same disposition.

Cosmic form traditions help people to experience the mystery of the universe as the unfathomable source and origin of all initial and ongoing formation in life and world. As we observed earlier, they may even use personalizing symbols to express this experience, but these are only used to symbolize certain felt nuances of their ultimately intrahuman and intracosmic experience. They are not meant to point to a personal power of creation and ruling authority objectively existing outside the cosmic realm and human experience.

Universality of the Predisposition for Presence to the Cosmic Mystery

The sense of a forming mystery, of the sacred, the holy, the numinous within life and universe, is potentially present as a predisposition to awe in the human life-form as such. Hence formation science—before its articulation in various form traditions—can use this universally present potency for awe in service of its universal theory of distinctively human formation.

At present we see in large numbers of people a growing concern for religious experience. Many seem disappointed with the functional-vital model of life that has been onesidedly fostered ever since the physical-scientific, technical, and industrial revolutions. Their transcendent dimension of life rises in protest, so to speak, demanding its acknowledgment and cultivation. This urgency leads to an awakening of the human predisposition of awe. From the distinctions we have made so far, it will be evident that such an awakening of the merely human experiential predisposition for awe is not necessarily identical with a personally appropriated transcosmic faith and form tradition. Yet this awakening may lead to a cultivation of the human awe disposition. Such cultivation may in turn benefit and foster among adherents of transcosmic traditions a movement of interiorization of transcosmic faith and form traditions.

Transcosmic Awe Disposition

The second facet of the transcosmic awe disposition is its orientation toward the personal or suprapersonal transcendent. This orientation is the central aspect that gives meaning to both the cosmic and the interformative aspects of the same disposition. Hence, the transcosmic awe disposition as a whole receives its name from this central facet, which transforms the cosmic and the intimate interformative dimensions profoundly and irrevocably. This orientation to a personal transcosmic mystery, a mystery to be adored and obeyed, transforms the merely human awe disposition and its forming impact on our life. The human life-form that unfolds in the light of a transcosmic form tradition adds something new to the human experience of the cosmic numinous in self and universe. The awe disposition is expanded by faith in a personal transcosmic power of formation that creates and rules the cosmos and the human form of life in independent glory and majesty.

Limited Transcendence of the Cosmic Awe Disposition

The human awe disposition disposes many people to appraise the forming mystery as only immanent in this cosmos. For them the mystery is not more than its epiphanies in this world; it does not exist outside its appearances in the universe. They may profess an agnosticism in regard to its possible objective personal external existence, saying that we simply cannot know. They may admit, however, to some transcendent quality of this cosmic mystery, albeit a limited one. They may maintain that it transcends each of its particular intracosmic manifestations but not the cosmos itself. Hence their innate transcendent form dimension is activated only to a limited transcendence experience. This limitation is due to their restrictive awe disposition. Their experience of ultimate transcendence is limited to a mystery that does not rise in glorious personal independence and power beyond this cosmos. Whether it does, agnostics say, we cannot know for sure. They do not believe in an absolute transcendence, in a personal power that creates, maintains, and rules the universe majestically in personal independence.

Fluent Transitions between Cosmic and Transcosmic Facets

There is not necessarily a rigid partition between the cosmic and the transcosmic aspects of the awe disposition. In many people who have developed them, both of these dimensions of transcendent presence flow into one another. Other people, who developed only a cosmic-human presence, may use words that seem to refer to a mystery that is personal. They say that the mystery, the holy, is caring, calling them forth, directing, disclosing itself, speaking inwardly. Such expressions could mean that their cosmic presence flows over in presence to a personal transcosmic mystery.

Their expressions *could* mean this, but they do not *always* mean this. Similar words may be used by people who are living exclusively in a cosmic human presence or by those who are moving into or are already in a disposition of transcosmic faith. The difference is that transcosmic believers would use such terms in a symbolic-realistic way, that is to say, as symbols pointing to a personal mystery really existing over and beyond the cosmos. Cosmic adherents, as in the Jungian faith and form tradition or in the Maslowian transpersonal psychology, could use the same idiom in a merely metaphorical fashion. They would not mean to say that these words refer to a transcosmic personal God. They want only to express their experience that the cosmic awe disposition gives rise to experiences of the cosmic formation mystery *as if* it were "calling forth," "directing their life," "speaking inwardly," "caring," and so on. The transcosmic believer, on the contrary, would say that the personal transcosmic mystery *is* personally calling forth, directing, speaking, demanding, ruling, revealing. For them such expressions are not merely "as if" metaphors but symbolic pointers to a personal God really existing as an almighty ruler beyond his cosmic epiphanies. They believe that this transcosmic reality can be described in such personalizing attributes, even if it cannot be exhausted by these symbolic pointers.

It is possible that in some cases the use of a similar language by certain adherents of cosmic form traditions signifies a subtle transition toward transcosmic presence. This transition may initially be prefocal and almost unnoticeable.

The use of the same expressions by both cosmic and transcosmic form traditions is an advantage for the language of formation science. It can use some of these expressions in its universal formation theory, leaving it up to readers or listeners to articulate their meaning in terms of their own form tradition.

Many symbols and metaphors cherished in cosmic spirituality can be meaningful for transcosmic believers. The immanent cosmic mystery dimension plays a basic role in their own spiritual life insofar as they are also aware of the epiphanic presence of the Most High within the universe. If their spiritual life approaches consonance, they are disposed to be present in awe to the formation mystery as simultaneously immanent and transcendent; as mystery at the core of our life and our world; and as being totally beyond the human life-form, its formation fields, and the cosmic horizons surrounding these fields. For them the formation mystery is both cosmic and transcosmic.

Contextual Appraisal of Cosmic or Transcosmic Meaning of the Mystery

Words such as holy, sacred, ground of being, and numinous express the formation mystery as cosmic, yet these same terms are also used to point to the transcosmic. Conversely, transcosmic terms, such as self-disclosing, inspiring, and life-directing, are metaphorically used to describe subjective aspects of the cosmic awe experience.

How do we distinguish the different meanings of these terms? We can recognize the intended meanings within their contexts. When Christians, for example, sing "Holy, Holy, Holy," we know what they mean from the whole context of their form tradition. It is clear to us that they do not refer exclusively to the hidden cosmic presence of the holy. Neither do they exclude this, but they affirm at the same time their faith in the existence of a personal transcosmic mystery to whom they pay homage in this hymn. Similarly when adherents of exclusively humanistic form traditions speak in awe about the direction the mystery discloses in their lives, we know from the context of their other communications that they do not refer to a transcosmic personal deity in an unequivocal revelation of the meaning of human life.

This contextual dependency on the meaning of similar sounding transcendent terms has proven advantageous for the terminology of a universal formation science. One purpose of this science is to provide a fundamental frame of reference for a variety of consonant form traditions without forcing them to abandon their own articulation of seminal concepts. Such a basic formation science may lead to the acknowlegment of some elementary commonality between various form traditions in regard to the distinctively human or spiritual formation of the human race.

The implicit denial of any commonality of spiritual form potency and aspiration in all human life-forms has been one of the causes of the absence of social justice, peace, and mercy on our planet. Form traditions that held themselves the only and exclusive repository of any wisdom of human life formation led their adherents to impose their views on others, by force if necessary. Such arrogance has been an enduring source of conflict, oppression, and persecution. Unfortunately the next war to be fueled by feuding religious (and/or ideological) form traditions may be the end of all wars and all form traditions. Hence, we feel the pressure to develop a universally acceptable formation science. This science should serve the distinctive humanization of all people. At the same time it should respect the autonomy of the various form traditions as long as they do not impinge on the human rights of others.

Cosmic and Transcosmic Facets of the Awe Disposition

To recapitulate: people of various form traditions use similar symbols and metaphors of transcendence with different meanings. These different meanings, however, do not necessarily exclude each other. This peculiarity of transcendent language facilitates for formation scientists the use of a terminology that is not offensive to, while being basically compatible with, a variety of form traditions. Such a language lends itself to further articulation by each unique form tradition, thereby fostering mutual respect and understanding.

The transhuman and transcosmic facets of our awe disposition enable us to appraise the mystery as the Totally Other. As long as the mystery is mainly appraised as an intracosmic mystery, we are inclined to transpose to it our own human pulsations, pulsions, ambitions, and aspirations. Or we may deify mere cosmic appearances. Polytheistic form traditions are illustrations of this tendency. Even when we appraise the mystery as transhuman, we are inclined, if our faith is still immature, to make it a mirror image of our own merely human imaginations, memories, and anticipations and their attendant feelings and strivings. However, the transhuman dimension points to a personal mystery that is uniquely and absolutely itself in relation to the human life-form. We must distinguish between our dissonant attributions to this mystery and its transhuman and transcosmic reality in impenetrable majesty.

Comparative Summary of Cosmic and Transcosmic Facets of the Awe Disposition

The forming mystery is omnipresent. It is immanent in the cosmic epiphanies as an all-embracing and all-pervading formation force. To make itself known within these cosmic epiphanies themselves, it endowed the human life-form with a predisposition for a basic awe experience in regard to the forming mystery in and behind all people, events, and things and their interactions.

The apprehension, appraisal, and affirmation of this cosmic mystery dimension alone is not sufficient for growth into a transcosmic awe disposition. The appreciation of the mystery dimension of the cosmos and of our intrasphere must be subordinated to the naming of a personal transhuman and transcosmic mystery who is the forming source of all human and cosmic epiphanies. This naming happens in metaphoric and symbolic words, rituals, and narrations. To acknowledge the forming mystery as transhuman and transcosmic demands that the human life-form identify it in its own personal impenetrable uniqueness, in its being different— totally other, essentially incomparable with any cosmic appearance or human experience.

Only after such acknowledgment is a personal interformative relationship possible between the formation mystery and the human life-form. The term *interformative relationship* does not imply that the human life-form can by itself give form to anything pertaining to the mystery. We call the relationship interformative in the sense that the transcosmic mystery can allow the free acts of the human life-form to influence its own transformative acts and modes of presence in relation to this life-form and its conditions.

For example, an effective prayer is a prayer that moves the heart of God, metaphorically speaking. Such a prayer is not the result of merely human initiative and self-exertion. It is, first of all, a gift of God. God gives this gift in such a way that it will only move him if we freely cooperate with this gift and actually pray wholeheartedly. In other words, he promises that our prayer, under the conditions set forth by him alone, will give form to his generosity toward us. He did not have to grant us this formative power of prayer in regard to his divine generosity. It is totally undeserved. However, once he does so, he is faithful to his promise and to this interformative potency with which he endowed us gratuitously. In this sense alone can we speak of interformation between a transhuman omnipotent mystery and the human form of life which has been freely created by this mystery and endowed with its gifts.

We may compare our personal encounter with the acknowledged mystery as it is in itself with our personal encounter with another human being. Formation science teaches that interformation as the effective encounter between us and another person presupposes the acceptance of the unique intrasphere of the other with its preformative roots, without transgressing this line of personal uniqueness. Without this acknowledgment and respect, no personal interformation between people is possible. This applies analogously to our interformative relationship with the mystery. We must respect its impenetrable oneness and the boundaries of its gift of interformation.

Lived Logic of the Spontaneous Formation of the Transcosmic Awe Disposition

The theistic awe disposition is made up of three basic coformants. We could call them briefly the cosmic, transcosmic, and interformative coformants. These coformants should not be apprehended and appraised in isolation from one another. Their mutually forming power can only be understood by an appraisal of their mutual interaction within the disposition.

The development of a formative disposition cannot be planned in advance by our functional intelligence as we can plan the development of a theological thesis or a practical project like building a house. We do not first construe intellectually a disposition in our mind in accordance with mentally defined principles and then execute it as a logical synthesis in a subsequent disposition.

Formative dispositions, including the disposition of transcosmic awe, grow out of our spontaneous life formation. Only when they announce themselves in our formation history can we critically appraise them. Such appraisal may have a correcting or complementing influence on the further unfolding of the disposition. The initial, spontaneous formation of a disposition, however, has a logic of its own—a lived logic of formation. The transcosmic awe disposition manifests a structure that gradually unfolds itself within a meaningful sequence.

Primary in the "human life-form as awe" is the spontaneous apprehension, appreciation, and affirmation of the mystery that announces itself via its preformative influence in the core dimension of the human intrasphere and correspondingly in its outer manifestations in the human formation field. This intraexperience of the cosmic mystery grants the human awe disposition its foothold in our humanness and earthliness. The awe disposition, thus specified, disposes people to a natural mystical experience.

This primordial stage of the awe disposition does not actually include or exclude the transcosmic structures that may refine this basic disposition. We may say, however, that the fundamental disposition of awe implies the potency to receive these structures. It points implicitly to something beyond itself, beyond this subjective experience of cosmic mystery. This pointing is potentially present in the transcendent dynamic itself of the awe disposition.

This potential transcosmic pointing becomes actual when the mystery is named as God, Father, Yahweh, or Allah. At that moment one becomes disposed to acknowledge the mystery as a personal transhuman and transcosmic presence behind its cosmic epiphanies. The simple cosmic awe disposition now develops into a more refined disposition. It disposes us to acknowledge the forming mystery both as an intimate human intraexperience of its cosmic epiphanies and as the transcosmic majesty of the totally other One who cannot be captured in any cosmic human awe disposition nor in the concepts, images, and feelings it engenders.

The subsequent refinement of the awe disposition into a disposition to interformation with the personal mystery may follow when this mystery freely invites the human life-form to such interformation. Openness to such an invitation is potentially inherent in the transcosmic awe disposition. The mystery grants the human life-form this latent form-receptive potency.

Transcosmic Awe Disposition and Transcosmic Form Traditions

What is the role of transcosmic form traditions in the theistic refinement of the cosmic awe disposition? Their part is indispensable, as we have learned from the formation history of humanity. Historically, it has only been through transcosmic faith and form traditions that people have refined theistically their cosmic awe disposition.

Formation science holds that we cannot explain distinctively human formation as a whole exclusively by means of the data and theories of one or another of its empirical auxiliary sciences. Human formation and its history is too profound and too complex to be approached exclusively in the light of contributions of the empirical sciences. The relevant contributions of these sciences should be critically integrated with the wisdom of consonant form traditions within an integrative science of formation. Only then can they serve a balanced formation of human life and world.

Formation science resists cultural anthropologism, psychologism, and sociologism. The suffix-*ism* indicates a movement that goes beyond the boundaries of these specialities in trying to explain, by means of specialized theories and findings, realities that cannot be covered adequately by the empirical sciences concerned. The movement attempts to explain the transcosmic awe disposition empirically through anthropological, psychological, or social events and influences. Formation scientists appraise critically the relevance of such findings and speculations for the consonant proximate formation of human life. They conclude that these reductionistic attempts inform us in fact only of the formative relevance of various empirical modes in which people may concretize, via their own awe disposition, their awe for the transcosmic mystery and its expression. However, this transcosmic mystery itself is communicated to them by transcosmic form traditions; it is not the direct result of mere psychological or sociological processes.

Indeed, a study of the transcosmic form traditions and their origin in time seems to indicate that the transcosmic facet of the awe disposition is something original given to humanity during its formation history. It opened for them a specific transcendent sphere of the human formation field that could not be explained exhaustively by any empirical science.

Formative Language of Form Traditions and Transcosmic Awe Disposition

Form traditions are communicated by formative language. The formative language of traditions coforms the formation field of their committed adherents. By assimilating the language of a transcosmic tradition, people receive and give form theistically to their awe disposition. Transcosmic language traditions do not ignore our everyday world. Such traditions, too, are filled with words and stories about the cosmos and about people, events, and things that are used metaphorically to point to the *transcosmic* mystery which cannot be comprehended in any worldly experience or concept. The evolvement of the theistic dimension of the awe disposition is not rooted in subjective experience. Theistic awe is based on a proclamation by faith and form traditions, which are traditions of the revealing word.

Formation by such traditions and their formative language disposes people to open up in awe to what cannot be experienced directly, to what goes beyond this life and world. Their words of proclamation intend precisely to signify this total transcendence. Intrahuman and intracosmic symbols play a central role in this theistic language, but they function only as significant pointers, not as exhaustive explanations. Nor does the name *God* for this mystery emerge from unaided human experience. The inspired naming itself makes the mystery present in its own unfathomable, suprapersonal oneness. In this pure givenness, it becomes a formative power in human life.

Transcosmic Awe Disposition and Celebration

The transcosmic dimension of the awe disposition disposes us to grateful celebration. Celebration is the festive expression of the awe-filled disposition of the human life-form to transcend itself, to rise above its actual and potential formation fields and their cosmic horizons toward the transcosmic presence. Celebration is a glorifying of the unparalleled sublimity of the suprapersonal mystery and its proclaimed names and consonant attributes. The human life-form does not celebrate in this sense what is encapsulated in mere human experience or what can be manipulated by magic or mastery. People celebrate, in the deepest sense of this word, only what transcends them absolutely and yet evokes their transcendent life dimension. Religious celebration appeals to this dimension as the potency to rise joyously above the acknowledged boundaries of life and world.

The deepest form-receptive potency of the human life-form is the transcendent potency to traverse all cosmic borders in receptive openness to a suprapersonal transcosmic mystery known only by proclamation.

Interformative Dimension of the Theistic Awe Disposition

The two first dimensions of the theistic awe disposition are thus interior experiential awe of the intracosmic epiphany of the formation mystery and the adoring awe of a transcosmic mystery, named and proclaimed as the personal God. Both dimensions together dispose people to a new kind of interiority, complementing the experiential inwardness of presence to the mystery's appearance in this world. The third dimension of the awe disposition is that of awe-filled, personal interformation between the transcosmic presence and the human form of life.

The source of this third dimension is neither the experience of the holy nor the primary narrating proclamation of the transcosmic mystery by theistic form traditions. Its source is a new interformative word. Interformative words have the power to constitute a relationship of mutuality. Only the mystery itself can institute such an interformative relationship by its totally free and undeserved word of invitation and dispose people to open themselves to this appeal in a new form receptivity. It is also only the divine power itself that can set the conditions under which it will allow the human life-form to influence its flow of formative grace. It is a true relationship of loving interformation but its initiation and continuation remains on the side of the mystery.

Christians believe that this third dimension of the awe disposition is evoked in its fullness by the Christian faith and form tradition. This tradition proclaims that Jesus initiated in fullness the interformative relationship between his Father and the human life-form as transformed in, with, and through him.

Dissonant Transposition instead of Consonant Personal Interformation

The condition of consonant interformation is that both participants apprehend, appraise, affirm, and confirm each other in their uniqueness, even if they cannot totally comprehend that identity. If this does not happen, the result can be what formation science calls "dissonant transposition" instead of "consonant interformation." In dissonant transposition the human life-form ascribes to another all kinds of subjectivistic images, memories, anticipations, and their attendant feelings and strivings, which are mainly the effect of its own pulsations, pulsions, ambitions, and aspirations. The same happens in the interformative relationship between the human life-form and the mystery as long as the suprapersonal God is not acknowledged in his own impenetrable oneness. In that case the interformative relationship becomes dissonant and deformative because of the unbridled subjectivism of one's experiential life, feeling, and fantasy.

The image of the mystery is bent to our subjective imaginations, pulsations, pulsions, ambitions, and aspirations. We refuse to accept in a spirit of form receptivity the objective language of theistic faith and form traditions insofar as they address the mystery as it is in itself. We slip into deceptive transpositions or even fall into religious illusions.

The acknowledgment of the mystery's absolute transcendence is the condition for a consonant relationship. To lead to union with the mystery, it presupposes the purification and illumination of imaginations, memories, and anticipations with their attendant feelings and strivings. Without such purification, we will impose our own pulsations, pulsions, ambitions, and aspirations on the mystery of divinity by dissonant transposition.

Exclusive Cultivation of Awe for the Cosmic Mystery

People may cultivate only the basic disposition of awe for the inwardly experienced cosmic forming mystery. They may experience a real sense of inner fulfillment. At privileged moments their intrasphere may feel bathed, as it were, in the subjective experience of the holy. Yet this experience is not sufficient for a personal, focal, and prefocal relationship of inter-formation with the suprapersonal Creator of the world. It is true that the human life-form is in the mystery and the mystery in it, but initially still in an undifferentiated substantial unity, not yet in a unity of increasing per-sonal likeness with its transcosmic personal source.

The fact that a natural experience of mystery is possible in many who do not believe in a personal God is not surprising to students of spirituality. The human life-form is, in its deepest being, divine. God is, cosmically speaking, substantially at one with the root of each unique human form of life. Hence the human person is capable of experiencing some aware-ness of an all-embracing mystery that cannot be named.

Formative Language and Interformative Awe Dimension

The awe disposition refines itself when a human life-form begins to speak about a personal mystery. The human life-form affirms itself as a personal "I" by positing the forming mystery in its speaking as a personal, totally other One who can potentially address this life-form as a cared-for yet personally responsible "you." The basic conditions for an interfor-mative relationship between the mystery and the human life-form are present now. Many prayers of celebration express this second dimension of the theistic awe disposition. In such texts God is glorified in the third person, as a "he," as the Most High, whose name one has learned through the proclamation of theistic faith and form traditions.

Finally, the disposition of awe-filled interformation becomes one's own when one knows oneself as a "you" addressed by this forming mys-tery, and when one in accordance with this divine word responds obedi-ently yet personally to this speaking Other. At that moment the personal interformative relationship between God and the human life-form be-comes in principle an integral part of the awe disposition.

The way to a consonant, actual, and personal interformation with the transcosmic mystery is long and laborious, filled with pitfalls, often lost and only to be restored with difficulty. It is for clarity's sake that we have described the attainment of the three dimensions of the theistic awe dis-position as a series of steps or phases. But we must be careful to avoid a "phasic" misunderstanding of the awe disposition, as if once one phase is achieved one can forget about it. In real life it is not that simple. No di-mension of the transcosmic awe disposition is a once-and-for-all gift and achievement. Each of the three coformants must be kept alive. Each of them contains far more treasures than one at first expected. New disclosures and implementations in one of the three dimensions benefit and transform the others. The human life-form must repeatedly return to each of them in new ways. One cannot close oneself up only in the interformative relationship without keeping alive and deepening the experience of the cosmic epiphany of the mystery. Classical spiritual writings recognize two dispositions of relationship to the mystery: the disposition of finding the Creator via his creatures and the disposition to seek the mystery as the totally Other in a cloud of unknowing, in the nakedness of faith

The personal interformative relationship with the mystery gives rise to a new interiority that implies a transformation of our intrasphere. And yet such intimate interformation can strike us after a while as illusive and chimerical. Interformation must be filled time and time again both by the inner experience of the cosmic epiphany of the mystery and by the transhuman faith in the proclaimed transcosmic mystery, which lifts the human form of life beyond the cosmos.

Conclusion

The transcosmic awe disposition can only emerge in its fullness by means of the formative language of transcosmic faith and form traditions. Typical of this language is that it transforms our awe disposition. The ongoing formation of the awe disposition will now be dominated by the absolute priority of the personal mystery. We become increasingly aware by purification and illumination of this disposition that *the mystery is*—it *is* prior to our apprehensions, appraisals, affirmations, images, memories, and anticipations with their attendant feelings and strivings. Insofar as the transcosmic disposition is not faithful in its acts to this absolute priority, it is liable to give form to an only "imagined" transcosmic mystery. This felt or imagined mystery is the distorted mirror image of the human life-form or some of its aspects. It is an object of subjective transpositions and dissonant attributions.

No amount of transcendent reflection about the human life-form, its formation field, and the horizons of this field, no depth or intensity of transcendent aspiration for the infinite, can by itself alone push through to the transcosmic mystery. The human life-form needs a purifying and illuminating recourse to the forming language of transcosmic faith and form traditions. These traditions offer the unfolding awe disposition the name of God. This proclaimed name purifies, illumines, and guides the awe disposition on our way to union with the mystery.

Transcosmic traditions give form to the awe disposition of their adherents, first of all, by means of official and popular rituals in their places of worship and in the family. The language of such forming rituals is condensed, compact, and concentrated. It is a selection of powerful crystallizations of the faith proclamation and the celebration it evokes. Such crystallizations in words, songs, prayers, music, aesthetic symbols, and movements do not aim at telling the whole story of the self-disclosure of the holy in utter detail. Nor is their purpose to communicate elaborate theological speculations. These crystallizations are chosen to make the mystery present in ways that actually initiate or engage here and now the transcosmic awe disposition of the faithful in all three of its dimensions. If the myths, movements, or symbols that coform a ritual became all-inclusive stories or theological explanations, they would lose their compact formative power for the awe disposition and its immediate activation.

Our critique of an experiential orientation is directed against the anxious hunt for exclusively private psychological religious experiences that are either strictly personal or shared only by a small idiosyncratic community. In a later volume we will discuss the Christian formation tradition and the transpersonal faith experiences that share in the proto-formative revelational and ecclesial experiences believed and cherished in both the faith and the form tradition of Christianity. These experiences are neither exclusively private nor merely psychological. They do not exclude psychological experiences, but they prevent us from making them the central concern or criterion of our spiritual life formation.

Afterword

Volume One of this series ended with a synopsis of the formation theory as construed so far on the basis of findings in this field and in related auxiliary sciences. We finished the synopsis with the distinction between the primary foundational life-form, which is the preempirical source of consonant life formation, and the secondary foundational life-form, which is the dispositional base of our actual empirical life formation.

Here in Volume Two the function of this secondary foundation and its formation dispositions has been clarified. We have discussed the secondary foundation in its connection with formation fields and dimensions, with formative apprehensions, appraisal, and affirmation, with formative imagination, memory, and anticipation, and with initial and ongoing formation history. We then considered the integrational forms of life, singling out the heart or core form and its enduring dispositions as decisive for the basic direction of the actual formation of our empirical form of life as a whole. This consideration showed the necessity of a reflection on the fundamental formation dispositions of the heart and their mutual interaction. The core disposition of awe was identified as central for consonant life and world formation, as the root of justice, peace, and mercy. The modes and expressions of the awe disposition, its relations to form traditions, its obstacles in a culture, and its evolvement within cosmic and transcosmic form traditions were examined.

In the next volume of this series, we will examine the other fundamental dispositions of the heart conducive to consonant life formation. These are the dispositions of consonance, congeniality, compatibility, compassion, appreciation, openness, detachment, obedience, simplicity, reverence, privacy, communality, firmness, effectiveness, gentleness, and social presence. The disposition of social presence will be given special consideration because of its crucial position in a science of spiritual *formation*. To give form in justice, peace, and mercy to life and world

251

distinguishes a spirituality with an emphasis on formation from other spiritualities that focus almost exclusively on the interior life. Formation science is committed to focal attention to the principles of formative and deformative social presence, to the dynamics of depletion, repletion, and restoration of this most important disposition and its impact on world formation. The final chapters of Volume Three will discuss the formative dispositions of social justice, peace, and mercy and will complete our examination of the theory of distinctively human formation.

In Volume Four the meaning and validation of formation science as one of the human sciences will be discussed. The research methodology of this science will be outlined and explained, and a complementary type of investigation, called articulation research will be discussed. Formation scientists who specialize in this research articulate the findings of their science in the light of one or more of the form traditions developed during the course of humanity's history.

Finally in Volume Five, we will consider, in the light of this exploration of articulation research, the role of form traditon as such in the formation history of humanity. This exposition will be followed by an articulation of the findings of formation science in the light of Christian faith and form traditions.

Bibliography

Books

Allers, R. *Self-Improvement*. New York: Benziger Brothers, 1939.

Allport, G. *Becoming*. New Haven: Yale University Press, 1955.

_____. *Personality*. New York: Henry Holt and Co., 1957.

Aquinas, Saint Thomas. *The Human Wisdom of St. Thomas*. Arranged by Joseph Pieper. Translated by Drostan McLaren, O.P. New York: Sheed and Ward, 1948.

_____. *In Aristotelis Librum De Anima Commentarium*. Edited by M. Pirotta, O.P. Editio Tertia. Taurini-Romae: Marietti Editori, 1948.

_____. *Quaestio Disputata de Anima*. Edited by P. Bazzi and others. Editio IX Revisa. Taurini-Romae: Marietti Editori, 1953.

_____. *Quaestiones Disputatae de Potentia*. Edited by P. Bazzi and others. Editio IX Revisa. Taurini-Romae: Marietti Editori, 1953.

_____. *Summa Theologica*. Literally translated by the Fathers of the English Dominican Province. New York: Benziger Brothers, 1947.

Aristotle. *The Basic Works of Aristotle*. Edited by Richard McKeon. New York: Random House. 1941.

Arnold, M. B. *Emotion and Personality*. New York: Columbia University Press, 1960.

Arnold, M. B., and Gasson, J. A., S.J., and others. *The Human Person*. New York: The Ronald Press, 1954.

Ayensu, E. S., and Whitfield, P. *The Rhythms of Life*. New York: Crown Publishers, 1982.

Bandura, A. *Social Learning Theory*. Englewood Cliffs, N.J.: Prentice-Hall, 1977.

Barnett, L. *The Universe and Dr. Einstein*. New York: William Sloane Associates, 1950.

Barret, W. *The Illusion of Technique*. Garden City, N.J.: Doubleday, 1975.

Becker, E. *The Denial of Death*. New York: Free Press, 1973.

Benedict, R. *Patterns of Culture*. New York: Houghton Mifflin, 1934.

Bentov, I. *Stalking the Wild Pendulum*. New York: Dutton, 1977.

Boelen, B. *Existential Thinking*. New York: Herder and Herder, 1971.

_____. *Personal Maturity: The Existential Dimension*. New York: Seabury, 1978.

Bois, S. *The Art of Awareness*. Dubuque, Ia.: William Brown, 1961.

Bonaventure, Saint. *The Journey of the Mind to God*. Translated by José de Vinck. Paterson N.J.: St. Anthony Guild Press, 1960.

Boros, L. *Living in Hope: Future Perspectives of Christian Thought*. New York: Herder and Herder, 1969.

Bossard, J. *Sociology of Child Development*. New York: Harper and Brothers, 1953.

Boulding, K. *The Meaning of the Twentieth Century*. New York: Harper and Row, 1965.

Bourke, V. J. *Will in Western Thought: An Historico-Critical Survey*. New York: Sheed and Ward, 1964.

Brazelton, T. B. *On Becoming a Family: The Growth of Attachment*. New York: Delacorte Press, 1981.

Bribbin, J. *Genesis*. London: Dent, 1981.

Buber, M. *I and Thou*. New York: Scribners, 1970.
Butler, C. *Western Mysticism*. New York: Harper and Row, 1966.
Campbell, A. *Seven States of Consciousness*. New York: Harper and Row, 1974.
Capra, F. *The Tao of Physics*. New York: Bantam Books, 1977.
_____. *The Turning Point*. New York: Simon and Schuster, 1982.
Carrington, P. *Freedom in Meditation*. Garden City, N.Y.: Anchor Books/ Doubleday, 1977.
Caseiello, J., S.J. *A Humane Psychology of Education*. New York: Sheed and Ward, 1936.
Chapple, E. *Culture and Biological Man*. New York: Holt, Rinehart & Winston, 1970.
Curle, A. *Mystics and Militants*. London: Tavistock Publications, 1972.
Davis, C. *Body and Spirit: The Nature of Religious Feeling*. New York: Seabury, 1976.
Dean, T., and Kennedy, A. *Corporate Cultures*. Reading, Mass.: Addison-Wesley, 1982.
de Caussade, J. P. *Abandonment to Divine Providence*. Translated by John Beevers. Garden City, N.Y.: Doubleday, 1975.
Dechanet, J. M. *Christian Yoga*. New York: Harper and Row, 1960.
DeGrazia, S. *Of Time, Work and Leisure*. New York: Twentieth Century Fund, 1962.
Deikman, A. J. *Altered States of Consciousness*. Edited by Charles Tart. Garden City, N.Y.: Doubleday, 1969.
Dewey, J. *Art as Experience*. New York: G. P. Putnam's Sons, 1934, 1959.
_____. *Experience and Nature*. New York: Dover Publications, 1925.
_____. *Human Nature and Conduct*. New York: The Modern Library, 1922.
_____. *On Experience, Nature and Freedom*. Edited by R. J. Bernstein. Indianapolis, In.: The Bobbs-Merrill Company, 1960.
Dunlap, K. *Habits, Their Making and Unmaking*. New York: Liveright Publishing Co., 1932.
Dupré, L. *The Other Dimension: A Search for the Meaning of Religious Attitudes*. Garden City, N.Y.: Doubleday, 1972.
_____. *Transcendent Selfhood: The Rediscovery of the Inner Life*. New York: Seabury Press, 1976.
Eliade, M. *The Sacred and the Profane*. New York: Harcourt, Brace and World, 1959.
Ellis, A., and Harper, R. A. *A New Guide to Rational Living*. Englewood Cliffs, N.J.: Prentice-Hall, 1975.
Ellul, J. *Hope in Time of Abandonment*. New York: Seabury, 1977.
Erikson, E. H. *Childhood and Society*. New York: W. W. Norton, 1963.
Farber, L. H. *The Ways of the Will*. New York: Basic Books, 1966.
Ferguson, M. *The Aquarian Conspiracy: Personal and Social Transformation in the 1980's*. Los Angeles: J. P. Tarcher, 1980.
Fingarette, H. *Confucius: The Secular as Sacred*. New York: Harper and Row, 1972.
_____. *The Self in Transformation*. New York: Basic Books, 1963.
Foster, R. J. *Celebration of Discipline: The Path to Spiritual Growth*. New York: Harper and Row, 1977.
Frankena, W. K. *Three Historical Philosophies of Education, Aristotle, Kant and Dewey*. Chicago, Ill.: Scott, Foresman, 1965.
Frankl, V. *Man's Search for Meaning*. New York: Pocket Books, 1974.
Fransen, P. *The New Life of Grace*. New York: Seabury, 1973.
French, R. M., Trans. *The Way of a Pilgrim and the Pilgrim Continues His Way*. New York: Seabury, 1968.
Freud, S. *The Ego and the Id*. London: Hogarth Press, 1927.
Friedman, M. and Rosenman, R. H. *Type A Behavior and Your Heart*. New York: Alfred A. Knopf, 1974.
Fromm, E. *Escape from Freedom*. New York: Farrar and Rinehart, 1941.
_____. *The Heart of Man*. New York: Harper and Row, 1964.
_____. *Man For Himself*. New York: Rinehart and Co., 1947.
_____. *The Sane Society*. New York: Farrar and Rinehart, 1955.
Fromm, E., Suzuki, D. T., and others. *Zen Buddhism and Psychoanalysis*. New York: Harper and Brothers, 1960.

Fuchs, O. *The Psychology of Habit According to William Ockham*. Louvain, Belgium: E. Nauwelaerts, 1952.
Goldstein, K. *Human Nature in the Light of Psychotherapy*. New York: Schocken Books, 1940.
_____. *The Organism*. New York: American Book Co., 1939.
Gouinlock, J. *The Moral Writings of John Dewey*. New York: Hafner Press, 1976.
Gratton, C. *Guidelines for Spiritual Direction*. Denville, N.J.: Dimension Books, 1980.
Guardini, R. *Freedom, Grace and Destiny*. New York: Pantheon, 1960.
_____. *The Virtues*. Chicago, Ill.: Henry Regnery Co., 1967.
Halacy, D. S. *Man and Memory*. New York: Harper and Row, 1970.
Hall, E. *The Dance of Life: The Other Dimension of Time*. Garden City, N.Y.: Doubleday, 1983.
_____. *The Hidden Dimension*. Garden City, N.Y.: Doubleday, 1966.
_____. *The Silent Language*. Garden City, N.Y.: Doubleday, 1959.
Harman, W. *An Incomplete Guide to the Future*. Palo Alto, Calif.: Stanford Alumni Association and San Francisco Book Co., 1976.
Haughton, R. *The Transformation of Man*. Springfield, Ill.: Templegate, 1967.
Heidegger, M. *Being and Time*. New York: Harper and Row, 1962.
Hennig, M. and Jardim, A. *The Managerial Woman*. Garden City, N.Y.: Anchor Press/Doubleday, 1977.
Herrigel, E. *Zen in the Art of Archery*. Translated by R. F. C. Hull. New York: Vintage Books, 1971.
Heschel, A. *God in Search of Man: A Philosophy of Judaism*. New York: Octagon Books, 1976.
_____. *Who Is Man?* Stanford, Calif.: Stanford University Press, 1965.
Hesse, H. *Siddhartha*. New York: Bantam, 1971.
Hora, T. *Existential Metapsychiatry*. New York: Seabury, 1977.
Howes, E. B., and Moon, S. *The Choicemaker*. Wheaton Ill.: The Theosophical Publishing House, 1977.
Hoyle, F., and Wickramsinghe, N. C. *Lifecloud: The Origin of Life in the Universe*. New York: Harper and Row, 1979.
Hughes, A. C. *Preparing for Church Ministry: A Practical Guide to Spiritual Formation*. Denville, N.J.: Dimension Books, 1979.
Huxley, A. *The Devils of Loudun*. New York: Harper and Row, 1971.
_____. *The Perennial Philosophy*. London: Fontana, 1958.
Irala, N. *Achieving Peace of Heart*. New York: Joseph F. Wagner, Inc., 1954.
James, W. *Habit*. New York: Henry Holt and Company, 1980.
_____. *The Principles of Psychology*. 2 Vols. 1890. Reprint 2 vols. Vol I. New York: Dover Publications, 1950.
Jacobson, E. *Progressive Relaxation*. Chicago, Ill.: University of Chicago Press, 1938.
Jantsch, E. *The Self-Organizing Universe*. Oxford and New York: Pergamon, 1980.
John of the Cross, Saint. *The Collected Works of St. John of the Cross*. Translated by Kieran Kavanaugh and Otilio Rodriguez. Washington, D.C.: I.C.S. Publications, 1973.
Johnston, W., ed. *The Cloud of Unknowing*. Garden City, N.Y.: Doubleday, 1973.
Johnston, W. *The Still Point*. New York: Harper and Row, 1970.
Jung, C. G. *Psyche and Symbol*. New York: Doubleday, 1958.
Kadloubovsky, E., and Palmer, G. E. Trans. *Writings from the Philokalia on Prayer of the Heart*. London: Faber and Faber, 1967.
Kestenbaum, V. *The Phenomenological Sense of John Dewey: Habit and Meaning*. Atlantic Highlands, N.J.: Humanities Press, 1977.
Kierkegaard, S. *The Concept of Dread*. Translated by Walter Lowrie. Princeton, N.J.: Princeton University Press, 1961.
_____. *Purity of Heart Is to Will One Thing*. New York: Harper and Row, 1956.
_____. *Sickness Unto Death*. Princeton N.J.: Princeton University Press, 1941.
Kilpatrick, F. P., ed. *Explorations in Transactional Psychology*. New York: New York University Press, 1961.

Kilpatrick, W. K. *Psychological Seduction*. Nashville, Tenn.: Thomas Nelson, 1983.
Kluckhohn, C., and Murray, H., and others, eds. *Personality, In Nature, Society and Culture*. New York: Alfred A. Knopf, 1953.
Knox, R. *Enthusiasm*. New York: Oxford University Press, 1950.
Korzybski, A. *Science and Sanity: An Introduction to Non-Aristotelian Systems and General Semantics*. Lakeville, Conn.: International Non-Aristotelian Library Publishing Company, 1948.
Lao-Tzu. *Tao Teh Ching*. Translated by John C. H. Wu. New York: St. John's University Press, 1961.
Lasswell, H. D. *Power and Personality*. New York: W. W. Norton, 1948.
Leach, E. R. *Rethinking Anthropology*. London: Athlone Press, 1961.
Lecky, P. *Self-Consistency*. New York: Island Press, 1945.
Leclercq, J. *The Love of Learning and the Desire for God*. New York: Fordham University Press, 1961.
Leech, K. *Soul Friend: A Study of Spirituality*. London: Sheldon Press, 1977.
Leonard, G. *The Transformation: A Guide to the Inevitable Changes in Humankind*. Los Angeles: J. P. Tarcher, 1981.
Levinson, D. J., and others. *The Seasons of a Man's Life*. New York: Alfred Knopf, 1978.
Lindworsky, J. *The Training of the Will*. Milwaukee, Wis.: Bruce Publishing Company, 1929.
Linn, D., and Linn, M. *Healing Life's Hurts*. New York: Paulist Press, 1977.
Lovelock, J. *Gaia: A New Look at Life on Earth*. London and New York: Oxford University Press, 1979.
Luce, G. G. *Body Time: Physiological Rhythms and Social Stress*. New York: Random House, 1971.
Luijpen, W. *Existential Phenomenology*. Pittsburgh, Pa.: Duquesne University Press, 1972.
Lynch, W. F. *Images of Faith: An Exploration of the Ironic Imagination*. Notre Dame, In.: University of Notre Dame Press, 1973.
_____. *The Integrating Mind*. New York: Sheed and Ward, 1962.
McClelland, D. *Personality*. New York: The Dryden Press, 1951.
McGinn, B. *Three Treatises on Man: A Cistercian Anthropology*, ed. Kalamazoo, Mich.: Cistercian Publications, 1977.
Maloney, G. *Inward Stillness*. Denville, N.J.: Dimension Books, 1976.
Mangalo, B. *The Practice of Recollection: A Guide to Buddhist Meditation*. Boulder, Col.: Praja Press, 1978.
Marcel, G. *The Mystery of Being*, 2 vols. South Bend, Ind.: Gateway Editions, 1977.
Marschack, A. *The Roots of Civilization*. New York: McGraw-Hill, 1972.
Martland, T. R. *The Metaphysics of William James and John Dewey*. New York: Philosophical Library, 1963.
Maslow, A. *Motivation and Personality*. New York: Harper and Brothers, 1954.
Matsagouras, E. *The Early Church Fathers as Educators*. Minneapolis, Minn.: Light and Life Publishing Company, 1977.
May, R. *Man's Search for Himself*. New York: W. W. Norton, 1953.
Mead, M. *Sex and Temperament in Three Primitive Societies*. New York: William Morrow and Co., 1935.
Meissner, W. *Foundations for a Psychology of Grace*. Glen Rock, N.J.: Paulist, 1966.
Merton, T. *Mystics and Zen Masters*. New York: Dell, 1961.
Metz, J. B. *The Advent of God*. Paramus, N.J.: Newman Press, 1974.
_____. *Poverty of Spirit*. New York: Paulist Press, 1963.
Miller, J. G. *Living Systems*. New York: McGraw-Hill, 1978.
Moltmann, J. *Theology of Hope*. London: SCM Press, 1967.
Monroe, R. *Schools of Psychoanalytic Thought*. New York: The Dryden Press, 1955.
Murchie, G. *The Seven Mysteries of Life*. Boston: Houghton Mifflin, 1978.
Murray, M. Paul of the Cross. *The Concepts of Self-Acceptance and Self-Respect in Karen Horney's Theory of Neurosis*. Romae: Typis Pontificiae Universitatis Gregorianae, 1961.
Muto, S. A. *Pathways of Spiritual Living*. Garden City, N.Y.: Doubleday, 1984.
_____. *Blessings That Make Us Be*. New York, N.Y.: Crossroad Publishing Co., 1982.

Nabert, J. *Elements for an Ethic*. Translated by William J. Petrek. Evanston, Ill.: Northwestern University Press, 1969.
Naranjo, C. *The One Quest*. New York: Ballantine Books, 1972.
Nuttin, J. *Psychoanalysis and Personality*. New York: Sheed and Ward, 1953.
Ornstein, R. *The Psychology of Consciousness*. New York: Pelican Books, 1975.
Otto, R. *The Idea of the Holy*. New York: Oxford University Press, 1958.
Park, D. *The Image of Eternity*. Amherst, Mass.: University of Massachusetts Press, 1975.
Piaget, J. *The Child's Conception of the World*. Translated by Joan and Andrew Tomlinson. New York: Harcourt, Brace, 1929.
Picard, M. *The World of Silence*. Chicago, Ill.: Regnery, 1964.
Pieper, J. *Leisure, The Basis of Culture*. New York: Mentor-Omega, 1952.
_____. *Prudence*. Translated by Richard and Clara Winston. New York: Pantheon Books, 1959.
Pfander, A. *Phenomenology of Willing and Motivation and Other Phenomenologia*. Evanston, Ill.: Northwestern University Press, 1967.
Polak, F. *The Image of the Future*. Translated by E. Boulding. San Franisco: Jossey-Bass, 1973.
Powers, J. M. *Spirit and Sacrament: The Humanizing Experience*. New York: Seabury, 1972.
Rahner, K. *Foundations of Christian Faith*. New York: Seabury Press, 1978.
_____. *Theological Investigations*. Vol. 3, New York: Seabury Press, 1974.
Reisman, D. *The Lonely Crowd: A Study of the Changing American Character*. New York: Yale University Press, 1961.
Ricoeur, P. *Fallible Man*. Translated by Charles Kelbley. Chicago, Ill.: Regnery, 1965.
_____. *Freedom and Nature: The Voluntary and the Involuntary*. Translated by E. Kohak. Evanston, Ill.: Northwestern University Press, 1966.
Rodriguez, R. *Hunger of Memory: The Education of Richard Rodriguez*. New York: Bantam Books, 1983.
Rokeach, M. *Beliefs, Attitudes and Values*. San Francisco: Jossey-Bass, 1965.
Roth, R. J. *John Dewey and Self Realization*. Englewood Cliffs, N.J.: Prentice-Hall, 1962.
Roton, Placide de. *Les Habitus: Leur Caractère Spirituel*. Paris: Labergerie, 1934.
Rulla, L. *Depth Psychology and Vocation*. Chicago, Ill.: Loyola University Press, 1971.
Rumke, H. C. *The Psychology of Unbelief*. New York: Sheed and Ward, 1962.
Sabbath, L. *The Radiant Heart*. Denville, N.J.: Dimension Books, 1977.
Scarf, M. *Unfinished Business: Pressure Points in the Lives of Women*. Garden City, N.Y.: Doubleday & Company, 1980.
Schachtel, E. G. *Metamorphosis*. New York: Basic Books, 1959.
Schafer, R. M. *The Tuning of the World*. New York: Alfred A. Knopf, 1977.
Scheflen, A. E. *Body Language and the Social Order*. Englewood Cliffs, N.J.: Prentice-Hall, 1972.
Schutz, A. *Collected Papers*. 2 vols. The Hague: Martinus Nijhoff, 1967.
Shapiro, D. *Neurotic Styles*. New York: Basic Books, 1965.
Sheldrake, R. *A New Science of Life: The Hypothesis of Formative Causation*. Los Angeles: J. P. Tarcher, 1982.
Sherif, M., and Cantril, H. *The Psychology of Ego-Involvements*. New York: John Wiley, 1947.
Simonton, C. and Simonton, S. *Getting Well Again*. Los Angeles: J. P. Tarcher, 1978 and New York: Bantam, 1978.
Sivananda, S. S. *Sadhana*. Delhi: Motilal Banarsidass, 1958.
Selye, H. *The Stress of Life*. New York: McGraw-Hill, 1956.
Sri Aurobindo. *The Life Divine*. Pondicherry, India: Sri Aurobindo Ashram, 1970.
Squire, A. *Asking the Fathers*. Wilton, Conn.: Morehouse-Barlow, 1976.
Stace, W. *Mysticism and Philosophy*. London: Macmillan, 1960.
Stotland, E. *The Psychology of Hope*. San Francisco, Calif.: Jossey-Bass, 1969.
Strasser, S. *The Soul in Metaphysical and Empirical Psychology*. Pittsburgh, Pa.: Duquesne University Press, 1957.

Strauss, E., and Griffith, R. *Phenomenology of Memory*, ed. Pittsburgh, Pa.: Duquesne University Press, 1970.

Streng, F. J. *Ways of Being Religious*. Englewood Cliffs, N.J.: Prentice-Hall, 1973.

Sullivan, H. S. *The Interpersonal Theory of Psychiatry*. New York: W. W. Norton and Co., 1953.

Suzuki, D. T., *An Introduction to Zen Buddhism*. New York: Grove, 1971.

Suzuki, D. T. and Fromm, E. *Zen Buddhism and Psychoanalysis*. New York: Harper & Brothers, 1960.

Suzuki, S. *Zen Mind, Beginner's Mind*. New York: Weatherhill, 1970.

Tart, C. T. *States of Consciousness*. New York: Dutton, 1975.

Terruwe, A. A. A. *The Neurosis in the Light of Rational Psychology*. Translated by Conrad Baars, M.D. Edited by Jordan Aumann, O.P. New York: P. J. Kenedy and Sons, 1960.

Teresa of Avila, Saint. *The Collected Works of Teresa of Avila*. Translated by Kieran Kavannaugh and Otilio Rodiguez. Washington, D.C.: I.C.S. Publications, 1976.

Thompson, W. M. *Christ and Consciousness*. New York: Paulist, 1977.

Tournier, P. *Guilt and Grace*. New York: Harper and Row, 1962.

_____. *The Meaning of Persons*. New York: Harper and Row, 1957.

Toynbee, A. J. *Change and Habit*. New York: Oxford University Press, 1966.

Trungpa, C. *Cutting Through Spiritual Materialism*. Berkeley, Calif.: Shambala, 1973.

_____. *The Myth of Freedom and The Way of Meditation*. Berkeley, Calif.: Shambala, 1976.

Ulanov, A., and Ulanov, B. *Religion and the Unconscious*. Philadelphia, Pa.: Westminister Press, 1975.

UNESCO. *Cultures and Time: At the Cross Roads of Culture*. Paris: UNESCO Press, 1976.

van Croonenburg, E. *Gateway to Reality*. New York: Seabury, 1971.

van der Leeuw, G. *Religion in Essence and Manifestation*. New York: Harper and Row, 1963.

Van Kaam, A., and Susan Muto. *Am I Living a Spitual Life?* Denville, N.J.: Dimension Books, 1978.

_____. *The Art of Existential Counseling*. Denville, N.J.: Dimension Books, 1966.

_____., and Kathleen Healy. *The Demon and the Dove*. Washington, D.C.: University Press of America, 1983.

_____. *The Dynamics of Spiritual Self Direction*. Denville, N.J.: Dimension Books, 1976.

_____. *Dynamisme du Quotidien*. Sherbrooke, Quebec: Les Editions Paulines, 1973. Paris: Apostolat des Editions, 1973.

_____., Bert van Croonenburg, and S. Muto. *The Emergent Self*. 1st American ed. Denville, N.J.: Dimension Books, 1968. (2nd rev. ed., 1968).

_____. *Envy and Originality*. Garden City, N.Y.: Doubleday, 1972.

_____. *Existential Foundations of Psychology*. Lanham, Md.: University Press of America, 1984.

_____. *Formative Spirituality*. Vol. 1, *Fundamental Formation*. New York, N.Y.: Crossroad Publishing Co., 1983.

_____. *Foundations of Personality Study*. Denville, N.J.: Dimension Books, 1983.

_____. *In Search of Spiritual Identity*. Denville, N.J.: Dimension Books, 1975.

_____. *A Light to the Gentiles*. Lanham, Md.: University Press of America, 1984.

_____. *Living Creatively*. Denville, N.J.: Dimension Books, 1978.

_____. *Looking for Jesus*. Denville, N.J.: Dimension Books, 1978.

_____. *The Mystery of Transforming Love*. Denville, N.J.: Dimension Books, 1982.

_____. *On Being Involved*. Denville, N.J.: Dimension Books, 1970.

_____. *On Being Yourself*. Denville, N.J.: Dimension Books, 1972.

_____., Bert van Croonenburg, and S. Muto. *The Participant Self*. Denville, N.J.: Dimension Books, 1969.

_____. *Personality Fulfillment in the Religious Life: Religious Life in a Time of Transition*. Denville, N.J.: Dimension Books, 1967. (Also in Vietnamese and Japanese.)

_____. *Personality Fulfillment in the Spiritual Life*. Denville, N.J.: Dimension Books, 1966.

_____., and Susan Muto. *Practicing the Prayer of Presence*. Denville, N.J.: Dimension Books, 1980.

_____. *Religion and Personality*. 1964. Expanded ed. Denville, N.J.: Dimension Books, 1980.

_____. *Religion et Personnalité*. Tournai, Paris: Casterman; Mulhouse: Editions Salvator, 1967.

_____. *Religione e Personalità*. Brescia: Editrice La Scuola, Officine Grafiche La Scuola, 1972.

_____. *Spirituality and the Gentle Life*. Denville, N.J.: Dimension Books, 1974.

_____., and Susan Muto. *Tell Me Who I Am*. Denville, N.J.: Dimension Books, 1977.

_____. *The Third Force in European Psychology*. Greenville, De.: Psychosynthesis Research Foundation, 1960. (Also in Greek.)

_____. *The Transcendent Self: Formative Spirituality of the Middle, Early and Late Years of Life*. Denville, N.J.: Dimension Books, 1979.

_____. *The Vocational Director and Counseling*. Derby, N.Y.: St. Paul Publications, 1962.

_____. *The Vowed Life*. Denville, N.J.: Dimension Books, 1968.

_____. *The Woman at the Well*. Denville, N.J.: Dimension Books, 1976.

Vergote, A. *Het Huis is Nooit Af*. Antwerp: De Nederlandsche Boekhandel, 1974.

_____. *The Religious Man*. Dayton, Ohio: Pflaum Press, 1969.

Vishnudevananda, S. *The Complete Illustrated Book of Yoga*. New York: Julian Press, 1960.

Vitz, P. C. *Psychology as Religion: The Cult of Self-Worship*. Grand Rapids, Mich.: William E. Eerdmans, 1977.

von Balthasar, H.U. *Does Jesus Know Us? Do We Know Him?* San Francisco: Ignatius Press, 1983.

_____. *The Glory of the Lord: A Theological Aesthetic*. Vol. 1, *Seeing the Form* (1–691). New York: Crossroad, 1983.

Von Dürckheim, K. *Hara: The Vital Centre of Man*. London: George Allen & Unwin, 1962.

von Hildebrand, D. *Transformation in Christ*. Chicago, Ill.: Franciscan Herald Press, 1974.

Watson, J. B. *Behaviorism*. New York: W. W. Norton, 1970.

Watson, L. *Lifetide*. London: Hodder and Stoughton, 1979.

Watts, A. *The Book: On the Taboo Against Knowing Who You Are*. New York: Random House, 1972.

_____. *The Way of Zen*. New York: Pantheon Books, 1957.

Webb, R. B. *The Presence of the Past: John Dewey and Alfred Schutz on the Genesis and Organization of Experience*. Gainsville, Fl.: Florida University Press, 1976.

Whitehead, E., and James. *Christian Life Patterns: The Psychological Challenges and Religious Invitations of Adult Life*. Garden City, N.Y.: Doubleday, 1979.

Whorf, B. *Language, Thought, and Reality*. New York: John Wiley, 1956.

Wickes, F. G. *The Inner World of Choice*. Englewood Cliffs, N.J.: Prentice-Hall, 1976.

Wojtyla, K. *The Acting Person*. Dordrecht, Holland: D. Reidel Publishing Company, 1979.

Zavalloni, R. *Self-Determination: The Psychology of Personal Freedom*. Chicago, Ill.: Forum Books, 1962.

Zerubavel, E. *Hidden Rhythms*. Chicago: University of Chicago Press, 1981.

Zilbergeld, B. *The Shrinking of America: Myths of Psychological Change*. Boston: Little, Brown, 1983.

Articles

Abernathy, W. J., and Hayes, R. "Managing Our Way to Economic Decline." *Harvard Business Review* 58 (July-August 1980):67–77.

Carrington, P. and H. Ephron. "Meditation and Psychoanalysis." *Journal of the American Academy of Psychoanalysis* 3 (1975):43–57.

Condon, W. S. "A Primary Phase in the Organization of Infant Responding Behavior." In *Studies in Mother-Infant Interaction*, edited by, H. R. Schaffer, New York: Academic Press, 1977.

Condon, W. S. and Sander, L. W. "Neonate Movement Is Synchronized with Adult Speech: Interactional Participation and Language Acquisition." *Science* 183 (January 1974): 99–101.

_____. "Synchrony Demonstrated Between Movements of the Neonate and Adult Speech." *Child Development* 45 (June 1974):456–462.

Cox, H. "The Pool of Narcissus: The Psychologizing of Meditation." *Cross Currents* 27 (Spring 1977):16–28.

Dumont, C. "Education of the Heart." *Monastic Studies* 12 (Michaelmas 1976):191–206.

Fallows, J. "American Industry: What Ails It, How to Save It." *The Atlantic* 246 (September 1980):35–51.

Frankl, V. E. "Determinism and Humanism." *Humanitas* 7 (Spring 1971):23–36.

Friedman, M. "Hope and Despondency: A Hasidic View." *Humanitas* 13 (November 1977): 291–305.

Gowan, J. C. "The Role of Imagination in the Development of the Creative Individual." *Humanitas* 14 (May 1978):209–225.

Gratton, C. "Approaching a Formative Context for Direction of the Original Self." *Studies in Formative Spirituality* 1 (February 1980):41–54.

Krippner, S. "Alterations in Awareness and Discovery of the Self." *Humanitas* 14 (May 1978): 243–254.

Meissner, W. W. "Notes on the Psychology of Hope." *Journal of Religion and Health* 12 (January 1973):7–29.

Merton, T. "Final Integration: Towards a Monastic Therapy." *Monastic Studies* 6 (All Saints 1968):87–99.

Munro, H. H. "The Unrest Cure." In *The Short Stories of Saki*, 140–147. New York: The Viking Press, 1946.

Navone, J. "Memories Make the Future." *The Catholic World* 204 (December 1966):149–153.

O'Donoghue, N. D. "Space and Time as Ethical Categories." *Continuum* 6:(Summer 1968):156–165.

Scarf, M. "Images That Heal: A Doubtful Idea Whose Time Has Come." *Psychology Today* 14 (September 1980):32–46.

Steindl-Rast, D. "The Environment as Guru." *Cross Currents* 24 (Summer-Fall 1974): 148–153.

Van Kaam, A. "The Addictive Personality." *Humanitas* 1 (Fall 1965):183–193.

_____. "The Addictive Personality." In *Phenomenology of Will and Action*, edited by Erwin W. Straus and Richard M. Griffith, 141–155. Pittsburgh, Pa.: Duquesne University Press, 1967.

_____. "Assumptions in Psychology." *Journal of Individual Psychology*: 14 (May 1958):22–28.

_____. "Assumptions in Psychology." In *The Science of Psychology: Critical Reflections*, edited by D. P. Schultz, 24–30. New York: Appleton-Century-Crofts, 1970.

_____. "Celebration of Consonance." *Envoy* 19 (March-April 1982):1–6.

_____. "Clinical Implications of Heidegger's Concepts of Will, Decision and Responsibility." *Review of Existential Psychology and Psychiatry* 1 (Fall 1961):205–216.

_____. "The Dynamics of Hope and Despondency in the Parents of Handicapped Children." *Humanitas* 13 (November 1977):307–316.

_____. "Education to Originality." In *Psychologia Pedagogica Sursum*. Barend Frederik Nel, 214–228. Stellenbosch/Grahamstad, South Africa: University Publishers and Bookseller, 1970.

_____. "Encounter and Its Distortion in Contemporary Society." *Humanitas* 2 (Winter 1967):271–284.

_____. "Existential Crisis and Human Development." *South African Journal of Pedagogy* 3 (July 1969):63–74.

_____. "Existential Psychology as a Theory of Personality." *Review of Existential Psychology and Psychiatry* 3 (Winter 1963):2–11.

_____. "The Field of Religion and Personality or Theoretical Religious Anthropology." *Insight* 4 (Summer 1965):1–8.

_____. "Form Traditon and Ritual." *Studies in Formative Spirituality* 3 (November 1982):411–426.

_____. "Harmony Unmatched in Time." *Envoy* 19 (March-April 1982):7.

_____. "Humanistic Psychology and Culture." *Journal of Humanistic Psychology* 1 (Spring 1961):94–100.

_____. "Human Potentialities from the Viewpoint of Existential Psychology." In *Explorations in Human Potentialities*, edited by H. A. Otto, 335–347. Springfield, Ill.: Charles C. Thomas, 1966.

_____. "Icon of the Living God." *Envoy* 18 (November 1981):173.

_____. "Joy and the Life of the Spirit." *Envoy* 19 (January-February 1982):1–5.

_____. "Motivation and Contemporary Anxiety." *Humanitas* 1 (Spring 1965):59–75.

_____. "The Moving Equilibrium of Joy and Concern." *Envoy* 19 (July-August 1982):1–5.

_____. "A Nimble Dance." *Envoy* 19 (September-October 1982):6.

_____. "Original Calling and Spiritual Direction." *Studies in Formative Spirituality* 1 (February 1980):7–41.

_____. "Personality, Personal Unfolding and the Aesthetic Experience of Literature," *Humanitas* 4 (Fall 1968):223–236.

_____. "Playful Before Your Face." *Envoy* 19 (January-February 1982):6.

_____. "Provisional Glossary of the Terminology of the Science of Foundational Spirituality." *Studies in Formative Spirituality* 1 (February 1980):137–155. 1 (May 1980): 287–304. 1 (November 1980):449–479. 2 (February 1981):117–126. 2 (May 1981):291–329. 2 (November 1981):498–540. 3 (February 1982):123–155. 3 (May 1982):293–319. 3(November 1982):453–471. 4 (February 1983):133–151. 4 (May 1983):265–279. 4 (November 1983):409–425.

_____. "Psychic Health and Spiritual Life," *New Catholic World* 219 (March 1976): 75–79.

_____. "A Psychology of the Catholic Intellectual." In *The Christian Intellectual*, edited by S. Hazo, 1–40. Pittsburgh, Pa.: Duquesne University Press, 1963.

_____. "A Psychology of Falling Away from the Faith." *Insight* 2 (Fall 1963):2–17.

_____. "Religious Anthropology and Religious Counseling." *Insight* 4 (Winter 1966): 1–7.

_____. "Structures and Systems of Personality." In *The New Catholic Encyclopedia,* 174–177. Washington D.C.: The Catholic University of America, 1966.

_____. "The Threefold Path." *Studies in Formative Spirituality* 2 (November 1981): 461–485.

_____. "Transcendence Therapy." In *Handbook of Innovative Psychotherapies*, edited by R. J. Corsini, 855–872 and 917–930. New York: John Wiley and Sons, 1981.

_____. "The Winter of My Heart." *Envoy* 18 (October 1981):191.

von Dürckheim, K. "La Meditation Comme Exercise Initiatique." *La Vie Spirituelle* 612 (Juillet-Août 1977):564–586.

Wallace, R., and H. Benson. "The Physiology of Meditation." *Scientific American* 226 (February 1972):84–90.

Unpublished Theses

Brownson, W. E. "The Concept of Habit in Dewey and Human Growth." Doctoral dissertation, Stanford University, Palo Alto, Calif., 1970.

Chappel, F., C.F.C. "Spirituality and the Re-creating Mode of Presence." Master's thesis, Institute of Formative Spirituality, Duquesne University, Pittsburgh, Pa., 1978.

Hanlon, M. C., S.C. "Custom: A Way of Life-Creative Renewal of Religious Living." Master's thesis, Institute of Formative Spirituality, Duquesne University, Pittsburgh, Pa., 1970.

Laferriere, A., S.A.S.V. "Spirituality and the Experience of Failure." Master's thesis, Institute of Formative Spirituality, Duquesne University, Pittsburgh, Pa., 1978.

Smith, J. B. "An Analysis of the Concept of Habit With Implications for Education." Doctoral dissertation, University of Pittsburgh, Pa., 1978.

Stott, B., R.S.M. "Spiritual Appropriation of the Past: From Resentment to Gratitude." Master's thesis, Institute of Formative Spirituality, Duquesne University, Pittsburgh, Pa., 1974.

Index

263